The Joy Of
Opera

Legendary Voices

'Nigel Douglas has written one of the most amusing, instructive and intelligent books about singers to have appeared for years ... Douglas's enthusiasm, sometimes tempered with a nice line in dry wit, is infectious.'

Sunday Telegraph

'No one in my experience has written . . . about singers and singing quite as Nigel Douglas does. What makes his assessments unique is his background of knowledge and professional experience, combined with the native literary and narrative endowment he brings to his subjects.'

Opera Quarterly, USA

'A vastly entertaining and informative read.'

BBC Music magazine

More Legendary Voices

'Again, he writes with perception, wit and real understanding born of his own experience as a tenor ... The book is so well written that one can enjoy every page.'

Sunday Telegraph

'This book is a must for anyone with the slightest interest in opera.'

Opera Now

'Nigel Douglas is almost uniquely placed to write about the great singers of the past ... For the expert he offers his wit and authoritative assessments of performances available on CD, for the novice graceful introductions explaining why these singers are so special and important.'

Financial Times

The Joy Of Opera

Nigel Douglas

ANDRÉ DEUTSCH

First published in Great Britain in 1996
This paperback edition published 2000, reprinted 2004 by

André Deutsch
an imprint of the
Carlton Publishing Group
20 Mortimer Street
London W1T 3JW

A catalogue record for this book is available from the British Library

ISBN 0 233 00005 4

Printed in Dubai

During my operatic career I have received guidance, encouragement, kindness and hospitality from many people in many countries. Some are no longer with us, others are. To all of them, with great gratitude, I dedicate this book.

Nigel Douglas

Few people could be better qualified to write an insider's view of the world of opera than Nigel Douglas. As a singer he has appeared throughout the world in a repertoire of over 80 tenor roles, he has directed numerous productions in London, Australia and continental Europe, he has presented over 300 of his own programmes for BBC Radio, and in recent years he has been in constant international demand as a lecturer. His previous books, *Legendary Voices* and *More Legendary Voices*, were greeted with exceptional critical acclaim on both sides of the Atlantic.

Contents

Acknowledgements

As usual I have many people to thank for their help in the preparation of this book. At the top of the list come Ilsa Yardley for her unstinting support and advice, Bobby Woodward for his brilliant research work, and Michael Dealtry, who has provided words of wisdom and practical assistance in equally generous measure. In Clare Chambers I have a copy editor with whom I have never had a cross word, and in Barbara Levy an agent who looks after all the bits with which I am not qualified to cope. Vivian Liff and George Stuart have allowed me to roam freely through their celebrated collection, Norman White has unhesitatingly provided me with anything I needed from his extensive archives, and Elizabeth Forbes and Peter Kemp have both been enormously helpful over the matter of illustrations. John Pennino of the Metropolitan Opera manages never to be too busy to respond to calls for assistance, and others to whom I am indebted include Mark Elyn in Illinois, Francesca Franchi of the Royal Opera House, Covent Garden, Dr Paolo Klun of La Scala, Milan, Richard Gregson and Christopher Raeburn, both of whom have helped to polish up my memories of many happy incidents in the not too distant past; and finally the father and daughter team of Eugene and Eugenie Hartzell, my infallible *Auskunftsquelle* for matters Viennese.

Illustrations

The author and publishers gratefully acknowledge the following for help in supplying and permission to reproduce the illustrations in this book; Austrian National Library; Clive Barda/Performing Arts Library; Bayreuth Festival; BBC Picture Archives; C. H. Beck'sche Verlagsbuchhandlung, Munich; Bridgeman Art Library; British Film Institute; Jeff Busby; Natale Chirulli; A. C. Cooper; Bill Cooper/Welsh National Opera; Richard Davies; Decca/G. Schikola; Zoë Dominic; EMI; Mary Evans Picture Library; Foto Saporetti; Guy Gravett; Harvard Theatre Collection; Mike Hoban; Hulton Getty Picture Collection; Karel Ješátko; Peter Kemp Collection; Mander & Mitchenson; Mansell Collection; Metropolitan Opera Archives, New York; Österreichischer Rundfunk; Bill Rafferty/English National Opera; Mark Ricaldone; Royal College of Music; Royal Opera House; Adrian Rowland; San Francisco Opera; Science Museum, London/Science and Society Picture Library; Julian Sheppard; Richard H. Smith; Stuart-Liff Collection; Sydney Opera House; Robert Tuggle Collection; Victoria and Albert Museum; Vienna City Museum; Votavafoto, Vienna; Welsh National Opera. We apologise for any inadvertent omissions in this list, which will be corrected in any subsequent edition of this book.

Introduction

'Opera; an exotick and irrational entertainment.'

Dr Samuel Johnson,
The Lives of the Poets

Though two and a half centuries have passed since it first found its way into print, I believe that if Dr Johnson were to reappear in our midst today and attend a performance of, say, Ligeti's *Le Grand Macabre* or Schnittke's *Life With an Idiot*, far from revising his opinion he might feel inclined to echo the memorable words of his contemporary, Clive of India, facing a parliamentary enquiry into allegations of corruption – 'By God, Mr Chairman, at this moment I stand astonished at my own moderation!'

Exotic? Most certainly, though one must bear in mind that in Johnson's day the word bore a more pejorative connotation than it does today, indicating something outlandish rather than merely strange, mysterious or evocative; perhaps he had just sat through an under-rehearsed performance of *The Beggar's Opera*. Irrational? Ah! yes, indeed. Not even the most committed operaphile would pretend that rationality enters into it. When someone is told that his mother is shortly to be burned at the stake and instead of hurrying off to rescue her he spends four and a half minutes announcing at the top of his voice that he is just about to do so; when ladies whose lungs are supposedly wasted with consumption still have enough breath to hurl their high B flats into the back row of the gallery; or when an American officer who speaks no Japanese marries a Japanese girl who speaks no English, so the two of them communicate by singing to each other in Italian, rationality clearly has nothing whatever to do with it. And why should it? Once the world's most heavenly voices have taken wing above a surging ocean of orchestral sound irrational events and unlikely situations achieve a justification all of their own. This is the glorious alchemy of opera.

Opera-mania, as I am well aware, is a disease to which some people are immune, but for those who have caught the bug, and it is a bug of formidable potency, words like 'exotic' and 'irrational' hold no fears. Is the power of music ever rational? Can people explain what is happening to them when they sit back listening to the slow movement of a Mozart piano concerto and the worries of the day gradually fade from the mind? Where does music come from, what part of one's spirit does it touch? Do questions such as these *need* rational answers?

To quote John Gay, the author of *The Beggar's Opera*, 'Variety's the source of joy', and although it was not the joy of opera which Gay had in mind at that moment, it is, I think, through the variety of its splendours that opera weaves its peculiarly powerful spell. One only needs to observe the multiplicity of opera-goers' reactions when attending the selfsame performance. Where one will leave the theatre enthusing about the beauty of the sets and costumes another can speak of nothing but the brilliance (or incompetence) of the conductor. Many may be impervious to any such considerations because the world's greatest tenor has been at work and in his shadow all else fades into insignificance; while others, lost in the melodies of Mozart or Puccini, may care but little who the conductor, the director, the designer or even the singers happen to have been – for them the music itself is all. In so diverse an art form the element of danger is ever present – there is so much which *could* go wrong and from time to time it does; but just occasionally those magical evenings do occur when every component seems to lose its individual identity and the vocal, the visual, the dramatic and the musical elements fuse into one overwhelming artistic and emotional experience. When a great bass-baritone has completed an inspired performance of Wotan's Farewell in *Die Walküre*, let us say, when Wagner's mighty orchestra has faded to the final pianissimo chord, and the conductor has laid down his baton, it is as if the house has momentarily been transported into a state of suspended animation. Drained but exalted, the audience instinctively observes a split-second's silence before great waves of applause come crashing forth from every corner, and whichever side of the curtain you happen to be on it is heady stuff. To the true operaphile there is no substitute.

To be fair, though, to Dr Johnson, the question of opera's irrationality was one which did indeed exercise the minds of the art form's earliest progenitors. When opera first came into being in the last years of the sixteenth century people were already well accustomed to the convention of characters in plays soliloquizing in blank verse – which is not, after all, a thing that many people are given to in everyday life – but the idea that they should express themselves in song was new and potentially disturbing. The transition was made possible by the mythological settings of the early operas. The earliest of all, *Dafne*, by Jacopo Peri, produced in Florence in 1598 (by which time Shakespeare was halfway through his oeuvre as a playwright), concerned the legend of Apollo and his pursuit of the nymph Daphne, whose chastity is preserved by the rather drastic measure of her transformation into a laurel bush. Now, Apollo, the god of music, could surely be excused for wooing his loved one in song; and as for Orpheus, the hero of the earliest opera which can be said to have maintained some kind of a place in the repertoire, Monteverdi's *Orfeo* of 1607, he was seldom known to express himself in any other manner. Gradually the intellectual debate about such niceties faded into a general acceptance that opera had come to stay, bringing its own set of conventions with it.

One contemporary of Dr Johnson's who shared his views on the opera was Lord Chesterfield, the statesman and diplomat whose twin claims to immortality lie in the fact that he gave his name to a novel form of sofa, and that he wrote an astonishing number of letters to his son about how to lead a virtuous life – a fact which has always struck me as ironical given that the son in question was the product of an extra-marital fling. 'As for operas,' his lordship wrote, 'they are essentially too absurd and extravagant to mention; I look upon them as a magic scene contrived to please the eyes and ears at the expense of the understanding.' However one may feel about the general tenet of this pronouncement, with the word 'extravagant' he has undeniably put his finger on one of the most regrettable facts of operatic life – good opera seldom comes cheap.

In the early days, when the presentation of opera was the exclusive preserve of crowned heads, it served as a showcase for the affluence of Europe's ruling families. Now that the private patronage of Emperors,

Kings, Dukes and Princes has been widely replaced by that of central and local governments, whose ultimate source of funding is the taxpayer, it is no surprise that opera should so often find itself flung into the political arena. 'Why should a single farthing of my taxes be spent on opera when I haven't the faintest intention of ever going to one?' – a question with which we in the operatic profession are drearily familiar. Back in my bachelor days my customary reply used to be 'Why should a hefty dollop of *my* taxes be spent on schools when I don't have any children?' As that particular argument is no longer available to me I have nowadays shifted to 'Why should I help finance the municipal baths when I hate swimming?' – less of a blockbuster as answers go, I admit, but the principle remains the same. A decision has to be reached as to whether or not the Arts, like schools, sports and so forth, are an essential part of life in a civilized community, and though nowadays there are few, if any, developed countries in which the ayes do not have it, the Muse of Opera, being an extravagant lady, is more prone than her sisters to feel the chill wind of controversy whipping round her ankles.

Many people, I know, assume that the high price of opera tickets and the vast sums of public money poured into so many opera houses are largely attributable to the excessive fees which are paid to the singers, a theory which most of us in the profession greet with a wry smile. The assumption is based, no doubt, on the publicity given to the earnings of a minute group of superstars, but the true cause of the high cost of opera lies in the sheer numbers of people participating in the performances. Even in those companies which cannot aspire to soloists of international fame any production of a reasonably 'grand' opera is likely to involve ten or so principal singers, a chorus of around forty, a conductor, an assistant conductor for off-stage cues, an orchestra of probably fifty or sixty, three or four stage managers, a score or so of stage hands and electricians, and a similar number of people at work in the costume, make-up and wig departments. Add to all this the expense of creating the sets and costumes for a production which may only be performed some thirty times over a five-year period and one begins to have an idea of the inflated scale of opera; and that is before one has even started to add such items to the equation as the costs of the company's administrative staff or the maintenance of a building which is expected to house between one and two thousand people safely and comfortably two or three hundred times a year.

Is it all justified? Well, to judge from the ever-increasing numbers of people who go to opera, buy operatic recordings or watch opera on television the answer has to be yes; it seems that the operatic bug is claiming more and more victims all the time. On social occasions thirty or forty years ago I used to dread that tried and trusted opening gambit 'What job do you do?', because the answer 'I'm an opera singer' would so often prove to be a total conversation-stopper; the best one could hope for was an embarrassed silence followed by some such riposte as 'Do you sing in your bath?', or, as an occasional variant, that most devastating of questions 'Should I have heard of you?' Nowadays it is far more likely that a lively debate will ensue. Whose fault was it *really* that the new production of *Aida* was such a disaster? Is it true that this new tenor is going to be the next Domingo? Is modern opera as difficult to learn as it is to listen to? Why do trendy directors insist on ruining everything? And increasingly often, with a glance at my receding hairline, What is the usual sort of age for a tenor to retire?

My intention in writing this book has not been to answer any such specific questions, but merely, after forty years in the operatic arena, to air a few random thoughts and reflections. Things, of course, look a little different from one side of the curtain than they do from the other, but I was an ardent opera-*goer* long before I dreamt of trying to become an opera-*singer*, and if anything I have written succeeds in shedding light on, stimulating interest in, or kindling enthusiasm for any aspect of the exotick and irrational entertainment known as opera I shall be content.

Nigel Douglas

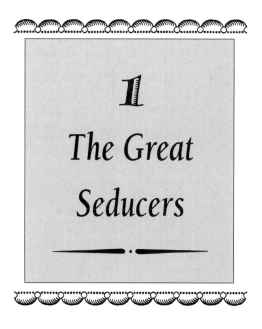

1

The Great Seducers

The plot of almost every opera ever written has as its mainspring, in some form or other, the power of love. Tragic love, comic love, doomed love, love triumphant, love sacrificial, secret love, heroic love, treacherous love, redemptive love, chaste love, very unchaste love indeed, illicit love with shattering consequences, they are all grist to the opera composer's mill; and every operaphile will stoutly maintain that the depiction of all this emotional turmoil is rendered infinitely more vivid by the potent admixture of music than would ever be possible through the spoken word alone. The ecstatic interweaving of the vocal lines in the moonlit love duet from *Don Pasquale*, the defiant fortissimo of 'Amor, amor! Infinito amor!' as Andrea Chénier and Madeleine de Coigny are led off to their rendezvous with the guillotine, Walther von Stolzing's ecstatic 'Parnass und Paradies!' at the climax of the *Meistersinger* Prize Song, the heart-breaking cadences of Pamina's farewell to life when she believes herself deserted by Tamino in *The Magic Flute* – what would be the impact of these and a thousand other examples like them if it were not for the inten-

DON GIOVANNIS
THEN AND NOW:

*Victor Maurel
(1848–1923).*

*John Forsell
(1868–1941).*

*Ezio Pinza
(1892–1957).*

*Paul Schoeffler
(1897–1977).*

Cesare Siepi with Mirella Freni, Covent Garden, 1964.

Gilles Cachemaille, Glyndebourne, 1994.

sity with which the music assaults the listeners' emotions? In the right hands music is the ideal medium for the portrayal of love in all its facets, and it always seems to me that it reaches a special peak of effectiveness when it is used to depict the stealthy skills of the seducer.

It would be hard to say whether, in opera, seducers outnumber seductresses or vice versa, but looking first at the male version of the species, the figure who dominates the scene is Mozart's Don Giovanni. He is a man who does not merely indulge in seduction when the mood is upon him, he devotes his life to it, and yet the remarkable thing is that during the entire action of the opera he never once achieves his goal. Both when he beams his charm onto little Zerlina with the irresistible 'La ci darem la mano', and when he serenades the chambermaid of one of his previous conquests, ('Deh vieni alla finestra'), Mozart places pure honey upon his lips, but ultimately it avails him nothing. Perhaps by the time we first meet the Don, just after he has badly bungled the seduction of Donna

Anna,* he is beginning to feel that the game is no longer worth the candle. Could the great seducer be growing bored with seduction? As his servant Leporello tells us, he has after all notched up a thousand and three successes in Spain alone, and perhaps subconsciously he realizes that that is enough to be getting along with.

The moral dilemma posed by making such a deeply evil individual as Don Giovanni into the 'hero' of any theatrical work is one which exercised commentators long before da Ponte and Mozart chose it as material for an opera. Back in 1676 the Don took his London bow in a play called *The Libertine* by Thomas Shadwell, and a hundred years later, in a publication entitled *The Companion to the Playhouse*, one of our early drama critics wrote: 'The villainy of Don John's Character is worked up to such a Height, as to exceed even the Limits of Possibility, and the Catastrophe is so very horrid, as to render it little less than Impiety to represent it on the stage.'

The fact remains, though, that in the operatic version, thanks largely to the charms of Mozart's music, this murderous and blasphemous seducer is the character who walks away with the lion's share of the audience's sympathy, especially if the singer undertaking the role is a performer of personal charisma. The same can be said of Verdi's most dedicated seducer, the young Duke of Mantua in *Rigoletto*. Morally there is nothing to be found in his favour; at least Don Giovanni has the courage to go to the Devil unrepentant of his sins, whereas the bravest thing we see the Duke undertake is, in the words of the doomed Count Monterone, to 'set his hound on a dying lion'. The Duke is vicious, selfish and cruel, a thoroughly bad lot, but even so opera-goers never really take against him for the good reason that he hardly ever opens his mouth without treating them to a marvellous tune. The airy elegance of 'Quest' o quella', with which he expounds the creed of 'I don't care who she is as long as she's pretty'; the ardour of 'È il sol dell' anima', with which he turns the head of the ingenue Gilda; the finely drawn cantilena of 'Parmi veder le lagrime', with which he laments the fact that his latest bit of fluff appears to have eluded him; the ebullience of 'Bella figlia dell' amore', with which

---

*It is currently fashionable to doubt whether it *was* bungled; indeed certain modern directors have Don Giovanni positively fleeing from an insatiable Donna Anna.

he chats up one of the local tarts; and above all 'La donna è mobile', the one the public waits for, ensure that this is a role which every star tenor itches to get his hands on. Not for nothing was it Caruso's choice for one important debut after another.

If one were wishing, however, to award to any single character the title of Opera's Nastiest Seducer there are candidates who can outdo even the Duke of Mantua. The Drum-Major in *Wozzeck* is an appalling creature, totally lacking the finesse which at least marks out the Duke as a master of his craft. The Drum-Major's method of seducing Wozzeck's common-law wife Marie is simply to strut around in front of her boasting about his unparalleled masculinity, and once he has got what he was after he wastes no time in letting Wozzeck hear all about it. I have myself sung both the Duke and the Drum-Major in my time and there is an undeniable pleasure to be had out of playing these thoroughly dreadful people. Perhaps it enables us performers to work some nasty streak out of our own personalities in a harmless manner – while also, of course, getting paid for doing so. Two other vile seducers in my own personal repertoire could, I think, be officially classified as operatic rarities. One was Ritter Hugo von Ringstetten in Lortzing's seldom performed *Undine* – he seduces and marries a water-sprite despite being already engaged to a high-born lady, who gets her own back by deciding to marry the King of Naples; and the other was a young bounder named Frank Innes in an operatic version, composed by Professor Robin Orr, of Robert Louis Stevenson's *Weir of Hermiston*. This opera was written for the Edinburgh Festival of 1975 and I was called upon at one point to express my true villainy by raping the innocent heroine in a churchyard. The director decreed that I should do so by forcing her against a tombstone, and that splendid bass Michael Langdon, who was playing the title-role, used to delight in telling the story that at one of the rehearsals he heard me complain to my victim (very politely, I hasten to add) 'This rape will never work unless you lift your left leg a little higher.' Whether I really said it or not I cannot recall, but – 'se non è vero, è ben trovato.'

In sheer nastiness, though, even creatures like Frank Innes and the Drum-Major must bow the knee to Puccini's arch villain, Baron Scarpia, head of the secret police, in *Tosca*. Before he ever appears we are put in the picture about him by the hero, Cavaradossi, who indulges in a tremendous outburst of rhetoric. 'Scarpia?' he cries. 'A bigot, a satyr, who conceals the lust of a libertine under the mask of piety, and, the instrument of his own lasciviousness, plays both the confessor and the hangman!' – a piece of advance publicity which the Baron lives up to with a vengeance. Having neither seen nor read the Sardou play on which the opera is based I find it hard to imagine how the full wickedness of the man could be truly conjured up without the assistance of the music. There is such an air of pernicious pseudo-piety about the vocal line which Puccini gives to Scarpia as he first approaches Tosca in the church of Sant'Andrea della Valle, and about the orchestral scoring too. 'Divine Tosca,' the hypocrite purrs, 'my hand awaits yours, your hand so small, not for purposes of gallantry, but to offer you some holy water.' The voice which I always have in my ear when I think of this passage is that of Tito Gobbi, happily preserved in two memorable recordings.* There is a patina of slime on the tone that he uses, insinuating, ingratiating and vile; and it is a vocal quality which makes way for something very much more forceful when the Baron employs his alternative method of seduction in Act II – submit to me, or your lover goes to the gallows.

It is perhaps unfair to pit the potency of mere mortal seductiveness against that of seducers invested with supernatural powers, but on an entirely different plane from Baron Scarpia, Peter Quint in Britten's *The Turn of the Screw* is another creature whom no one in his right mind would wish to have around the house. In his sinister attempts to seduce the two young children, Miles and Flora, Quint is assisted by the fact that he is no longer flesh and blood, but a ghost who can come and go as he pleases. It is a major contributory factor to the air of creepiness which this piece engenders that neither in Henry James's original story nor in Myfanwy Piper's cleverly adapted libretto are we ever actually told what Quint had done to the children while he was still alive, though the inference is plain enough that his motivation in haunting them is of some eerily erotic nature. It seems unlikely that it is merely their souls which

---

*The full set of *Tosca* with Callas, di Stefano and Gobbi, conducted by Victor de Sabata, on EMI *CDS 7 47175 8* still takes a lot of beating. The other, with Callas, Bergonzi and Gobbi conducted by Georges Prêtre on EMI *CMS 7 69974 2*, also has much to recommend it, notably the stereo recording, but it finds Callas in less comfortable voice.

A supernatural seducer. Peter Pears as the ghost of Peter Quint strikes terror into Jennifer Vyvyan as the Governess in The Turn of the Screw, *La Fenice, 1954.*

he wishes to possess; he leaves that sort of thing to Mephistopheles in Gounod's (or Boito's) *Faust*. Certainly, as far as Faust himself is concerned, there is no ambivalence in the air. The operatic Faust, unlike Goethe's somewhat subtler creation, is little more than a thoroughly dirty old man, and when Mephistopheles asks him what it is that he is after – 'La richesse?', perhaps, or 'La gloire?' – Faust makes no bones about his true ambitions. He wants his youth back, and for one reason only. 'A moi les plaisirs,' he cries, 'Les jeunes maitresses! A moi leurs caresses, A moi leurs désirs!' One can only assume that the first time around he must have muffed his chances, but now, with Mephistopheles to pave the way for him, the attempts of the rejuvenated Faust on the virtue of the fair Marguerite could scarcely go awry. The poor girl does not stand a chance, though I do think that it speaks volumes in Faust's favour that despite the guarantee of victory he still takes the trouble to woo her with those two jewels of the seducer's art 'Laisse-moi, laisse-moi contempler ton visage' and 'O nuit d'amour, ciel radieux'.

Faust's little bit of dirty work may have had a catastrophic effect on the life of poor Marguerite (pregnancy, infanticide, death sentence, madness), but there is another seducer to be found in the pages of French opera whose influence was further-reaching even than that. In Daniel Auber's *Masaniello, ou La muette de Portici* (*Masaniello, or the Dumb Girl of Portici*), Alfonso, the son of the Spanish viceroy of Naples, is denounced by Fenella, the 'Muette' of the title, as her seducer; and the moment she chooses for the revelation of this shocking conduct (transmitted for obvious reasons in mime) is the occasion of Alfonso's marriage to a Spanish princess named, as Spanish ladies tend to be in the world of

The eponymous hero in Auber's Masaniello, ou La muette de Portici, *as portrayed by Mario (1810–1883).*

opera, Elvira. Fenella's fisherman brother Masaniello uses this outrage as his cue to stir up an insurrection (this parat of the story is based on historical fact), and although he ultimately both fails and dies the patriotic fervour engendered by the opera's crowd scenes during a performance in Brussels on 25 August 1830 transmitted itself with such immediacy to the public that the flame of revolution leapt, so to speak, over the orchestra pit, and into the auditorium. Students rushed from the theatre calling down imprecations on the heads of the Dutch who currently ruled over them, the student riot developed into a full-scale revolt, within two months a provisional government was appointed, and the following year Belgium was reconstituted as an independent country. Thus did the actions of one operatic seducer transcend the normal limitations of life upon the wicked stage – let no one underestimate the power of the Muse of Opera.

La muette de Portici is a typical example of the shifting fashions of operatic taste. One of the earliest of the French grand operas which held such sway in the nineteenth century, it was a tremendous favourite wherever it was performed, and in Paris alone it achieved no less than five hundred performances in its first fifty years. The last of *La muette's* stupendous *coups de théâtre* consisted of Vesuvius erupting in the background while the luckless Fenella commits suicide by casting herself from a lofty crag, a dénouement whose effectiveness did not pass Richard Wagner by when he started pondering a suitably cataclysmic finale for his *Ring* cycle. Apart from one production by the Berlin Staatsoper in 1953, however, and another in Wiesbaden in 1983, I am not aware that *La muette* has been performed since the war, and with one or two exceptions, such as *Le Prophète* and *L'Africaine*, whenever the mammoth operas of Giacomo Meyerbeer, which followed in its wake, have been dusted off and set before post-war audiences they too have failed to find favour.

One opera, on the other hand, which has noticeably benefited from the swings of public taste is Verdi's *Falstaff*. It seems to grow in popularity year by year, and for a welcome change it offers us a seducer whose exceptional poundage can scarcely be said to have an ounce of real evil in it. Sir John is the only character in the opera who still believes in his attractiveness to women – 'Siete un gran seduttore,' Mistress Quickly mischievously remarks while the trap is being baited, 'You are a great seducer'; and back comes the lofty reply 'Lo so. Continua', 'I know. Carry on.' When the fat knight dons his finery and steps forth for the undoing of Mistress Ford we are treated both visually and aurally to one of the great scenes of comic opera, culminating in the ineffable 'After you', 'No, after you', 'Well, let us go together' exit for Falstaff and Ford, the former blissfully unaware that his companion is the husband of the very lady he has undertaken to seduce.

The richest harvest of ineffectual seducers *à la* Falstaff is to be found in the pages of classical operetta. There it would not do for genuine villains to be given their head – operetta is not the place for broken hearts and shattered lives. Seducers in operetta are principally required to make idiots of themselves and to repent their foolish ways, one of the earliest examples of the genre being provided by no less a figure than Jupiter, king of the gods, in Offenbach's *Orpheus in the Underworld*. In the course of trying to settle the awkward question of whether or not Euridice should be restored to the arms of her husband Orpheus, Jupiter takes a fancy to her himself, and decides to resort to those skills as a quick-change artist for which he earned such a reputation in classical mythology. Disguised as a tiny golden fly he pops through the keyhole while she is taking a bath, and engages her in a duet which, to me at least, marks the high point of the entire score. As Richard Traubner puts it in his book *Operetta – A Theatrical History,** 'A situation right out of boulevard *vaudeville* is set by Offenbach in the style of the Académie Nationale de la Musique', and the plumper the baritone who buzzes around pretending to be a minuscule insect the more engaging is the overall effect. Eisenstein in *Die Fledermaus* is another prototypically ham-fisted seducer – he goes one further even than Falstaff by attempting to seduce his own wife, whom he fails to recognize at a masked ball. The Duke of Urbino in *Eine Nacht in Venedig* (*A Night in Venice*), and Count Balduin von Zedlau in *Wiener Blut* (*Vienna Blood*), are two more examples of Straussian 'heroes' who spend the evening laying siege to various ladies and, Don Giovanni-like, failing dismally at each attempt. The character who comes closest to achieving his goal is that other arch-seducer from *Die Fledermaus*, the fatuous Alfred. He, being by profession an operatic tenor, has no doubts

---

*See bibliography.

about how to break down feminine resistance – you fill your would-be victim with champagne and then you sing to her. Had it not been for the untimely arrival of the prison governor, Colonel Frank, who knows how Act I might have ended?

Of all the soi-disant seducers in operetta, though, my personal favourite is Henri, the teenage naval cadet in Richard Heuberger's *Der Opernball* (*The Opera Ball*). His problem is that he believes himself to be 'un gran seduttore' when he is in fact not a seduc*er* but a seduc*ee*. To his intense excitement he receives an anonymous invitation, apparently from some mysterious aristocratic lady, to an assignation at the masked ball which is held every year in the Paris Opéra – no such thing has ever happened to him before. He is to present himself at midnight by the great clock, which he duly does, trembling with anticipation. A few moments later the lady arrives, heavily disguised – she is in reality Hortense, a pert young chambermaid – and great is his perturbation when this glamorous personage informs him that she has reserved a *chambre séparée*. There, she assures him, over an intimate champagne supper they can open their hearts to one another, and as the inexperienced youth begins to realize that one thing looks likely to lead to another he almost faints from a combination of cold feet and thumping heart. As Heuberger's infinitely seductive melody expands, however, so too does Henri's aplomb, until at last he is totally convinced that it is he, the man of the world, who is luring her, the defenceless female, into the *chambre séparée*.

Henri may be fooled, though we are not, as to who is the true seducer in that particular scenario; seduction is far from being a male preserve, so let us now turn our attentions to the female of the species. Operatic seductresses are not, on the whole, as deeply steeped in evil as are so many of their male equivalents. Some of them, certainly, would be uncomfortable people to have dealings with, and at the top of that list I would feel inclined to place Richard Strauss's Salome. She is one of those characters who are incapable of perfect realization, as Strauss himself recognized when he said that she required 'the voice of an Isolde in the body of a schoolgirl'. She also needs to be a dramatic soprano who is both willing and able to radiate erotic allure while performing the Dance of the Seven Veils, something which the original Salome, Marie Wittich, stoutly (in the circumstances an appropriate word) declined to attempt. 'I am', she said,

Maria Ewing as Salome, Covent Garden, 1988. Unlike Marie Wittich she had no qualms about unveiling herself in public.

'a respectable woman', 'Ich bin eine anständ'ge Frau',* and eventually the problem was solved by bringing on a dancer to perform the celebrated striptease. It is a solution which was still widely in use until quite recently and it certainly made the dance less embarrassing than it can occasionally become, but the sight of a chunky soprano disappearing behind one side of a screen and a slinky ballet dancer emerging moments later from behind the other also calls for a mammoth suspension of disbelief. Nowadays it is a matter of pride for any artist who sets her sights on the role of Salome to turn herself into a proficient terpsichorean, and it is per-haps no coincidence that in recent years the role has become the almost

---

*By an amusing coincidence this expression was just about to become one of the most familiar in the German language, as it is the title of a popular number in Lehár's *The Merry Widow*, which received its premiere in Vienna on 28 December 1905, three weeks after *Salome* had burst upon the scene in Dresden.

exclusive reserve of a certain type of very fit and athletic American soprano.

Salome is really a double-seductress. Her purpose in shedding her seven veils is to seduce Herod into granting her heart's desire, the head of John the Baptist, but before Herod has even made his first entrance Strauss devotes some of the most suggestively erotic music ever written – a description which is still valid after ninety years – to the scene in which the depraved young princess attempts to seduce John (Jokanaan) himself. Unfortunate girl – I feel that while some may be born depraved and others, like her mother Herodias, may achieve depravity, she has had depravity thrust upon her. With a nymphomaniac mother and a lecherous, fratricidal stepfather she cannot be said to have enjoyed the advantages of a stable family background, and it was bad luck for her that right at the moment of her sexual awakening a creature as fascinating as John the Baptist should have crossed her path. In one of Richard Strauss's later operas, *Arabella* (1933), we meet a young lady whom I would feel inclined to describe as opera's most practically minded seductress. This is Zdenka, younger sister of the eponymous heroine, and for reasons which are far-fetched even by operatic standards her parents bring her up and pass her off as a boy. The ostensible justification for this is that her father, the impoverished Count Waldner, cannot afford to 'bring out' two girls in Viennese society and the elder, Arabella, has the prior claim. The truth of the matter, I suspect, is that Strauss was always at his happiest writing for the soprano voice, and ever since the days of Mozart's Cherubino Germanic audiences have had a special partiality for the sight of shapely girls in men's attire. Be that as it may, there is assuredly more to little Zdenka than meets the eye. She is aware that a young officer named Matteo is smitten with her sister Arabella but that Arabella's inclinations lie elsewhere. She therefore surreptitiously passes Matteo a letter which purports to be an offer of an assignation from Arabella, and to contain the key to Arabella's hotel bedroom. In fact it is Zdenka's key, she having long ago formed a passion for Matteo, and so well does she play her role that when Matteo leaves her room again and finds out whose bed he has actually been sharing he professes himself altogether satisfied with the episode and he and Zdenka become engaged. A happy ending, then, to her machinations, but it is an unexpected way for a lady to behave, especially one so young.

Another of German opera's great seductresses who can, perhaps, like Salome be said to have been at least as much sinned against as sinning, is Alban Berg's Lulu. As in the case of *The Turn of the Screw* much is hinted at in this opera rather than stated. What was the true nature of Lulu's early dealings with the elderly newspaper editor Dr Schön? Was she his victim, or was he hers? What does the relationship between her and the tramp Schigolch consist of? Is he really her father or is he simply yet another moth who flutters round her flame? Her seductions take place in an atmosphere of vacuous detachment; they are fleeting episodes in which for some unspecified reason she seems obliged to indulge. There is scarcely a single male member of the cast who does not either lust after her, or marry her, or both, none of which seems to concern her very much. One aspect of this detachment of Lulu's provides my own most vivid memory of the opera's first British production.* It was mounted by the Welsh National Opera during the season of 1970/71, and I was making my debut with the company in the role of the young composer, Alwa. One of the hardest scenes I have ever had to perform was the final duet between Lulu and Alwa, during which he launches into a hymn to the glories of her anatomy, lying beside her on the floor and, as he dedicates a separate musical form to each of her limbs, exploring the area in question with his hands. I have no doubt that most male members of the public regarded this as an enviable task, especially in view of the fact that my Lulu was the altogether delectable young American soprano Carole Farley, and I would have agreed, had it not been for the scene's excruciating vocal and musical demands. There was one phrase for which, try as I might, I simply could not find the right note – the orchestra at that moment was playing every semitone in the scale except the one I needed – and eventually Carole, blessed with the gift of perfect pitch, offered to help me out. Thus it came about that in every performance, just as these steamy proceedings were reaching their climax, the great seductress lay back with an innocent smile on her face, humming a perfect C natural. I sometimes wondered what would happen to me if I should find myself singing the role elsewhere, but luckily I never did.

---

*The opera was still in its uncompleted form. The British premiere of the completed version took place at Covent Garden in 1981.

Most detached of operatic seductresses, Lulu lies back and lets it happen. Karen Armstrong with Erik Saedén as the tramp Schigolch.

It is only to be expected that when Venus, the goddess of love, makes her appearance on the operatic stage we will be treated to a rather special exposition of the art of seduction, and when the composer who presents her happens to be Richard Wagner we are unlikely to be disappointed. In the opening scene of *Tannhäuser* Venus is At Home to the minstrel of that name, and the bacchanale which she stages for his diversion features such exotic attractions as bathing naiads, reclining sirens and dancing nymphs. As if this were not enough, when Wagner revised the opera for Paris he also incorporated the Three Graces (not known for the modesty of their attire), a platoon of cupids and a generous supply of fauns and satyrs. Tannhäuser, however, like Aschenbach in *Death in Venice*, is an artist who has trouble reconciling the two sides of his nature, the Apollonian and the Dionysian; when he is with Venus he yearns for the life of his mortal peers and when he is with his mortal peers he infuriates them with his blasphemous ravings about the sensuous delights of life on the Venusberg. During the opening orgy he is in the former of these two moods. Venus, aware of his restlessness, piles on the pressure by summoning up a magic grotto and, to a ravishing accompaniment of divided strings, suggests that he and she should there surrender to the joys of love. As is, I think, only to be expected, when Tannhäuser, impervious to all the trouble she has taken, insists that what he really wants is to be allowed to go home Venus becomes extremely angry. German is a splendid language for invective, and with the words 'Zieh hin! Wahnbetörter!', more or less 'Be on your way, you lunatic!', Venus gives him a piece of her mind. This is no ordinary lovers' tiff, however, and when Tannhäuser plays his trump card by invoking the name of the Virgin Mary Venus and her whole entourage disappear magically from sight.*

If Tannhäuser is a complex character, what can we say of Kundry, the evil seductress in Wagner's last stage work, *Parsifal*? One of the most enigmatic figures in the whole of opera, Kundry is the woman who laughed at Christ on the cross and is now condemned to live for eternity playing a strange double role as temptress and harlot in the castle of the wicked magician Klingsor, and as slave and penitent in the neighbouring kingdom of the Holy Grail. It was she who seduced Amfortas, king of the knights of the Grail, as an indirect result of which he has suffered ever since from an agonizing wound in his side, a wound which nothing can heal, while year by year the brotherhood of knights sinks further and further into a state of leaderless torpor. When their longed-for rescuer Parsifal returns from a seemingly endless pilgrimage Klingsor sets Kundry to work – 'Der festeste fällt', he crows, 'sinkt er dir in die Arme', 'the most resolute falls when he sinks into your arms.' Kundry's method of breaking down Parsifal's resolve is an original one; she plays upon the guilt he feels for having deserted his mother and thus brought about her death. As her lips touch his, however, for the fatal kiss her seductive powers produce a very different result from that to which she is accustomed. In a flash the scales fall from his eyes, he realizes the fearful consequences of sinful longing and the price which Amfortas has had to pay

---

*Venus makes many appearances in opera, particularly in those of the baroque era, which were much given to divine personages descending from the sky. The least respectful treatment she ever received was predictably at the hands of Jacques Offenbach; in *Orpheus in the Underworld* she makes her first appearance tottering home to Olympus at crack of dawn, very much the worse for wear after a night on the tiles.

Marie Wittich (1868–1931) as Kundry at Bayreuth. Despite her Wagnerian physique she was also chosen to create the role of Salome at the Dresden Hofoper in 1905.

for yielding to Kundry as he himself almost has. She, aware that her erotic spell has failed her, indulges, like Venus before her, in a vicious spurt of anger, but when she summons Klingsor to her aid and he hurls at Parsifal the holy spear which, with Kundry's aid, he had previously stolen from Amfortas, the spear hovers in the air above Parsifal's head, Parsifal seizes it and Klingsor and his castle crumble to dust.

As we can see, there is nothing straightforward about Wagner's seductresses – like many of his other characters they are richly steeped in symbolism. If we turn, though, from the works of the formidable German to those of most French composers we find a gallery of seductresses who have not a jot of symbolism in their make-up – they are merely very, very sexy. The chromatic slitherings of Carmen's entrance song, for instance, the arrestingly provocative *habanera*, instantly establish that Bizet's gipsy girl is trouble on two legs. Fascinating, tantalizing and predatory, she puts

Grace Bumbry toys with her admirers: Carmen, *Salzburg, 1966.*

her cards right on the table. 'If I take a fancy to you watch out for your-self!' she sings, but the hapless Don José, although forewarned, turns out to be hopelessly unforearmed. One glance from her and he is on the slip-pery slope; it is a descent which leads to the destruction of them both. The comparative failure at its first appearance of an opera as compelling in every department as *Carmen* seems with hindsight to have been inexplic-able; it is one of the great tragedies of operatic history that Bizet never lived to see the piece on which he himself had pinned all his hopes triumph over its early critical rejection to be universally hailed as a masterpiece. Like so many masterpieces it was innovatory. Members of the chorus grumbled about being expected to act as individuals instead of just standing around in a block, members of the orchestra complained that parts of the score were unplayable, and most of the press found the plot too shocking to be suitable for public performance. They should be around today.

No less enticing than Carmen, and ultimately even more destructive, is Saint-Saëns's biblical temptress Dalila, better known in the Anglo-Saxon world as Delilah. Saint-Saëns always strikes me as one of the most remarkable figures in French music. An infant prodigy pianist who made his official debut at the age of ten in the Salle Pleyel playing concertos by Mozart and Beethoven, after which he offered as an encore to play by heart whichever of Beethoven's thirty-two piano sonatas the audience might prefer; an organist who was described by Liszt as 'the greatest in the world'; a scientist who wrote several highly regarded treatises on astronomy and designed his own telescope; champion of Bach, Handel and Mozart, none of whom were fully appreciated in French musical circles at that time; and, last but not least, a composer whose output spanned an unprecedented period, from his earliest songs, written when he was five, to his final chamber and piano pieces produced not long before his death eighty years later.* It is ironical that the principal ambition of this brilliant polymath was to succeed as an operatic composer, yet of his dozen operas *Samson et Dalila* was the only one to establish a place in the repertoire – and that had originally been conceived as an oratorio.

Moreover, even *Samson* had to wait seven long years before anyone would pluck up the courage to stage an opera whose story had been garnered straight from the Bible, and then it was not the director of one of the French opera houses who took the plunge, but Franz Liszt in Weimar. Thereafter *Samson* rapidly established itself as an international success and the title-roles became sought-after territory for leading dramatic singers; there are certainly few parts for a mezzo-soprano more rewarding than that of Delilah. The score's most famous number is her aria 'Mon coeur s'ouvre à ta voix', or 'Softly awakes my heart', and as the voluptuous melody entwines the luckless Samson in its seductive web it is little wonder that he becomes as powerless in Delilah's hands as Don José does

---

*One of Saint-Saëns's more esoteric distinctions was to become the first composer of note to provide music for a silent film, *The Assassination of the Duc de Guise*, in 1908.

in Carmen's. This is, however, but one of three great solos accorded to our lethal temptress. 'Amour! Viens aider ma faiblesse!', with which Delilah invokes the power of Love to assist her in her treacherous scheme, provides another powerful example of Saint-Saëns's skilful intermingling of vocal and instrumental resources for the creation of theatrical atmosphere; while in the hands of the right performer the first of the three, 'Printemps qui commence', can be as effective as either of the others. In my book *More Legendary Voices** I describe one particular recording of this passage as being possibly 'the most blatantly sexy piece of singing ever recorded by an operatic diva', and I feel no reason to revise my opinion. This is the version by that captivating Spanish artist Conchita Supervia,† and the fact that there is something kittenish about her vocal quality – she was not one of your monumental mezzos – only adds to the sensuality so vividly evoked by the composer. It is a performance drenched in eroticism.

Jules Massenet, six and a half years Saint-Saëns's junior, was another French composer who possessed a well-developed knack for the musical depiction of feminine allure. Not usually regarded as a musician of such exceptional attainments as Saint-Saëns he was nevertheless much more successful in selecting the right material for operatic treatment, and in the 1990s several of his pieces which had gradually fallen into neglect – *Don Quichotte*, for instance, and *Chérubin* – seem to be coming back into favour. One which has faded, however, from its previous popularity is *Thaïs*, the story of a courtesan so irresistible that the whole city of Alexandria has been, as the cenobite monk Athanaël sees it, seduced and corrupted by her lascivious goings-on. Alas, poor Athanaël, who persuades himself that he is seeking her out in order to recall her to the path of virtue and religious faith, recognizes too late that his obsession with her has its roots in a very much more basic instinct. In the course of converting her from her life of sin he falls irretrievably under her sexual spell, and as she ascends to heaven he is left below to wrestle with his own pri-

---

*See bibliography.
†In fact she recorded the aria twice. Her 1927 version, sung in Italian, can be heard on Lebendige Vergangenheit *CD 89023*, and her 1931 version, in the original French, on Nimbus *NI7836/7*. Both are equally spellbinding.

vate hell. The one passage in the score which is likely to be familiar to audiences today is that evocative orchestral interlude known as the 'Méditation', but it is very much to be hoped that the emergence of some glamorous soprano capable of following in the footsteps of the great stars of the past who delighted in playing the title-role – Sybil Sanderson, Mary Garden, Louise Edvina, Geraldine Farrar, and Maria Jeritza, to mention but a few – may lead to an overdue revival in the fortunes of *Thaïs*.

Possibly the most bizarre of all seduction scenes in the annals of French opera is that which occurs in Act III of Meyerbeer's *Robert le diable*. Robert, though he does not know it, is the son of a shady character named Bertram, one of those people who, like Kaspar in *Der Freischütz*, enjoy some special relationship with the Devil. It becomes vital to Bertram's plans that Robert should appropriate a certain holy cypress branch which grows above the tomb of Ste Rosalie in a dilapidated cloister. This sacrilegious deed must be performed by moonlight, and to lend Robert some moral support Bertram calls up from their graves the ghosts of all those nuns who, in their lifetimes, had broken their vows of chastity. A right numerous and spirited bunch these nuns turn out to be; and when Robert's determination appears to waver they dance around him, led by their abbess, with many a seductive suggestion, sex, drink and gambling being the main items which are apparently theirs to offer. Thus encouraged he seizes the branch, whereupon there is a mighty clap of thunder and (to the public's deep disappointment, I feel sure) these jovial shades disperse.

I have left my favourite seductress to the end. In the novel by Abbé Prévost, and in the two operas by Massenet and Puccini, the figure of Manon Lescaut is one which stirs my sympathy. With Manon her seductiveness is not a calculated means to an end, as it is with Delilah, nor is it a dangerous game which she happens to enjoy playing, as is the case with Carmen. It is simply one of Manon's little weaknesses, to be classed alongside her love of fine clothes and expensive jewellery. She never intends any harm to young des Grieux, things just work out that way, and if he was a lost man from the moment when his path crossed hers that was not really her fault, was it? She cannot quite remain faithful to him – apart from anything else he has no money – but neither can she quite let him go. In other words, where some operatic seductresses emerge as monsters

An irresistible Manon.
Victoria de los Angeles
prepares for action,
Covent Garden, 1950.

Manon is nothing worse than fallibly human. In our enlightened age I would never dare to say 'Frailty, thy name is woman!' unless Shakespeare had said it first, but had Hamlet had Manon in mind I would understand why he felt the way he did.

The funny thing is that in the case both of *Carmen* and of the two Manon operas the real protagonist is not the female figure of the title so much as the male figure who falls victim to her. The real tragedies are the tragedies of Don José and of the Chevalier des Grieux; they are the characters who undergo a dramatic transformation, while Carmen and Manon remain what they have always been, catalysts for another's destruction.* In the Puccini opera, *Manon Lescaut*, it is in the Act II duet starting with

---

*It is interesting to note that Prévost's novel is in fact entitled *Histoire du Chevalier des Grieux et de Manon Lescaut*. As far as an opera is concerned ladies' names, it seems, are best for the box-office.

the words 'Tu, tu amore? Tu?' that we see Manon's fatal fascination at work. She has left des Grieux in order to be installed as the mistress of an elderly nobleman, but during the old man's absence from home des Grieux arrives to reproach Manon for her infidelity. She admits her fault, but surely des Grieux can see that she has done it all for him? All these riches, all this luxury, 'Tutto è per te', 'it is all for you.' 'Son forse della Manon d'un giorno meno piacente e bella?' she asks – 'perhaps I am less pleasing and beautiful than the Manon of a little while back?' To which, with all the passion of which Puccini was such a master, des Grieux replies 'O tentatrice! È questo l'antico fascino che m'accieca!', 'O temptress! This is the old fascination which is blinding me.' It is a tremendous scene,* the fulcrum of the opera which first placed Puccini firmly on the operatic map, but even so it takes second place in my personal affections to the equivalent passage in Massenet's *Manon*.

In Massenet's version of the story des Grieux's irrevocable capitulation occurs in Act III Scene 2, set in the seminary at St Sulpice. Des Grieux, who is intent on taking holy orders, has just preached his first sermon, but we soon find out that he still has some way to go before he can achieve inner peace; when he is left alone he delivers himself of the aria 'Ah! fuyez, douce image', 'Ah, flee, sweet image!', an impassioned plea that he should be freed from the entrancing visions of Manon which still haunt his mind. The very opposite occurs – Manon appears in person and once again 'the old fascination blinds him'. In the course of this chapter I have referred to numerous heady examples of the power of seduction expressed in musical terms, but I know of none more compelling than the melody with which Manon breaks down the last bastions of des Grieux's faltering resolve. 'N'est-ce plus ma main que cette main presse?' she murmurs, 'N'est-ce plus ma voix?' – 'Is it not still *my* hand which yours is pressing? Is it not still *my* voice?' 'Ah! regarde moi!' she continues, 'N'est-ce plus Manon?' – 'Ah, look at me! Am I no longer Manon?'

The melody is gentle, suggestive and cajoling. There is no hint of aggression or of evil in it: this is the siren voice of the 'eternal feminine',

---

*Anyone interested in the crème de la crème of Puccini singing would be well advised to listen to this scene with Jussi Björling as des Grieux on RCA Victor *GD 60573*.

soothing, all-pervasive, irresistible. If Manon could have encountered Don Giovanni which of them, I wonder, would have gained the upper hand?

2

Thirsty Work

Ah, make the most of what we yet may spend,
Before we too into the Dust descend;
Dust into Dust, and under Dust, to lie,
Sans Wine, sans Song, sans Singer, and – sans End!

Edward Fitzgerald
The Rubáiyát of Omar Khayyám

Poets are much given to emphasizing the interrelationship between wine and song, and they are indeed prime factors in an easily traceable chain of cause and effect – singing creates thirst, thirst is quenched by wine, wine leads to merriment, merriment leads to song. Not all song, of course, needs to be of the operatic variety, but opera and wine do have many characteristics in common; they are both to be counted amongst the good things of life, they are both of a heady and intoxicating nature, both are capable of a significant impact on their consumers' emotions, and both, at their best, have a regrettable tendency to cost a great deal of money. The connection, however, goes deeper than this. Thirst appears to create a mystical union between singers and their public – to judge from the eagerness with which audiences head for the bar during the interval, listening to opera seems almost as thirst-inducing an activity as singing in it. During an average opera evening at Covent Garden in the summer months the catering department of the Royal Opera House expects to work its way through four or five dozen bottles of champagne, five or six dozen of white wine, and half a dozen bottles of spirits, plus ten times as much soft drink as they would have needed a decade ago. During the winter months the picture understandably changes. The inner man requires a warmth which even music cannot provide, the demand for white wine declines and sales of red wine and coffee register a strong upward trend.

One intriguing point is that on ballet evenings, whether in winter or in summer, the sale of champagne falls off dramatically, possibly indicating that opera possesses a greater power for relieving its supporters of any such pedestrian instinct as thrift, but more probably, I suspect, reflecting the higher status of opera as a vehicle for business entertainment. At Glyndebourne, that other great Mecca of corporate sponsorship, it is impossible to analyse the intake of alcohol as at least half the audience provide their own, but the lawn during the long dinner interval is habit-

Opera as a social event: Glyndebourne, 1939.

ually enlivened by the popping of important-sounding corks, and to many people a Glyndebourne evening unaccompanied by at least one well-chosen vintage would scarcely be a Glyndebourne evening. As regular patrons learn with time it is advisable on these occasions to avoid the heavier styles of wine, because one inevitable consequence of too rich a feast, especially during a heatwave, is an increase in the number of nodding heads thereafter. My own head, I have to confess, has been known to feature amongst the nodders – not for nothing does the Theatre Director La Roche open his role in Richard Strauss's *Capriccio* with the words 'Bei sanfter Musik schläft sichs am besten', 'to gentle music one can sleep one's best' – but I comfort myself with the thought that at Glyndebourne there is a noble precedent. When I was an undergraduate and first becoming seriously involved in the world of opera I had the good fortune to be invited to numerous performances by Glyndebourne's founder, old Mr John Christie. I would be placed beside him in the family's box, where the only duty imposed on me in return for this generosity was to ensure that during the second half of the performance even if he were to snooze he should do so inaudibly.

There are, of course, many operas in which wine is an essential ingredient not only in the interval but also during the action. Sometimes it is merely as an adjunct to a meal. Don Giovanni, for instance, shortly before his departure to a destination so hot that it is hard to imagine any drink that would be of use to him, washes down his supper with an 'eccelente marzimino', made from a type of vine which, under its modern spelling of Marzemino, still features prominently amongst the wines of Trentino in Northern Italy; while in the second act of *Tosca* Baron Scarpia, whose 'poor dinner' is so regrettably interrupted by Cavaradossi's screams from the torture-chamber, prefers a 'vin di Spagna', a sip of which he is gracious enough to offer the victim's beloved 'per rincorarvi' – 'to revive your spirits'. This will have been a top-of-the-market Rioja or Navarra, one must assume – the sybaritic Scarpia would be scarcely likely to have settled for your run-of-the-mill Spanish Red – whereas the wine with which the penniless poet Rodolfo revives the ailing Mimì during their first encounter in *La bohème* is likely to have been something of an altogether humbler nature. It was certainly strong enough to do the trick, though. Mimì restricts herself to a more than modest intake; 'poco, poco,'

The most vicious of operatic wine lovers. Henri Albers (1866–1925) as Baron Scarpia.

she insists, and in any case she is only allowed three beats of 'Andante moderato' in which to drink it, but it brings her fainting fit to an impressively rapid conclusion, giving her the strength to leave the room, blow out her candle, come back in again, drop her key, sing an aria and steal the tenor's heart, all within a dozen pages.

Another opera in which Bacchus is called upon to accelerate Cupid's work is Verdi's *La traviata*. As the chorus expresses it, 'le cure segrete fuga sempre l'amico licor', which can be approximately rendered as 'the quickest cure for secret sorrows is a drop of the right stuff', and certainly the shy and hesitant Alfredo becomes a different fellow after he has been persuaded to lead the company in one of opera's catchiest drinking songs. Here again we are left in ignorance of the actual type of liquor which is under offer, but as the hostess, Violetta, is a Parisian *poule de luxe* it seems safe enough to assume that her guests would long since have turned elsewhere for their entertainment if she were in the habit of providing anything less than a respectable marque of champagne. It is certainly champagne which lubricates that other celebrated display of vanishing inhibitions, the finale to Act II of Johann Strauss's *Die Fledermaus*.* 'Let all pay homage to the King of Wines,' the company sings, 'King Champagne the first'; and so powerful is the monarch's sway that when the philandering Gabriel von Eisenstein finds his various amorous indiscretions coming home to roost, he is able to shrug off all personal responsibility. 'The champagne is to blame for everything,' he explains – and gets away with it. The same somewhat tendentious plea is put forward at the end of another Strauss operetta, *Wiener Blut*, by Graf Balduin von Zedlau, Ambassador from the German province of Reuss-Schleiz-Greiz to the Congress of Vienna, when he is sufficiently maladroit to be caught by his wife *and* his mistress in dalliance with a sexy shop-girl; though in this instance an even more potent excuse is eventually settled on than the influence of champagne – that of Viennese Blood.

Needless to say, composers of Verdi's and Strauss's skills had no difficulty in setting the racy events of their various party scenes to music which sweeps the audience along with its gaiety and panache; for a more detailed musical depiction of the workings of alcohol on the human system we should turn to that matchless late flowering of Verdi's genius, the score of *Falstaff*. When the curtain rises on Act III it reveals a man with as jaundiced a view as it is possible to imagine of the entire human condition. Sir John Falstaff, after setting out in his most fantastic finery to woo the lovely Alice Ford, has ended up being dumped in the River Thames in an outsized basket of dirty linen. He is cold, he is wet, his faith in his fellow creatures is at its lowest ebb – until the landlord of the Garter Inn brings him a tankard of mulled wine. 'Let's mix a little wine with all that Thames water,' Falstaff sings, downing the life-giving draught, and the strings depict for us in miraculous fashion the fat knight's sensations as once again warmth and optimism start coursing through his veins. While he muses on the wondrous speed with which wine manages to rise from the lips to the brain, bringing light to one's eye and bathing one's thoughts in a golden glow, a soft trill is to be heard gently suffusing the orchestral accompaniment. Gradually it swells with Falstaff's burgeoning

---

*The most inebriated of all the principals in *Fledermaus*, the jailer Frosch, never gets his hands onto the champagne. The secret of his relentless bonhomie lies in a flask of slivowitz.

Mulled wine restores the fat knight's humour. Donald Maxwell as Verdi's Falstaff, Welsh National Opera, 1993 (dir. Peter Stein).

vigour until it reaches a triumphant fortissimo, filling the whole opera house with the old man's renascent *joie de vivre*. As the critic Ernest Newman put it, 'we seem positively to see the new life within him rising from a faint trickle to a mighty flood.'

Sir John's mulled wine is likely to have been some form of claret, rather than the sack, or sherry, which was his staple diet, and though claret clearly had the power to make *him* feel better disposed towards mankind in general there is another operatic drinking scene in which it inspires less charitable thoughts towards one section of mankind in particular. When Captain Vere in Benjamin Britten's *Billy Budd* invites the First Lieutenant and the Sailing Master of HMS *Indomitable* to join him in his cabin for a chat about the conduct of the war against France he gingers up their somewhat faltering conversation with a couple of toasts, passing round

The officers of HMS Indomitable enjoy a drink and a chat. Captain Vere (the author) Mr Redburn (Julian Moyle) and Mr Flint (Brian Drake) in Michael Geliot's production of Billy Budd, Welsh National Opera, 1972.

the table one of those splendidly reassuring flat-bottomed ship's decanters. The first toast, as the officers expect, is to 'The King! God bless him!', and in no time these two bluff sea-dogs, normally so in awe of their scholarly captain, start to let their hair down. 'Don't like the French,' declares Lt Redburn, 'their notions don't suit us, nor their ideas.' 'Don't like the French,' agrees Mr Flint, 'don't like their bowing and scraping, don't like their hoppity skippity ways.' There is a moment of embarrassment when the Captain urges them both to refill their glasses, this time in order to toast the French, but great is his guests' relief when the second half of the toast turns out to be 'Down with them!' The whole scene has been conceived with marvellous cleverness both by the librettists and the composer; within a dozen pages the virtues and limitations of these three protagonists have been subtly revealed, and I fancy that Captain Vere would have spotted the irony, though the other two would not, in the fact that all this francophobia is washed down with a fine French wine.*

Not every operatic wine-bibber enjoys such heartening effects as old Sir John Falstaff or the officers of the *Indomitable*. Turiddu in Mascagni's *Cavalleria rusticana*, for instance, lives (briefly) to regret his over-indulgence. His drinking song, 'Viva il vino spumeggiante', is driven by a sense of desperation as he becomes ever more aware that his infatuation with the lovely Lola is likely to lead him onto the point of her husband's avenging knife. This time there's no doubt as to the nature of the wine in question; it is one of those fiery Sicilian reds which Turiddu himself describes to his mother as 'generoso', thus displaying a succinctness which certain professional wine-writers might do well to emulate. 'Troppi bicchieri ne ho traccanati', 'I knocked back too many glasses of it,' he rue-fully observes before going out to meet his adversary in single combat. He does not return, and as the alcohol content of Sicilian 'vino da tavola' often reaches 16 per cent or more he probably never knew what hit him.

Turiddu's is a self-induced disaster, but very often in opera it is the wicked baritone who uses the lure of drink to engineer the tenor's down-fall. When that arch-villain Iago turns to plotting the destruction of the luckless Cassio in Verdi's *Otello* he plays upon what Shakespeare describes as his victim's 'very poor and unhappy brains for drinking'. This time Verdi comes up with a Brindisi which is as creepy and insidious as Alfredo's in *La traviata* was boisterous and merry, the slithering chro-matics on the cry 'Beva, beva!', 'Drink, drink!', sounding more like a threat than an invitation. Running Iago close for sheer nastiness of pur-pose, and also using a drinking song to promote his evil designs, is Kaspar, one of the foresters in Weber's *Der Freischütz*. He is in league with the forces of darkness and he is intent on corrupting his colleague Max, for whom things are not going well. Poor Max, confident until recently of winning the hand of the fair Agathe by defeating all comers in a shooting contest, has suddenly lost the ability to hit even the proverbial barn door, and Kaspar, who spots him trying to console himself with a tankard of beer, berates him for wasting his time on such a lowly tipple. Wine is what

---

*My enjoyment of Tim Albery's widely admired production of *Billy Budd* for the English National Opera in 1988 was somewhat dented by the fact that this partic-ular scene went for nothing, the officers sitting in a meaningless row, as if in a dentist's waiting-room.

Max needs, declares Kaspar, and damn the expense – but what the unfortunate fellow actually gets is wine laced with an unspecified additive from a little flask which Kaspar keeps in his pocket. This inexplicably enables Max to bring down an eagle of unprecedented proportions which has been hovering like a speck in the sky far out of any normal rifle's range, a bull's-eye which in turn brings down a heap of trouble onto Max's head.

Another opera which puts up a strong case in support of Kaspar's dismissive views on beer as a drowner of sorrows is Janáček's *The Cunning Little Vixen*. Janáček is a composer who, like so many others of startlingly original genius, has been slow to establish himself as a popular favourite outside his own native country, but whose name is now happily less inclined than it was to be regarded by the general public as synonymous with 'difficult modern music'. As far as Great Britain is concerned this welcome change can be largely attributed to a series of productions by the Sadler's Wells Company in the 1950s and 1960s, often under the proselytizing baton of that great Janáček champion Sir Charles Mackerras, and to a subsequent series of brilliant co-productions for the Welsh National Opera and Scottish Opera with David Pountney as their director and Maria Björnson as their designer. One of the *Vixen*'s principal themes is the habitual tendency of human beings to become bogged down by their frequently imaginary problems while the inhabitants of the natural world, the animals and the insects, simply follow their instincts and fulfil their humble cycle of birth, life and death, a pattern of regeneration as clearly preordained as that of the changing seasons. The spiritual numbness of the humans in the piece (always excepting Harasta the poacher) is achingly expressed by Janáček in the course of two scenes set in the local pub. With every glass of beer that they consume the Forester, the Schoolmaster and the Priest become more and more negative, the Priest dwelling on an incident from his past when he was accused of molesting a girl, the Schoolmaster pining for the gorgeous Terynka, to whom he has never even summoned up the courage to address himself, and the Forester obsessed with thoughts of the vixen which he had caught as a cub and which has outwitted him and escaped. Meanwhile Harasta, like the animals a creature of instinct, shoots the vixen and marries Terynka . . .

The degree to which Janáček's three protagonists lack the native hue of

Beer fails to relieve the gloom. John Dobson, Robert Tear, Thomas Allen and Gwynne Howell in The Cunning Little Vixen, *Covent Garden, 1990.*

resolution cannot, of course, be entirely blamed on their drinking habits, but just in case *Freischütz* and *The Cunning Little Vixen* may appear to be damaging to beer's reputation as a life-enhancing beverage, I am happy to say that there is another opera which makes worthy amends. *Martha*, by Friedrich von Flotow, despite the popularity of the tenor aria 'Ach, so fromm' (better known by its Italian title of 'M'appari'), is rather out of fashion nowadays,* which is a pity, as it contains a great deal of delightful music (some of it less superficial than one might suppose) and at the same time presents an illuminating picture of us Britons as other people saw us back in the mid-nineteenth century, and to a certain extent still do. The role of the honest young farmer Lyonel who turns out to be the long-

---

*The only professional production which I can remember in Britain in recent years was one by Nicholas Hytner for the New Sadler's Wells Opera Company in the mid-1980s. Hytner did not quite trust the piece to work on its own terms, and by making it excessively jokey robbed it of some of its charm, but it provided a nice night out all the same.

A classic Met cast of 1916 recalls the joys of life in Merrye Olde England. Margarete Ober, Giuseppe de Luca, Enrico Caruso and Frieda Hempel in Martha.

lost son of the banished Earl of Derby used to be a particular favourite both of Caruso's and of Gigli's – as many an old photograph reveals, anyone looking less like a typical English aristocrat than those two resplendent tenors would be truly hard to imagine – but it falls to the bass, Lyonel's sturdy and down-to-earth foster-brother Plumkett [*sic*] to sing the praises of British beer. The brand which he especially favours is dark brown porter ale, the beefy elixir which enables John Bull to keep his fists up on land and sea despite the blanket of fog under which the British nation is popularly supposed to spend three-quarters of its existence. 'Hurra! dem Hopfen, hurra! dem Malz' sings Plumkett, 'Hurrah for hops and hurrah for malt!' – though in real life I have yet to meet a German who does not vastly prefer his own national product to anything brewed in Britain.

Operatic heroes are not, of course, under any obligation to stick to one form of drink or another. It does not have to be a straight choice between

The butcher's boy and the baker's daughter lace Albert Herring's lemonade with a fatal dose of rum. Frederick Sharp and Nancy Evans in the original production at Glyndebourne, June 1947.

wine and beer, and as a mixer of tipples it would be hard to beat Benjamin Britten's Albert Herring. A guileless Suffolk lad, securely tied to his mother's apron strings, he is chosen to be King of the May in Loxford's traditional festival because there is not a single young lady in the entire town of sufficiently spotless reputation to become May Queen. Unfortunately Sid, the local wag, hits on the bright idea of helping Albert cope with his shyness at the presentation ceremony by lacing his lemonade with rum. Later in the evening, alone in his mother's fruit and vegetable shop, Albert muses on the qualities of that heavenly elixir – 'But *Oh!* the taste of that lemonade! Wonder how it's made?' It was evident, too, that the winsome Nancy, who had never taken a blind bit of notice of him up till now, was beginning to look at him in a manner he had never experienced before. 'Why did she stare', he sings, 'each time I looked up at her?'; and it was one of Britten's priceless gifts, not shared by many composers of the post-war period, to be able to crown these decisive moments with the kind of melody which haunts the listener's ear. For Albert the penny drops at last. There is more to life than slaving away at his mother's beck and call; chaps like Sid don't let other people mess up their lives. In his pocket are the twenty-five sovereigns which were his prize for being King of the May – and off he goes to blue as much of it as he can on a pub-crawl of Rabelaisian indulgence. Starting with a glass of old-and-mild in The Dog and Duck he progresses to a tumbler of naval rum chased with whisky and gin, after which he starts a fight and is chucked into the gutter to sober up. Having done so he decides to sample the wares of The Horse and Groom, which rapidly results in his reintro-duction to the gutter. The upshot of it all is that when he comes home in the morning he is a new man, able to revolutionize his existence with the unprecedented words 'That'll do, Mum!'. Thanks to a humble tot of rum, in one glorious night of debauchery Albert has found independence.

Nemorino gets his courage up. Gigli at the age of 62, Teatro San Carlo, Naples.

A comparable figure to Albert is the peasant lad Nemorino in that most touching of Italian comic operas, Donizetti's *L'elisir d'amore*. Not quite such a downtrodden figure as Albert at the beginning of the piece, he is nevertheless totally out of his league when he tries to compete with the hectoring Sergeant Belcore for the hand of the local belle, Adina. Besides her stunning looks Adina has had an education; she can read, and ironically this is what leads to the solution of Nemorino's problem. He hears her reading aloud to her girlfriends the fascinating story of 'la crudele Isotta', 'the cruel Isolde',* who treated the love-sick Tristan with disdain until the intervention of a magical love potion bound her to him for life. It so happens that on the very same day a garrulous quack named Dr Dulcamara visits the village peddling potions of his own. They will deal with every affliction known to mankind, he declares, their beneficial properties extending from the extermination of bugs and rodents to the restoration of a youthful glow to cheeks now wrinkled with age. When Nemorino asks him whether he stocks the elixir which did such wonders for Queen Isolde it turns out that Dulcamara does indeed personally distil it. Handing Nemorino a small bottle of cheap Bordeaux he warns him that it needs twenty-four hours to take effect – by which time the good doctor will be out of reach – and down Nemorino's throat it goes. As in the case of Albert and Nancy, Adina is amazed by the sudden air of self-confidence which Nemorino displays. Her interest is aroused, and one thing leads to another, leaving even Dulcamara convinced that there must be more to his elixir than meets the eye.

When we turn from imaginary magic potions to the real thing many an opera presents itself for consideration. The herbal recipe employed by Oberon and Puck, and so exquisitely depicted in musical terms in Britten's *A Midsummer Night's Dream*, sadly fails to qualify as a potion, because it is squeezed onto the victims' eyelids, not poured down their throats, but in another of the Shakespearean operas, Gounod's *Roméo et Juliette*, the protagonists drink deep, and with very dire results. Seldom

---

*It is really more correct to refer to her in English as Iseult or Iseut, but I feel that Wagner's spelling, at least as far as opera-goers are concerned, is the one under which she will be most familiar.

Opposite *The author, as old mad Hauk, enjoys himself with three celebrated interpreters of Emilia Marty in Janáček's* The Makropoulos Case. *Elisabeth Söderström, Welsh National Opera, 1979 (dir. David Pountney).*

Bottom left *Josephine Barstow, English National Opera, 1989 (dir. David Pountney).*

Bottom right *Anja Silja, Glyndebourne, 1995 (dir. Nikolaus Lehnhoff).*

have good intentions gone more spectacularly awry than those of Frère Laurent, he who administers the fatal sleeping-draught, and though in the opera the sequence of drinking, sleeping, waking and dying has been changed from that in the play – the very worthy objective is to have the two lovers both conscious at the same time so that they can sing a final love duet – the poor Friar is still left with a lot of explaining to do.

Although Juliette actually ends by stabbing herself it is unquestionably the taking of the sleeping-draught that has led to her dying so young, but as if to underline the wide range of such nostrums available in the world of opera we encounter in Janáček's penultimate masterpiece, *The Makropoulos Case*, a potion with exactly the opposite effect. Its heroine, an opera star named Emilia Marty, is no less than 337 years old, having had an elixir of youth forcibly tried out on her when she was sixteen, on the orders of Emperor Rudolf II in Prague. Based on a play by the Czech dramatist Karel Čapek the opera is a fascinating (and occasionally humorous) study of the emotional state of someone whose journey through life has become meaningless, precisely because it is a journey without a destination – the normal destination of death. Feeling that the ageing process has at last begun to take a grip on her Emilia returns to Prague, where the formula is hidden, to take a second dose of the elixir. During the course of the opera, however, she becomes aware that what she really craves is not a further extension of her barren and burdensome existence, but rather that it should be allowed to terminate. Richard Strauss once said that only first-rate composers know how to end their operas, and I would be inclined to consider Janáček, alongside Puccini, Britten and Strauss himself, as one of the greatest of the twentieth century's writers of final scenes. Even he, though, seldom brought down a curtain more masterfully than with Emilia's last great monologue; as the only existing copy of the formula goes up in flames she herself turns at last to dust and ashes.

I often feel that men of old must have known a great deal more than we do nowadays about the properties of certain herbs; how else would magic potions have become such an essential feature of ancient myths and sagas? Be that as it may they are without doubt a godsend for operatic librettists, enabling the action to take all manner of unlikely twists and turns – they are the oil, as it were, that lubricates the plot's machinery – and no one made more effective use of them than Richard Wagner. In the first act of *Die Walküre*, for instance, Sieglinde has no trouble at all in putting her husband Hunding so soundly to sleep that she and her incestuous twin Siegmund are able to indulge in one of opera's most extended and ecstatic duets, fortissimo high A naturals and all, without the slightest fear of waking him. In *Siegfried* the most magical liquid is not in fact a herbal potion, but the blood of the dragon Fafner – Siegfried licks it off his fingers and it saves his life by enabling him to understand not only the warning song of the Forest Bird, but also the murderous intent behind the blandishments of the treacherous Mime.* In *Götterdämmerung*, however, we are back with a very handy double-action hallucinatory potion, presumably of herbal origin. One draught of it causes Siegfried to fall instantly in love with Gutrune and, as if that were not enough, to become totally oblivious of his newly acquired bride Brünnhilde, who is patiently waiting back home behind a protective wall of impenetrable fire.

Powerful as these potions clearly are, none of the Wagnerian magic drinks has etched itself more deeply into musical history than that which Isolde's faithful attendant Brangäne hands to her mistress in the first act of *Tristan und Isolde*. Wagner scholars differ in the extent to which they attribute the composer's source of inspiration for *Tristan* to his infatuation with Mathilde, the wife of his wealthy patron Otto Wesendonck, or to his encounter with the philosophy of Arthur Schopenhauer. Both doubtless played their part in bringing about a frame of mind in which Wagner felt out of sorts with the extrovert Siegfried, in whose creation he was currently immersed, and in impelling him to set aside his work on *Der Ring* and turn to a totally different tonal and emotional realm, that of *Tristan*. The fact that he was living as the Wesendoncks' guest and neighbour (in Enge, just outside Zürich) made even Wagner, not normally hesitant in such matters, feel that his chances of consummating his latest passion were slender – a source of frustration which accorded well with Schopenhauer's pessimistic theory that as ideals and the chance of their fulfilment are usually separated by a yawning gulf, the only possibility of

---

*I long ago made a mental note not to drink any dragon's blood – the gift of hearing what people are thinking rather than what they are saying is one I am happy to do without.

Victim of a love potion. Ludwig Schnorr von Carolsfeld (1836–1865) created the role of Tristan, and died six weeks later.

happiness lies in the suppression of all aspirations and desires. A couple of years before starting work on *Tristan* Wagner wrote in a letter to Franz Liszt that as he himself had never enjoyed the true happiness which love can bring – he was presumably careful to hide the letter from his current wife Minna – he wished to erect a monument to 'this most beautiful of dreams', and to do so in the form of an opera in which love should be totally sated. A longing as all-consuming as that which takes possession of Tristan and Isolde, however, transcends the possibility of human fulfilment and is only able to find its ultimate expression in the perfect solution of death ('Sich sehnen und sterben'); and for the weaving of so complex an emotional web Wagner found the tenets of contemporary musical theory quite simply too constricting. With the famous 'Tristan chord', F, B, D sharp, G sharp, in the third bar of the Prelude we are on our way towards the new world of atonality.

I wonder if I am alone in feeling that there is an element of cheating in this whole Tristan and Isolde business? A love which has inspired one of the most compelling of all operas, which has been the catalyst for so revolutionary a development in Western musical technique and which, via an unprecedented number of learned commentaries, has launched upon the world a greater flood of German compound words than any other operatic theme that I can think of ('egoistischsinnliches Besitzergreifen-wollen', 'Seelenzerstörende Selbstverklärungserscheinungen', and many another mellifluous gem) should surely be a love whose flame has been lit by natural causes – eye should meet eye, heart should speak to heart, the combustion should be spontaneous. The Tristan–Isolde *coup de foudre*, however, is drug-induced, and I do not think that that is quite fair. It is true that as a result of past events too involved to be expounded here they *are* already in love, but neither of them has admitted the fact, and when they drink to one another out of the cup which Brangäne brings them they believe themselves to be drinking poison. It is, in other words, sup-posed to be a suicide pact, but Brangäne, unable to face the prospect of losing her beloved mistress, hands them instead a love philtre which Isolde's mother had thoughtfully provided in order to make Isolde's impending marriage to Tristan's uncle, the elderly King Mark, less dreary than it otherwise might have been. C'est magnifique, mais (in my opinion at least) ce n'est pas l'amour.*

On the subject of poison, I wish that librettists would have introduced the stuff more often, because when it comes to killing off a singer there is quite simply no more user-friendly method. The best actor in the world cannot make the extensive final utterances of a character such as Massenet's Werther dramatically convincing when he has just shot him-

---

*Apropos my earlier reference to *L'elisir d'amore*, in the *Viking Opera Guide* John Deathridge makes the interesting point that 'Wagner probably knew the opera, as it was in the repertoire of the Dresden Court Opera when he was conductor there in the 1840s'. I scarcely imagine that it could have been the frivolous Adina who struck the first spark in Wagner's imagination, steering his footsteps towards the work which was to stretch his formidable talents to their musical and emotional limits, but it is a nice idea.

self point blank with a pistol, whereas after the ingestion of a slow-acting poison one can sing one's adieux, addios and leb' wohls as often as one feels inclined, without raising a titter. I am of course aware that it was Goethe, not Massenet's librettists, who originally decided on a bullet for the sorrowful Werther, but just now we encountered an example of Shakespeare being improved upon for operatic purposes, and if you can tinker with him surely you can tinker with anyone. Nor is the time factor the only advantage to a well-chosen poison; there is also the fact that it can be cancelled out. A person cannot become un-shot or de-stabbed, but when Donizetti's Lucrezia Borgia finds that her husband has poisoned Gennaro (her son by a previous marriage, though he himself is not aware of the fact) she promptly administers an antidote and he is up and about in no time, singing as lustily as ever. Admittedly it is only a reprieve. When Lucrezia livens up a ball in the second act by wiping out every male on the guest list she inadvertently re-poisons Gennaro along with the others. Again she offers him an antidote, but this time, having discovered meanwhile whose son he is, he prefers not to take it.

And so to the question which I think I must have been asked by members of the public more often than any other except 'Do you sing in your bath?' – 'When opera singers drink on stage what is it that they are drinking?' Well, there is no hard and fast rule about this; different opera houses favour different harmless liquids. To simulate red wine Ribena is the best solution, and it is interesting to note that no other red currant drink will do – only Ribena, diluted to the correct degree, produces exactly the right colour. For white wine one usually encounters some version of apple juice, though in the early days of my career on the continent of Europe I remember occasionally coming up against that old theatrical standby cold weak tea, and not enjoying it. For beer the commonest recipe is burnt sugar mixed with water, which funnily enough is not as disgusting as it sounds, and as for champagne several prominent manufacturers offer a stage version of their own. It bears no resemblance to their genuine product, being nothing more than a form of ginger beer, which at least makes some sort of pop when opened on stage and puts up a reasonable pretence of fizzing in the glass. The bottles and the labels, though, are indistinguishable from the real thing, making the whole operation a feasible form of advertising for the company in question. Moët et Chandon, I would

Opera's most frustrated drinker. The author as Herodes in Salome, *English National Opera North, 1985 (dir. Joachim Herz).*

say, emerge as the brand leaders, but I remember that when I directed *The Merry Widow* at Sadler's Wells some years ago I enquired whether we might, as a form of indirect sponsorship, be supplied free of charge by that most merriment-inducing of all widows, la Veuve Clicquot – a suggestion which met with the importer's full co-operation.

In any case, whatever the liquid on offer, there are moments when we singers are heartily grateful for a production which obliges us to pick up a glass and drain it. Singing is undeniably thirsty work, the mouth is often open, the air in certain opera houses can be terribly dry, and even in comparatively static pieces the combination of the bright lights and the heavy costumes can be very dehydrating. It is no problem if you are singing a role which allows you the occasional exit to the wings, but when you are on stage for the whole of an act, perhaps in midsummer and in some intemperate part of the world, the all-important throat can become parched. In energetic pieces such as the Viennese operettas, where one is often called upon during a ballroom scene to round off a love duet with a brisk waltz or even a csárdás, the appearance of the host with some such words as 'Now, my dear Count, how about a glass of champagne?' can be very welcome indeed, and one slips up a quick prayer of thanks for the thoughtfulness of the author. The most perversely *un*accommodating scene in my personal repertoire occurs, though, not in an operetta but in an opera, Richard Strauss's *Salome*. Herod, who has been throwing himself around in a state of feverish agitation for quite a while, and who usually has the burden of a heavy cloak and a great thick wig to contend with, sings at one point 'Oh! oh! Bringt Wein! Mich dürstet', 'Oh! oh! Bring wine! I'm thirsty!' A splendid idea, especially as Herod has already announced that the vintage on that particular evening's menu is 'a delicious wine, sent me by Caesar himself' – but alas, when it is brought Strauss does not give his tenor time to drink it.

Another favourite question is 'Do you ever take a little nip to bolster your courage before you go on stage?' My answer to this has to be that in thirty-five years in the opera business I have known perhaps a couple of dozen singers who have trodden that particular primrose path, but generally speaking they have not lasted long. A singer's nerves are there for a purpose, they key you up and set the adrenalin flowing. If you are so scared of going on stage that you need an artificial stimulant there is something wrong; one little whisky soon becomes two, two become half a bottle, and then you are in real trouble. As with everything else in life, however, there are exceptions. At one stage of my career I sang frequently with a certain well-known bass whose breath as he leant conspiratorially towards me at a certain moment late on in the piece would, I think, have been inflammable, but whom I never knew to miss a single cue. One of the most glorious singers ever to grace the operatic profession, the immortal Jussi Björling, was sometimes so drunk on stage that colleagues could not believe that he would get through the performance – and yet he invariably did so, singing like a god and never making a vestige of a musical mistake. On the whole, though, that carefree motto 'Bevi e canta', 'Drink and sing', which appears on so many wine-jugs in Italian tourist shops, should be reversed as far as opera singers are concerned. Our motto needs to be 'Canta, e poi bevi', 'Sing, and then drink.'

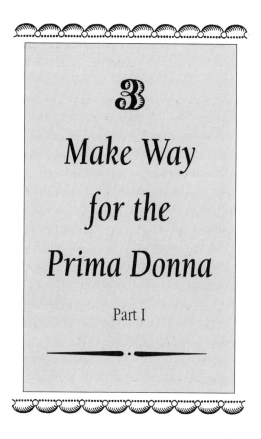

3

Make Way for the Prima Donna

Part I

When the Canadian baritone George London first heard that he had been cast alongside the temperamental Maria Callas in Puccini's *Tosca* he was filled with foreboding. Such was her reputation for trouble-making that when they met at their first rehearsal he was prepared for anything. To his surprise he found her to be everything he most admired in a fellow singer – she was 'a trouper, a fanatic worker, a stickler for detail' – and they understood each other perfectly. This, however, was not how the newspapers, or indeed George London's friends, wished it to be. Reports appeared in the press that the two stars had had a falling-out and when London attempted to reassure people that this was not so his words fell on deaf ears. They required Callas to be 'tempestuous' and 'fiery', and that was how it was going to be. 'And I believe', wrote London in a magazine article, 'that this is a good thing. It brings back a long-lost atmosphere of operatic excitement. There is nothing that can fire opera-goers – and send them to opera box-offices – so surely as the desire to see a genuine member of that sublime species, the prima donna.'

Amen to that, but what exactly do the words 'prima donna' signify? Originally the term, meaning literally 'first lady', simply attached to any member of the fair sex who undertook a starring role in opera, but owing to the high proportion of such ladies who, over the years, have established a reputation for excessively wilful tendencies the general public has long understood the expression differently. Anyone of a demanding disposition is liable to be dubbed a 'prima donna' whether or not she has ever set foot on an operatic stage, a fact which makes it difficult in the modern world to describe those singers who are bona fide prima donnas (or, if one wants to be pedantic, *prime donne*) but who do not indulge in what is commonly perceived to be prima donna-ish behaviour. It has been my good fortune to work alongside many operatic ladies of outstanding ability – names such as Elisabeth Söderström, Janet Baker, Anja Silja, Josephine Barstow, Heather Harper and Anneliese Rothenberger come to my mind – but I have never known any of them indulge in tiresome tantrums, and to brand them as 'prima donnas' would be to risk an entirely false impression. So what should one call them instead? The title 'leading lady' smacks of inter-war musical comedy, and the word 'star' has become debased by its application to anyone appearing for more than ten seconds in a TV soap opera. It is a problem.

In any case, semantics aside, we all know what George London meant, and for the purposes of this chapter when I use the expression 'prima donna' it is likely to be with reference to one of those larger than life ladies (often in the literal sense) who possess that extra *je ne sais quoi* (or sometimes, to be more accurate, *je sais exactement quoi*), which enables them to leap from the arts pages into the spicier areas of the international news. Over the years the qualities which have enabled them to do this have generally been, in no strict order of potency, a propensity for quarrelling with managements, a propensity for quarrelling with tenors, an unusually energetic love life, a tendency to cancel performances at a whim, a generally exotic lifestyle, and an aversion to anyone who says 'no'. Those who combine all these attributes are serious headline material and there is no doubt at all that despite George London's entirely accurate assessment of her attitude towards her work Maria Callas still remains *the* prima donna of the post-war world.

Callas drove her eccentricities to the point of self-destruction, and, tragic as this was, it is easy enough to see how it came about. She carried two particularly heavy burdens, a talent of awesome proportions and a superhuman inferiority complex. It was this latter which, in the opinion of that celebrated impresario of the recording industry Walter Legge, 'was the driving force behind her relentless, ruthless ambition, her fierce will, her monomaniacal egocentricity and insatiable appetite for celebrity. Self-improvement, in every facet of her life and work, was her obsession.' For a few short years Callas was able to thrill operatic audiences in a manner all her own, and her recordings, though to the discriminating ear many of them display at least superficial signs of those technical faults which led to her premature decline, still outsell those of any other soprano. I heard her many times throughout her career and though there were only two occasions on which I was entirely won over by her – one was a *Trovatore* at Covent Garden, the other a *Lucia* in Vienna – her unpredictability was part of her fascination. A voice which, while she was still in her twenties, had been used for such 'blockbuster' roles as Isolde, Brünnhilde and Turandot, and was then transformed into a totally different instrument, honed to the classical *bel canto* lines of Bellini and Donizetti, must by definition have been a fierce animal to tame, and the horrifying nervousness from which she habitually suffered before performances, her nails sometimes drawing blood from the hands of those she clung to in the wings, can surely be taken as a sign of her desperate insecurity. She was a person who could only give of her best in an atmosphere of extreme tension and if that were missing she would create it.

This kind of supercharged personality would have been enough in itself to make Callas a hotly debated figure within the ranks of her profession, but there were other factors which elevated her (if that is the right word) to the status of an international celebrity. One was the relentless warfare which she waged against operatic managements whose attitude did not suit her, and which resulted in her becoming *persona non grata* at La Scala, Milan, the San Francisco Opera, the Vienna State Opera and the

Metropolitan Opera to name but a few. The skirmishes which attracted the greatest publicity were those she engaged in with Rudolf Bing, manager of the Met, who cancelled her contract for twenty-six performances in 1959. The principal bone of contention was Bing's requirement that she should appear as Violetta in *La traviata* between two performances as Lady Macbeth, a role which represents an entirely different type of vocal challenge. As always there was a valid artistic point behind Callas's intractable attitude, but in charging head-on at Bing she did herself no favours. His press statement was a masterpiece of veiled invective, opening as follows: 'I am not prepared to enter into a public argument with Mme Callas because I fully realize how much more skill and experience she has than I do in such matters. Although her artistic qualifications are the subject of violent debate between her friends and her enemies, it is well known far and wide that she has the gift of bringing her undeniable histrionic talent into her business dealings.' Certain American columnists decided that the best way to make capital out of the ensuing brouhaha was to come down on Callas's side, and one of them, a certain Harry Golden, expressed the opinion that Bing, along with every other impresario who trades in artistic talent, 'should learn to suffer'. Referring to Callas as a star 'who has brought excitement back to the opera with a gift of warming the bones of us who love New York and the Met', he concluded by posing the question 'Who is this Rudolf Bing?' Well, there lies the rub – he was a man who was able to slam the stage door at the Met, and opera singers do need stages on which to sing. Callas could fire back as many salvos as she liked – 'I'm the only one who has the nerve to do things right,' she declared in another publication, referring to the Met's sloppy rehearsal practices. 'The others are afraid to do anything. They're too afraid of losing their jobs to fight for principle, to fight for what they know is right. I'm not afraid. I'm doing this for passion, not for fame or money' – but she never sang at the Met again.

It was, in any case, the stuff of which a certain sort of fame is made, and it was reinforced by the second factor which provided the press, especially in Italy, with constant copy on the Callas theme, namely the happy circumstance that her career exactly coincided with that of another great soprano, Renata Tebaldi. I have been assured by many people who were well acquainted with both these ladies that there was no personal

The future scourge of operatic managements as she looked at the age of 13. Maria Callas with her mother.

animosity between them, but there is almost nothing which enables the media to keep stoking the fires of public interest more efficiently than a feud, and so a feud there had to be. One Italian magazine came up with a veritable scoop when it published back-to-back interviews with the two divas, which reveal step by step how insidiously the seeds of discord were sown. In answering the opening question 'What do you think of the fact that Signora Callas is called "the Devil" and Signora Tebaldi is called "the Angel"?' both ladies side-stepped with humour and adroitness. Then the knife was elegantly slipped between the ribs. 'But did you not describe la Tebaldi as "having no backbone"?' Callas was asked, to which she replied that the phrase had appeared in an article in *Time*, but not attributed to her. Anyone wishing to parade this as propaganda was either acting in bad faith or did not understand English. The question put to Tebaldi, however, was 'Do you suppose that this offensive assessment corresponds to the thoughts of la Callas?', a trap into which Tebaldi unfortunately fell. 'I do and I am sorry about it,' she was reported as having replied. 'I may perhaps have no backbone, but I have something else which Signora Callas does not; I have a heart.' Whether or not this may have left Callas feeling that the game stood at 0—1 against her I am unable to say, but some time later a British newspaper quoted her as declaring that to compare herself with Tebaldi would be 'like comparing champagne with cognac. No – champagne with coca-cola!'

It is not, however, only the press which revels in a feud such as this, because the principal attraction of opera to many an enthusiast is the depth to which it stirs the listeners' passions, and for adding fat to the fire of passion there are few finer ingredients than partisanship. During my student days in Vienna it was virtually *de rigueur* to be a Callas man or a Tebaldi man, but with us it was only a matter for friendly debate, while for certain sections of the Italian public it was a *casus belli*. In 1955 a group of 'Tebaldiani' brought a performance of *Andrea Chénier* at La Scala to a temporary standstill when Callas hit a less than perfect high B flat, and a fortnight later there was a similar fracas during a performance of *Medea* in Rome. It must have been hugely annoying for those who had come to enjoy the opera, but it was grist to the newshawks' mills.

For newsworthiness, however, even these lively events faded into insignificance when compared with ingredient number three in the emergence of Maria Callas as, at least for a while, the most widely discussed woman in the world; newspaper readers who would never have dreamt of spending an evening in an opera house or a banknote on a Callas recording were riveted by reports of her sexual goings-on. Married early in her career to a middle-aged industrialist from Verona, Callas's personal life had largely evaded the spotlight until rumours became rife that she and the multi-millionaire Greek shipowner Aristotle Onassis were more than just good friends. In June 1959 Onassis and his wife gave a sumptuous party at the Dorchester Hotel after the first night of *Medea* at Covent Garden, with Callas as the main attraction and the rest of the guest list reading like a gossip columnist's dream. From the British political establishment (Lady Churchill, Mr and Mrs John Profumo, Christopher Soames, Mr and Mrs Duncan Sandys) via the arts (Lord and Lady Harewood, Margot Fonteyn, Cecil Beaton) to the international plutocracy (the Aga Khan, Stavros Niarchos) and the world of the silver screen

(Douglas Fairbanks, Charlton Heston, Gary Cooper) Onassis had cast his net wide. At the end of July came the famous cruise on board the Onassis yacht *Christina*, with Sir Winston Churchill amongst Callas's fellow passengers, and by the end of September both Callas's husband and Onassis's wife were filing for divorce.

According to several people who were close to her during this period Callas, in her middle thirties, was like a girl who had just discovered sex for the very first time. There is certainly little doubt that her new role in the heady world of what used to be known as 'international café society' rapidly proved itself to be incompatible with the professional dedication required of a world-class operatic soprano, and there is equally little doubt that Onassis's subsequent maltreatment and eventual desertion of Callas had a great deal to do with the fact that she died, lonely and withdrawn, at the age of only fifty-three. It had been eight years since she last set foot on an operatic stage, and it was the ultimate tribute to the drawing powers of a true prima donna that on that occasion – *Tosca* at Covent Garden in June 1965 – hundreds of people had queued for forty-eight hours on the off-chance of a standing-room ticket. The story of Maria Callas would in itself make electrifying material for an opera – but how on earth would one cast the title-role?

Since the death of Callas there has been no other prima donna to rival her reputation as 'the Tigress', but looking back in the annals of opera we find several others who could at least have run her a close second. One of these, Caterina Gabrielli by name (1730–1796), was described by a contemporary writer in the following evocative terms: 'At the age of forty-five Caterina Gabrielli, a coloratura vocalist who had secured the admiration of various continental sovereigns, made her appearance in London. The most dangerous syren of modern times, she was wonderfully capricious, and neither interest nor flattery, nor threats nor punishment had any power to control her.'

As far as punishment is concerned one might feel that Callas's rejection from so many potential places of work was punishment enough, but that would have been a bagatelle to Gabrielli. As the critic Rupert Christiansen relates in his highly diverting book *Prima Donna*,* she man-

---

*See bibliography.

aged to have herself twice committed to prison, once by the Viceroy of Sicily because of her insolent insistence on singing in his opera house so quietly that no one could hear her, and once for calling the Infante of Parma, to his face, an 'accursed hunchback'. No whit abashed she made a practice of giving daily performances for the entertainment of her fellow prisoners, doubtless letting fly for their benefit with considerably more gusto than she had for the Viceroy and his guests. The quality of her singing when she could be bothered to make the effort can be judged from the fact that on one occasion the celebrated castrato Gasparo Pacchierotti burst into tears while singing with her and rushed from the stage, stricken with panic at finding himself in competition with such a stupendous vocalist. At the peak of her career Gabrielli took a year off work in order to devote herself to the joys of love with a besotted young aristocrat (who must, incidentally, have been quite a man, as Gabrielli was credited with a copious list of conquests, and to keep her quiet for a year was no mean feat), and yet such can be the spell of a *prima donna assoluta* that despite all these shenanigans the eminent English musical historian Charles Burney was able to refer to her as 'the most intelligent and best bred virtuosa with whom I had ever conversed'.

It is strange how often, in tales of operatic ruction, the city of Parma plays a part. Not only has it been the scene of many a singer's demise at the hands of a merciless public, as well as the scene of one of Gabrielli's incarcerations, but it was also the birthplace of a lady who must by all accounts have been well worth a place beside Callas and Gabrielli in the tigress stakes. This was Francesca Cuzzoni (1696–1778), another vocalist of astounding quality who triumphed in London in several of Handel's operas but whose contrariness was such that on one occasion the composer was moved to threaten her with defenestration if she did not sing what he had written. Cuzzoni was another prima donna whose fire was stoked by the existence of a deadly rival – Faustina Bordoni, perfectly cut out for the role of 'Angel' to Cuzzoni's 'Devil'. Cuzzoni was vulgar in appearance, badly dressed and untalented as an actress, whereas Faustina (as she was always known) had all the advantages of an upper-class background, physical beauty and personal charm. As Cuzzoni was a soprano and Faustina a mezzo theirs was a feud which gained extra piquancy through the fact that they frequently appeared in the same performance, something which could never have happened to Callas and Tebaldi. It is easy enough to imagine the sense of expectation in the auditorium of the King's Theatre, London, whenever a Cuzzoni aria was to be immediately followed by one from Faustina, or vice versa; hardened 'Cuzzonists' and 'Faustinians' refused to drink in the same taverns or to enter each others' houses, let alone applaud the rival faction's heroine. Eventually, on the evening of 6 June 1727, during a performance of Bononcini's *Astianatte*, egged on, it would appear, by the barrage of conflicting boos and bravas, the two ladies came to blows on stage. The management must have regarded Cuzzoni as the prime instigator because it was she who was dismissed, but not for long; King George II, who ascended the throne the following week and was evidently a Cuzzonist at heart, threatened to withdraw his patronage unless she was reinstated. In the end, however, poor Cuzzoni was the loser. After a hideous decline in her fortunes she ended her days in Bologna as a penniless button-maker – at least the rumour that she was to be beheaded for poisoning her husband turned out to be a fabrication – while Faustina, happily married to a successful composer and with two talented daughters to warm her heart, lived, loved and admired by all, to the ripe old age of eighty-four.

If Cuzzoni v. Faustina was the pre-eminent feud in eighteenth-century opera, that between Grisi and Viardot must rate as the most subtly fought contest of the following hundred years. Giulia Grisi (1811–1869) was a tremendous favourite both in Paris and in London, an artist of the highest quality, and such notices as the following, which appeared in the *Illustrated London News* in June 1850, used to greet her with almost monotonous regularity: 'It is in the union of face, figure, personal beauty, expression, voice, gesture, facility and power of vocal execution, and intensely dramatic declaration, that Grisi's Norma has distanced all her competitors, and that physically and artistically it stands forth as the perfect conception of histrionic genius.'

Grisi had a highly colourful aunt, a famous contralto named Josephina Grassini, to whom was attributed the rather remarkable achievement of having slept with both Napoleon *and* Wellington (though never, one imagines, at the same time), with Lord Castlereagh thrown in for good measure; and it was not only in her operatic prowess that the niece emulated the aunt, because in due course young Giulia bore an illegitimate

A famous partnership on and off the stage. Giulia Grisi and Mario amuse themselves on their terrace posing as Leonora and Manrico in Il trovatore.

child to Lord Castlereagh's son. Later, however, she formed a lasting alliance with the outstanding tenor of the day, an aristocratic Italian who, feeling that his family should not be besmirched by association with the wicked stage, preferred to exist under the single name of Mario; and it was Mario who became Grisi's secret weapon in her war of attrition against Pauline Viardot (1821–1910).

Viardot, the great Spanish-born mezzo-soprano, daughter of tenor and teacher Manuel García and sister of the brilliant but short-lived Maria Malibran, presented no great threat to Grisi in the florid Italian repertoire but was distinctly her superior in the new-fangled concoctions of Monsieur Meyerbeer. When Viardot made her stage debut as Rossini's Desdemona at Her Majesty's Theatre in 1839 Grisi decided that it would be preferable if in future the newcomer stayed on the far side of the English Channel, and she managed to keep her away from London until

1848. When Viardot did eventually return it was to sing the role of Amina in *La sonnambula* at Covent Garden, a great mistake, as this had been a Grisi *tour de force* in her younger days. The tenor cast as Viardot's partner was none other than the great Mario, who, strange to say, was obliged to withdraw at extremely short notice owing to a sudden 'indisposition', his place being taken by a gentleman named Flavio who had no time to rehearse, and of whose further career I have been unable to find any trace. In such circumstances as these Viardot had little chance to shine, but she was nobody's fool – not for nothing were men of the stature of Gounod and Berlioz to be numbered amongst her ardent admirers, while Turgenev became positively enslaved by her – and later in the season she neatly squared her account.

On 3 August 1848 Viardot was granted a benefit performance. The opera was to be Meyerbeer's *Les Huguenots*, an ideal vehicle for Viardot's dramatic talents, and the demanding role of Raoul was to be taken by

Above left
Pauline Viardot (1821–1910) as Fidès in Le Prophète, *a role which Meyerbeer rewrote and extended specially for her, with Mario as Jean . . .*

Above . . . *and as an old lady, composing and teaching in Paris.*

Mario. On the very morning of the gala he was once again obliged to withdraw, but, surprise surprise, Madame Grisi would be prepared to sing the title-role in *Norma* for her rival's benefit if that opera could be substituted. At this point I would like to hand over the narrative to Harold Rosenthal, author of *Two Centuries of Opera at Covent Garden*:

> Viardot thanked Grisi for her courtesy and kindness and then asked whether the costumes and scenery were ready to play either opera. On being informed that this was the case, she told the management that Gustave Roger, the French tenor who had been singing in other operas during the season, was still in London, and that she would ask him to play Raoul in place of the indisposed Mario. 'But', she added, 'if he cannot do that *Norma* can of course be given instead, but I will sing Norma.' Roger agreed to appear and sang Raoul in the original French, not having learnt it in Italian. Viardot, on her part, demanded a copy of the French words and, during the times when she was not on stage, quickly memorized as much of the French text as she could, taking up the role in that language from about half-way through the opera.

The upshot of all this was that the great duet 'O ciel! Où courez vous' in Act IV engendered an unprecedented atmosphere of excitement in the house, with Viardot and Roger being called repeatedly before the curtain; but perhaps it is scarcely necessary to add that Roger never sang the role at Covent Garden again.

To find another lady who used her elbows with the same determination as Giulia Grisi one has to put the clock forward half a century and hail that redoubtable Australian Nellie Melba. Melba! The mere mention of the name is enough to conjure up the essence of a bygone age, when the sun never set upon the British Empire, when the lights of the Covent Garden stage would be reflected from the boxes and the stalls by the twinkle of a million diamonds, when Monsieur Escoffier, head chef at the Savoy Hotel, would crave the diva's permission to bestow her name upon his latest creation, and when Their Majesties the King and Queen would indicate to the management of the Royal Opera that they wished the current season to include a performance of Puccini's *La bohème* with Madame Melba and Signor Caruso in the leading roles. It may be tactless to add that once King George V had ascended the throne the principal reason why *La bohème* remained a royal favourite was that it was the shortest opera in the repertoire, but there we are.

Throughout this most brilliant period in the history of Covent Garden, a period of true star singers as well as of stunning social éclat, Nellie Melba, born Helen Mitchell, daughter of a Scottish building contractor who had emigrated to what many regarded as a scarcely civilized colony in the furthest corner of the world,* did not merely sing at the Royal Opera, she reigned over it. Never before in the whole history of the place had any singer had a permanent dressing-room of his or her own, but Melba did, and on the door was a notice reading 'MELBA. SILENCE! SILENCE!' How did she do it? First and foremost, of course, in her capacity as a peerless vocalist. She combined a remarkable purity of tone – 'silvery' was the favourite epithet amongst those attempting to describe its quality – with a technique which came disarmingly close to perfection. The American writer Robert Tuggle sums up her status in his book *The Golden Age of Opera* when he tells us that she 'provided the vocal standard by which New York critics measured all singers'; and though the opinion was occasionally expressed that a certain glacial quality stood between her and the ideal embodiment of a Mimì or a Traviata, Melba's recordings still leave no doubt of the degree to which, in purely vocal terms, practice had made perfect. To take but one brief example from the hundreds which present themselves in her recordings, anyone wishing to know the meaning of the phrase 'evenness of scale' could scarcely do better than listen to the climactic phrase of Mimì's aria 'Donde lieta uscì', in which, on the words 'se vuoi serbarla a ricordo d'amor', the melody climbs over the space of an octave and a third and Melba crowns it with a high B flat identical in ease and quality to the low G from which the ascent began.

In the story of Melba's personal ascent, however, vocal supremacy was only part of the secret. She saw herself as some kind of uncrowned queen and by the blatancy with which she demanded to be treated as one, not only in the world of opera but wherever she went, nine times out of ten

---

*Melba's habit of claiming that she had 'put Australia on the map' did not always go down well in her native land.

from her admiringly
Nellie Melba
1903

Butter would not melt in her mouth . . . The redoubtable Nellie Melba in Faust.

she succeeded. Many are the tales of her performing such high-handed actions as moving all the furniture in a hotel lobby if it struck her as having been ineptly arranged, and then, when asked by the management to desist, silencing their protests with the imperious announcement 'I am Melba!' Largely through the patronage of Lady de Grey, a prominent London hostess whose husband was a member of the Covent Garden committee, Melba established a foothold in the normally unassailable bastions of London Society, and it is one of the many fascinating contra-dictions in her personality that she combined being an appalling snob – a failing to which she herself readily confessed – with the retention of more than a dash of her native earthiness. 'What's this bloody thing?' would be her usual unladylike comment at rehearsals when flinging into the wings some article of stage decoration which had failed to take her fancy, and it was certainly not with the hauteur of a *grande dame* that she confronted

Sir Thomas Beecham on one particular occasion which he recalled with relish in his memoirs. He had just taken over the management of Covent Garden after the First World War, and as the building had been used for some time as a storehouse it had required extensive redecoration.

> It was a few weeks before its opening [Beecham recalled] that an angry figure stormed into my office and asked what the deuce I meant by painting her room green. It was Nellie Melba, and very upset she seemed to be. I had never before come into working contact with this imposing personality, although I had heard something of her autocratic ways; and considering the best method of defence here to be attack, I pretended not to remember who she was, and asked what the deuce *she* meant by entering my office unannounced, adding that I knew nothing of private ownership of rooms in the building.

This, needless to say, 'produced a fresh explosion of wrath', but it is not insignificant that the final result of the colloquy was an offer by Sir Thomas to have the room repainted in any colour of the diva's choice.

It doubtless added to the mystique of the Melba persona that at the age of thirty she became the mistress of the twenty-two-year-old Duc d'Orléans, Pretender to the throne of France, despite the fact that by then she had become what most men would call an imposing figure of a woman rather than an alluring one. It was a discreetly conducted liaison – Melba was not yet divorced from an Australian whom she had married before the days of her fame – but London Society was aware of it, and that sort of thing does no harm to a prima donna's standing. One way and another Melba's influence grew, and it gradually became noticeable that other sopranos engaged by the Covent Garden company tended not to be re-engaged if they scored too great a success in what might be broadly regarded as the Melba repertoire.

One such was that darling of the Vienna opera, Selma Kurz, who dazzled the London public with her Gilda in *Rigoletto* in 1904, but who, to quote Harold Rosenthal once again, 'never became a permanent fixture there, for she was too popular for Melba's liking ... and things were made none too easy for her'. Perhaps it is fair to add, however, that Kurz herself was not above the occasional caprice. When she undertook the role of

Oscar in *Ballo* at Covent Garden she was pulled up by the conductor, Luigi Mancinelli, for indulging in the trick (one which had virtually become her trademark in Vienna), of sustaining a trill on the last high note of the aria 'Saper vorreste' while walking slowly round the entire perimeter of the stage. Having promised not to do so in performance she went ahead on the erroneous assumption that in the presence of an audience the conductor would be obliged to give in. Mancinelli, however, left her stranded by bringing in orchestra and chorus dead on the beat, and in the words of Percy Pitt, musical adviser to the company, 'the slanging matches which ensued were unprintable, but the diva never sinned again, at least not at Covent Garden.'

It would be a mistake, though, to suppose that it was only rival sopranos who came up against what might nowadays be termed 'the Melba factor'. The tenor John McCormack, moving forward to join her for a curtain call at the end of a Covent Garden performance, was stopped in his tracks by the curt injunction 'In this house nobody takes bows with Melba.' At least she did allow McCormack to sing there; the stentorian young baritone Titta Ruffo was not so fortunate. Due to apear with her as Rigoletto in 1903 Ruffo created such a sensation at his only rehearsal – in which Melba declined to participate, preferring to observe the proceedings from a box – that he received an ovation from the chorus and orchestra. The next day, however, he found that his name had been removed from the posters, Melba having informed the management that he was too young to sing with her. Ruffo demanded to see the director and expressed himself, as he himself later described it, 'in such imaginative Italian' that the director threatened him with legal action, whereupon the disgruntled baritone shook the dust of London from his feet and never entered the Royal Opera House again.

When such an incident as this occurs it is only human, I feel, to fantasize over methods of revenge, but in his wildest imaginings Ruffo could never have dreamt up an opportunity as ideal as that which subsequently presented itself. Eight years later Melba stopped off in Naples on her way home to Australia and heard Ruffo, by now the most highly paid baritone in the world, in Meyerbeer's *L'Africaine*. A couple of days later he was due to be singing the title-role in Ambroise Thomas's *Hamlet*, and with the air of one bestowing an infinite favour Melba offered to undertake the role of Ophelia. The director of the Teatro San Carlo, doubtless envisaging record box-office receipts, begged Ruffo to agree, but Ruffo sent back the message, with strict instructions that it should be delivered verbatim, 'Signor Ruffo considers that you are too old to sing with him.' In fact Ruffo and Melba *were* subsequently cast together, and in *Rigoletto* too, in Philadelphia. There are no records of any untoward eruptions, but I somehow doubt whether Ruffo took much trouble to curb his enormous voice during their numerous duets.*

Even amongst her rival coloratura sopranos there was one whose native talent was so phenomenal that Melba was powerless to damage her. This was Luisa Tetrazzini, the Florentine Nightingale,† and of all the divas of those distant days she is the one whose personality, combined with the recorded evidence of her astonishing vocal skills, I find the most appealing. She was a person who grabbed life with both hands and shook it into the shape she wanted. After a minimum of vocal training she was capable of such flights of pyrotechnical coloratura that she regularly drove audiences frantic with enthusiasm, and the reckless abandon with which she would scatter her high E flats around the auditorium seems to have characterized every aspect of her existence. Even her professional debut was a case in point. Just as a performance of *L'Africaine* was due to start in the Teatro Pagliano, Florence, in 1890, the conductor came before the curtain to announce that the soprano due to sing the daunting role of Inez had been taken ill; there was no alternative but to send the audience home. Up leapt the nineteen-year-old Tetrazzini from the stalls and called out 'I know the role by heart, I'll sing it for you!' This led to a brisk exchange

---

*Lest I should be accused of painting too grim a picture of the great Nellie I would like to redress the balance by quoting an intriguing indication of the degree to which she was adored by the public. The *Morning Post*'s euphoric review of her farewell performance at Covent Garden before a temporary return to Australia in 1914 ends with the words: 'The enthusiasm of the reception continued to the end, and even when the majority of the audience had gone away there were still enthusiasts left in the gallery to cheer and call "Coo-ee".'

†This was her universal nickname, although on one occasion a San Francisco critic, impelled no doubt by an admirable desire to tell the truth as he saw it, expressed the opinion that although she did indeed sing like a nightingale 'she looked more like a pigeon'.

'I am old, I am fat, I am ugly. But I am still Tetrazzini!'

of views between the conductor, who was understandably sceptical, and various members of the public, who felt that this self-confident young lady should be given her chance. Eventually it was agreed that Tetrazzini should be allowed two days' rehearsal in which to convince the conductor that she was up to the task; she succeeded and on day three the performance took place. So great was Tetrazzini's triumph that she was invited to repeat the role in the Teatro Argentina in Rome, where word of an astounding new talent reached the ears of no less a personage than the Queen of Italy. Within a few weeks of taking her first steps on a public stage the fledgling diva was honoured by a summons to sing in the royal palace.

During the next few years Tetrazzini devoted a considerable amount of her time to the harvesting of fame and fortune in South and Central America. According not only to her own highly imaginative memoirs but also to innumerable reports in the local press, Brazilian millionaires, Mexican matadors and Argentinian presidents were to be numbered amongst her devoted slaves, and though she tended to be accompanied on these expeditions by companions who were generally referred to as her 'managers', but also from time to time as her 'husbands', there was inevitable speculation that some of the costliest pieces of jewellery which she acquired in that part of the world had not been donated only as a tribute to her singing, sensational as that indubitably was. In her young days there was a certain sauciness about Tetrazzini which was particularly fetching to those gentlemen who preferred the fuller figure, and there is little reason to doubt the reputation which she acquired for inviting members of the opposite sex to her dressing-room before performances in order to help her relax. It was part and parcel of her uninhibited attitude towards life, as was her habit of throwing a kiss to the audience when making her first entrance in an opera or joining in the applause for one of her partners on stage. Although one can sympathize with Richard Aldrich, critic of *The New York Times*, when he wrote 'Much that she does cannot meet with serious approval', the sheer quality of her singing, combined with her self-evident determination to give the public its money's-worth, placed her somewhere beyond the normal criteria of critical assessment.

Nowadays, when a famous soprano may jet into London or New York unobserved in order to do perhaps a couple of days' recording before jetting off again to her next assignment, it is difficult to envisage what used to be involved in the arrivals and departures of a diva such as Luisa Tetrazzini. In an excellent biography Charles Neilson Gattey* describes her arrival in San Francisco for a series of concerts when 'cheering crowds lined Market Street all the way from the Ferry Building to the Palace Hotel', and nothing bears more cogent witness to the special love affair which she conducted with the population of that fair city than the extraordinary story of her open-air concert on Christmas Eve 1910. A stage

---

*See bibliography.

was erected outside the *San Francisco Chronicle* building, at the junction of three main streets, and without the assistance of any form of amplification Tetrazzini sang to a crowd which had been expected to number one hundred thousand, but which eventually swelled to around a quarter of a million. To many she was nothing more than a distant dot in a huge white hat, but even those who were too far away to hear the orchestra claimed to have heard every note she sang.

The role in which Tetrazzini conquered both London and New York was Violetta in *La traviata*, and it would be hard to exaggerate how spectacularly those conquests were achieved. Despite her undeniable triumphs elsewhere these two cities, so vital for anyone wishing to break into the topmost bracket of international stardom, had persistently cold-shouldered her. She was already thirty-six when she received her first grudging contract from Covent Garden – one which the General Manager, Harry Higgins, would have wriggled out of had she not stuck to her guns and threatened to sue him – and her debut was regarded as such a non-event that the critics had not even been invited to attend. Unknown to Tetrazzini, though, when Higgins heard her first cadenza in the final scene of Act I and realized that he had on his hands, as he put it, 'a real *leggiero-spinto* with breadth and purity of tone such as I had dreamed of all my life', he rushed to the telephone and rang every influential paper in Fleet Street. By the time the curtain went up on Act II numerous reporters had tumbled out of their cabs and into the opera house, and the next day Tetrazzini was front-page news. After this the only way for Covent Garden to satisfy the public's clamorous demand for tickets was to mount a special series of Sunday concerts; Melba, who detested Tetrazzini, habitually referring to her as 'that dwarf', was in Australia and powerless to intervene.

Another immediate result of Tetrazzini's Covent Garden debut was an invitation from Oscar Hammerstein to join his Manhattan Opera Company in New York, where even Richard Aldrich felt obliged to admit that her reception was 'almost unparalleled in New York's operatic history'. The critic of the *New York Press* reported that her final E flat above high C was 'produced with so great an ease and freedom that persons possessed of the sense of absolute pitch almost doubted their senses', and for good measure she capped the note in question – her last utterance in

Queen of a million Victorian hearts. Adelina Patti as Gounod's Juliette.

Act I – by indulging in *her* favourite trick. Bending down after she had struck the high E flat she gathered up the long train of her dress and strolled into the wings, holding that astounding note until she had disappeared from sight.

There was, of course, much more to the Tetrazzini phenomenon than the mere ability to hit notes which others could not reach. As her recordings reveal, when she indulged in her dazzling flights of *fioriture* she did so not with the mere clockwork precision familiar from so many other coloratura sopranos as they set forth on their flights into the stratosphere, but with a tremendous rhythmic impulse which puts theatrical flesh and blood onto even the flashiest passages. It seems to me that the twentieth century has seen few, if any, singers with a natural vocal talent to rival

Tetrazzini's, and when the German soprano Frieda Hempel once expressed much the same opinion to Tetrazzini herself she received a delightfully succinct reply. Glancing down at where her waistline should have been, the diva replied 'Well, Friedelina, some singers gotta da figure – but Tetrazzini gotta da voice!'

By the time she undertook her later concert tours Tetrazzini most assuredly no longer 'hadda da figure', but audiences all over Britain and America capitulated to her as happily as ever. She would come trotting onto the stage at a brisk pace, arriving before her public, as Ivor Newton, her regular accompanist, later recalled in his memoirs, 'breathless and panting'. As the audience had invariably overflowed onto the platform she would recover herself by walking round shaking people's hands and kissing any young children who happened to be within reach. 'Her friendliness and warmth', Newton continued, 'would bring the entire hall to a state of excitement before she had sung a note,' and then, when she felt ready to break into song, she would grasp the end of the long rope of pearls which she wore round her neck and throw it over her shoulder as a signal to Newton that it was time to begin.

During the course of her career Tetrazzini earned gigantic sums of money, but thanks to her absurdly extravagant lifestyle, her incurable generosity, her immediately recognizable vulnerability to confidence tricksters of every hue, and her unfortunate decision to take a third (official) husband late in life who was little more than half her age (and, to judge by the wedding photographs, certainly not one third of her weight), eventually all the money and all the jewels disappeared. Being the sort of person she was, however, she accepted the rough as she had the smooth, and by all accounts her indomitable sense of humour held up to the end. She earned a precarious living letting out lodgings to singing students in Milan, and she was never short of friends who would drop in for a gossip. Often she would be asked what state her voice was in, where-upon she would waddle to the piano, strike a chord and let fly with a dazzling arpeggio capped by a high C of undiminished splendour. 'Ah!' she would chuckle when she saw the amazement on people's faces, 'sono vecchia, sono grassa, sono brutta', 'I am old, I am fat, I am ugly' – and then, with all the old panache, 'ma sono sempre la Tetrazzini!', 'but I am still Tetrazzini!'

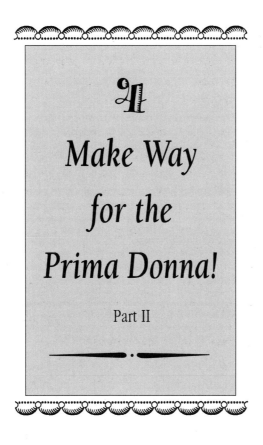

Make Way for the Prima Donna!

Part II

Physical allure may have played no part in the later chapters of the Tetrazzini story, but in that of the American prima donna Geraldine Farrar (1882–1967) it was a vital ingredient. A rare combination of talent and glamour enabled her to become, along with Caruso, the Metropolitan Opera's greatest box-office attraction over a period of sixteen seasons, but it is doubtful whether she would have achieved all that she did had she not also possessed a highly developed flair for self-promotion. From an early age, resolutely supported by both parents, she benefited from an unshakeable belief in herself. When, as an unknown teenager, she had her portrait taken by the leading Parisian fashion photographer of the day she demanded professional rates on the grounds that fame was only just around the corner, and she was right. At the age of nineteen she made a successful debut as Marguerite in *Faust* at the Hofoper Berlin, and within a short time it became a known fact, both to the Berlin public and to the American press, that she had won the heart of the Kaiser's son and heir. In due course a scurrilous Berlin paper, *Die Welt am Montag*, came out with remarks injurious to Miss Farrar's moral reputation, and its editor, a certain Herr Kohn, found that he had her father to deal with. Mr Farrar, a strapping gentleman with a considerable reputation as a baseball player, determined, in the words of one American newspaper, 'to avenge his daughter in the old-fashioned American way. Forcing his way into Herr Kohn's residence, he dragged that distinguished molder of public opinion out of bed and kicked him about the apartment until he begged for mercy.'

In her memoirs Farrar presents her relationship with the Crown Prince

as having been an innocent dalliance between 'two children' (though it did not exclude the occasional 'warm handclasp' or 'a few furtive kisses'), but it certainly did no harm to the process of putting her on the map. Tetrazzini's are not the only singer's memoirs which need to be taken with a hefty pinch of salt – why, after all, should politicians and military men be the only people who in retrospect never made a mistake? – and Farrar's are doubtless no less suspect than most others, but at least she went to the trouble of thinking up a highly original form in which to present them. Every second chapter is written as though it had been dictated to Farrar by the spirit of her dead mother, a device which cunningly enables Farrar to write such things about herself as 'this astounding daughter of mine', 'Geraldine left her dressing room, a blonde vision of youth and beauty', or 'Her next role was Juliette – and what a vision she was!' Understandably, perhaps, neither mother nor daughter touched upon the most vital episode in Farrar's emotional life, namely her passionate affair with Toscanini. This was a relationship which started badly. At a rehearsal soon after his arrival at the Met Toscanini repeatedly criticized Farrar, who pointed out to him that in her capacity as a star she was not accustomed to such treatment; back came the reply that Toscanini only recognized the existence of those stars which God had placed in the sky. It soon became evident to Farrar, however, that she gave her finest performances when Toscanini was in musical charge, and so besotted did he become with her that when, after seven years, she broke off their relationship because he was not willing to leave his wife and marry her, Toscanini deserted the Met altogether rather than suffer constant reminders of the love that he had lost.

Farrar was a prime example of that intriguing phenomenon, the woman whose glamour appeals as strongly to other women as it does to men. Her social activities featured prominently in the women's magazines – where is Farrar buying her clothes this season? who is Farrar's new hairdresser? – and her fan club consisted largely of boisterously enthusiastic young females known as the Gerryflappers. Their activities were considered by some to be inconsistent with the dignity of the Metropolitan Opera, and when Farrar herself was persuaded by Cecil B. de Mille to star in a series of silent films there were those who began to question her true commitment to the operatic muse. One of her film roles was that of Carmen, a part which she continued to sing regularly at the Met, but when she started introducing into the operatic version such Hollywood touches as slapping, scratching and biting her Don José, even Caruso, that most obliging of tenors, is said to have taken exception. She remained, however, in the words of Gatti-Casazza, the general manager of the Met, 'the "beniamina" (pet child) of the Metropolitan public', and when, in 1922, she decided to end her association with the company her farewell performance was marked by displays of affection on the part of the audience unparalleled in the whole history of the house.

Farrar was a very fine singer – recordings such as her meltingly feminine Marguerite, her incisively characterized Butterfly and her zestful Carmen bear eloquent witness to that – but the atmosphere at the old Met was nothing if not competitive, and her dominant position there could scarcely have been maintained by vocal means alone. To quote Gatti once again, 'she had a will of iron and succeeded always in triumphing over all obstacles', the obstacles in question occasionally taking the form of younger competitors. One such appears to have been the Italian mezzo Gabriella Besanzoni, engaged by the Met in 1919 after building a powerful reputation in South America chiefly for her prowess in the role of Carmen. Besanzoni was at the time the inamorata of the pianist Arthur Rubinstein, whose autobiography contains a vivid account of the hostility she encountered at the Met. 'They have a German contralto,' she told him, 'the Matzenauer,* the most venomous creature I ever met . . . she told strange tales about my artistic capacity . . . that my Carmen pleased not for my singing but for my indecent gestures which excited the men in the audience. Farrar, who sings Carmen here, helped her spread these lies.' Whether this was true or false it is a fact that Besanzoni only survived one season at the Met, and that she was never given her chance as Carmen, a part, as Rubinstein puts it, ' "owned" by the beautiful Geraldine Farrar, who would have let herself be shot before yielding it'.

Funnily enough it was a special source of pride with Gatti that he ran so civilized a company that even rival prima donnas could be persuaded to lay down their arms and opt for peaceful coexistence. As a classic

---

*Margarete Matzenauer, Hungarian by birth, was a Met stalwart for nineteen years, appearing frequently in the Wagnerian repertoire.

Emmy Destinn (1878–1930), apparently fearless as well as 'indefatigable'.

example he was known to quote the case of Farrar and the great Czech-born soprano Emmy Destinn, who had loathed each other at the Berlin Opera, continued to loathe each other at the Met, never once exchanged a word of greeting, and yet managed to alternate in the selfsame roles without ever causing the management a moment's bother. It would have been asking too much of Farrar, however, not to have the occasional dig at Destinn in her memoirs, and one such is her account of how Destinn came to be Berlin's first Salome. Richard Strauss, we are assured, was anxious that Farrar should undertake the task, emphasizing how effective she would be half naked in the Dance of the Seven Veils, but she was sensible enough to recognize that the role would wreck her voice; 'so the indefatigable Destinn sang it' – Farrar is gracious enough to add that she did so 'superbly' – 'and looked like a misplaced *Walküre*'.

I have a sneaking feeling that in choosing that word 'indefatigable'

Farrar may have been indulging in a touch of innuendo. Destinn was a woman of an unusually passionate nature, passionate in her singing – it was the emotional impact of her performances which made her, both at Covent Garden and at the Met, the most admired of all sopranos of her type – passionate in her patriotism – her devotion to the Czech nationalist cause resulted in the Austrian authorities interning her in her own castle during the First World War – and passionate in her relationships with the opposite sex. Word had it that her performances, like Tetrazzini's, used to benefit from a brisk bout of physical arousal shortly before curtain up,* and certain wags used to refer to her long-term lover, the French-Algerian baritone Dinh Gilly, as 'la forza della Destinn'. There are differing theories as to how her relationship with Gilly eventually ended. According to one, Gilly, trapped on Destinn's country estate at the beginning of the war, was offered his freedom by the Austrians if he would promise not to fight for France. This he declined to do and was moved to an internment camp, while for Destinn a replacement fell, quite literally, out of the skies – a young aviator crashed in her grounds, she nursed him back to health and married him. According to another, Gilly simply decided that he would prefer the internment camp after discovering Destinn in the arms of a lusty young woodman. Whichever version is correct (if either) Gilly did indisputably lose his appetite for prima donnas. While appearing as supporting artist on one of Tetrazzini's post-war concert tours he treated Ivor Newton to his views on the race in general. 'They should all be burnt at the stake!' he exclaimed. 'I detest them all. I lived with one for five years.'

Once a gentleman had taken Destinn's fancy he was not long left in doubt as to her requirements, and it is Arthur Rubinstein once again whom we have to thank for a vivid account of her no-nonsense approach. After a performance of *Salome* at the Châtelet in Paris Rubinstein was invited to join Destinn and her sister for supper in their hotel suite, a meal which both the ladies attended in their dressing-gowns. Rubinstein paid Destinn one extravagant compliment after another, even going so far as to

---

*It is fair to add that this particular label, like the familiar tale of buxom Toscas bouncing back into view after the death fall from the Castel Sant'Angelo, has been hung round many a soprano's neck.

say that his own phrasing of Chopin had been influenced by her mastery of *rubato*, but instead of purring with pleasure at such praise Destinn leapt up in fury, flung her champagne glass into the fireplace, and screamed 'All right, all right, I know I am a good singer, but I am also a woman!' Her sister, recognizing an exit cue when she heard one, calmly withdrew, and Rubinstein's surprise at this sudden turn of events was intensified, once the diva had disrobed, by finding that a brightly coloured tattoo of a boa constrictor entwined one of her legs from the ankle to the upper thigh. I have never quite understood how this fact had not become evident to one and all during the Dance of the Seven Veils, but who am I to doubt the word of Arthur Rubinstein?

It is perhaps the ultimate tribute to Destinn's vocal artistry that although photographs do on the whole lend conviction to Farrar's 'Valkyrie' jibe she was never short of amorous pursuers, both of the welcome and the unwelcome variety. A newspaper interview from June 1914 offers an interesting insight into one of the more tiresome side-products of operatic stardom:

> 'I have only one objection to the role of Butterfly,' declared Mme Destinn, 'and that is that it seems to have too great an attraction for those people who write love-lorn letters to singers. I have received a great many such unwelcome billets-doux.' She produced one faded letter, which read as follows: 'Most Radiant Madame Butterfly Destinn! Do not imagine that I am in any sense a Japanese when I tell you that you are the most lovable oriental I have ever laid eyes on. One glance at your glorious beauty across the footlights has thrown me into the hysterics of a great and genuine passion, and I hereby fling my heart at your small feet, and also offer you my hand and my fortune. If you will have me, we shall make a pilgrimage to Japan, and there you shall dwell by my side in Geisha costume for ever!'

As the writer of this remarkable document was a well-known American millionaire, Destinn's contemptuous dismissal of his suit offers a reassuring indication that although Farrar may have been justified in calling her 'indefatigable' she was not entirely unselective.

The country later to be known as Czechoslovakia was responsible for more than one thorn in the flesh of Geraldine Farrar. When she withdrew

Adored by the public, dreaded by many a leading tenor. Maria Jeritza (1887–1982), 'the Viennese thunderbolt', as Maria/Marietta in Korngold's Die tote Stadt.

from the Met she had only just passed her fortieth birthday, and the principal reason for this premature retirement was the arrival on the scene of an obstacle over which even she did not possess the power to triumph – 'the Viennese thunderbolt', Maria Jeritza. Born in fact in the city of Brno (Brunn), Jeritza grew up to personify everything which the public looks for in a thoroughbred prima donna. She was glamorous, capricious, and controversial, a star whose mere presence on the stage sent an electric current through the house, a woman who could make her own rules, never out of the headlines, frequently in the law courts, adored by the operatic publics of Vienna, London and New York, and dreaded by numerous leading tenors. She was tall and blonde, and blessed with a pair of startlingly bright blue eyes, and so numerous are the stories of her outrageous goings-on that it is sometimes hard to remember what stature she attained as a performer; not for nothing were the two leading opera composers of the day, Puccini and Richard Strauss, to be numbered amongst her most devoted admirers.

The juiciest of the operatic scandals in which Jeritza loomed large was the Great Vienna Spitting Incident of 1925. This occurred in the State Opera during a performance of *Die Walküre* while Wotan and his wife Fricka were conducting their somewhat extended discussion on the subject of marital fidelity. Jeritza was in the wings waiting to come on as Sieglinde, and according to the Fricka, Maria Olczewska, she was making audibly derogatory remarks, something which seems entirely likely as Olczewska, who was engaged to the baritone singing Wotan, had been known to express her suspicions that there was something going on between her fiancé and the winsome Miss Jeritza. Several times Olczewska hissed at Jeritza to keep quiet, but to no avail, so eventually she worked her way to the side of the stage and spat at her. Unfortunately her aim was at fault and the person in the line of fire was an innocent bystander, the mezzo Ermine Kittel. I feel disinclined to believe press reports that Kittel fainted from the shock – as a fully armoured Valkyrie she was, after all, well protected – but the upshot of the affair was that Olczewska was dismissed from the Opera while Jeritza survived without even a reprimand.

Jeritza's most famous visiting card was the role of Tosca, and the moment everyone waited for was the Act II aria 'Vissi d'arte', which she invariably sang lying on her front flat out upon the floor. She loved to tell the story of how this tradition had been established. During a rehearsal attended by Puccini the baritone singing Scarpia had pushed her harder than she expected, whereupon she had slipped and fallen, bumping her nose in the process. Fearing that she had a nose-bleed, instead of standing up again she decided to sing the aria right there as she was, whereupon the delighted composer leapt up from his seat in the stalls and called out 'Brava Maria! This was an idea from God! Never sing the aria any other way!' So beguiling is this version of the story that it would be a shame to give any credence to the eminent director Wilhelm von Wymetal, who used to claim that the idea had been his own and that he and Jeritza had spent quite a while working on it. Be that as it may it was principally, though perhaps not exclusively, her handling of the aria which earned for Jeritza the nickname of 'la prima donna prostrata'.

Jeritza's first role at the Met was one of many which she had created in Europe, Marie/Marietta in Korngold's *Die tote Stadt*. Her success was enough to persuade the critic Deems Taylor that 'New York had found the thing dearest to its heart – a new personality', but it was when she followed this up with her celebrated Tosca that the thunderbolt really struck home. Even Gatti, who had experienced every famous Tosca since the opera was first written, was moved to write that after the 'Vissi d'arte', 'the theatre broke out in a demonstration the equal of which I can scarcely recall'. Not only Farrar but also that haunting operatic tragedienne Claudia Muzio took it as a signal that the Met was no longer the right address for them, though Farrar could not resist the temptation to include in her memoirs one well-aimed Parthian shot. Jeritza, she found, had adopted a pose of 'unashamed abandon', and she went on to say: 'From my seat in the stalls I obtained no view of any expressive pantomime on her pretty face, while I was surprised by the questionable flaunting of a well-cushioned and obvious posterior.'

Tosca was also Jeritza's chosen vehicle for her Covent Garden debut four years later, and as this followed shortly after The Great Spitting Incident and the ensuing furore in the international press, public interest ran high. Tickets changed hands at eight times their face value and an all-night queue formed outside the gallery. Nor was the audience disappointed. As the *Manchester Guardian* put it 'Tosca panted round the room like a tigress in a paroxysm of terror and fury, and there were distinct signs of hysterics amongst the audience.' For her next Covent Garden role, Giordano's Fedora, Jeritza indulged in a typically extravagant whim. She announced to the press that she would be wearing all her own jewellery, and as it was valued at a sum which would nowadays be well over a million pounds several of the gentlemen on stage during the chorus scenes were not members of the cast, but private detectives employed by her insurance company. It was in this same role of Fedora that Jeritza first embarked upon one of her most widely publicized tiffs with a tenor, claiming that during a performance at the Met she had been roughly handled by Beniamino Gigli. Matters came to a head shortly afterwards when they were cast together in *Tosca* and there was an altercation about the acknowledgement of applause. Jeritza elected to step in front of the curtain, call for silence, hold a handkerchief to her tear-stained face and announce to the public 'Mr Gigli not kind to me.' By a happy coincidence it was a broadcast performance.

Jeritza remained a prima donna right up to the end of her very long life. During the Hitler years she settled in the United States – the last two of her four husbands were both wealthy Americans – and when she returned to Vienna in 1950 to raise money for the rebuilding of the State Opera by appearing once again as Tosca it was immaterial to the public that she could no longer sing the role. At sixty-three she still performed the 'Vissi d'arte' lying on the floor, and late that night she was to be found scattering autographed photographs onto the crowds of worshippers who had gathered beneath her hotel balcony. In her late eighties she was still to be seen at the opening night of every Met season, swathed from neck to ankle in white mink, a living reminder to the audience of what it had once meant to be a prima donna. One little anecdote from her old age, told to me by the American soprano Beverly Sills, sums up the role of 'the sublime species' as Jeritza evidently saw it. While Sills was still in her *Wunderkind* days she sang at a party where Jeritza was amongst the guests, and after her performance Jeritza presented her with a gold toothpick, a weird thing to give to a child. 'You must become a character,' Jeritza explained. 'You must make people talk about you. After we have all eaten you pick your teeth with this gold toothpick and you'll see – everybody will be talking about you!'

Viewed superficially, the desire to attract attention at all costs may seem one of the more trivial attributes of the true prima donna, but Jeritza knew whereof she spoke. There were other sopranos at the Met who, viewed purely as singers, were indubitably Jeritza's superiors. Claudia Muzio was one, and she was a fabled actress too – I well remember Dame Eva Turner telling me that amongst the sopranos of her time Muzio made 'the most unforgettable impression of all'. Rosa Ponselle was another. Some years ago I asked the soprano Nanette Guilford, who had sung regularly at the Met during the 1920s and '30s, how Jeritza's voice compared with Ponselle's, and back came the answer like a pistol shot. 'Would you compare Woolworth with Cartier? Jeritza had a good voice, but Ponselle's was the most beautiful voice that anyone ever heard!' And yet,

Below '*A mass of carefully dis- organised auburn hair*'. The bewitching Conchita Supervia (1895–1936).

Below right Supervia in her role as châtelaine at her British husband's country home in Rustington, Sussex.

and yet . . . No opera manager, especially not one as hard-nosed as Gatti-Casazza, will pay a star singer one penny more than he or she is worth in box-office terms, and it is interesting to note that in the Met season of 1921–2 the Woolworth voice was earning $1,500 per performance to the Cartier's $625. Geraldine Farrar, who also knew the value of attracting attention, received the same fee as Jeritza, while Muzio, who liked to live her life in anonymity, received only $800.

If a talent for attracting attention is one *sine qua non* of all true prima donnas, the knack of getting their own way is certainly another, and just as the personalities of the different ladies vary, so too do the techniques which they employ. Some use the bludgeon, others prefer guile, but now I would like to turn to one whose most devastating weapon was her charm. The epithet most commonly applied to the Spanish mezzo-soprano Conchita Supervia (1895–1936) was 'enchanting', and to judge from Ivor Newton's description of her it was the *mot juste*:

Unusually beautiful, with large expressive eyes, a small nose and the most beautifully shaped mouth I have ever seen, she had a mass of carefully disorganised auburn hair, and the sort of figure, all curves and charm, that Latin taste adjudges to be perfect. She was always intensely alert and possessed of apparently inexhaustible vitality. Her gaiety, good temper, sympathy and charm cloaked a keen intelligence and adamantine will-power. To be with her was to inhabit a land of cloudless happiness; waiters and railway porters leapt devotedly to her service and everywhere men stopped to admire her as she passed.

As far as the 'adamantine will-power' is concerned I have little doubt that those who had the running of Covent Garden in those days would have concurred. In 1934 Sir Thomas Beecham and Mr Geoffrey Toye, respectively artistic director and managing director of the Royal Opera, made the mistake of trying to slip a fast one past Supervia, and they lived to regret it. They engaged her for Carmen and for the title-role in Rossini's *La Cenerentola* (*Cinderella*), and from the outset she made it a condition of the engagement that she would not have to touch the former until the latter, which is written in a totally different vocal style, was over and done with. Toye, however, feeling that it would be a risk to introduce a new singer in an unfamiliar opera at the beginning of the season, announced *Carmen* as the opening attraction. This proved the catalyst for a deluge of letters from Supervia, all expressed with the utmost courtesy, but leaving no room for doubt that Toye was up against an immovable object. Regarding her contract with Covent Garden as null and void Supervia signed up with a film company; the Royal Opera was left with an extravagant new production of *La Cenerentola* on its hands and the only mezzo in the world worthy to play the title-role had slipped through their fingers. In the end Toye was reduced to attending on Supervia late one night in the Mayfair Hotel and imploring her to help them out. This she graciously agreed to do, by singing two performances of *La Cenerentola* at the end of the season.

Despite all the annoyance to which she had been subjected Supervia arrived for the rehearsals radiating good will towards all and sundry. One day Sir Thomas, who was conducting, wanted to know exactly how much music would be required for the entrance of the crystal coach. As the coach was not yet available for a trial run Supervia came up with the perfect solution; 'Sir Thomas, Geoffrey!' she cried, 'come and be my snow-white ponies!' So it came about that these two lofty personages were to be seen trotting round the stage with a grave demeanour, lifting their knees in the approved dressage fashion, followed by Supervia, whip in hand, while the rehearsal pianist timed them on a stopwatch. I cannot help feeling that Supervia must have been itching to put the whip to its proper use – Jeritza, I imagine, might well have done, but Supervia's was a more conciliatory style. Asked soon afterwards in a newspaper inter-view what were the essential ingredients for a successful opera production she replied, 'One only needs one or two *esprits animateurs*. At Covent Garden we have two such spirits – the adorable Sir Thomas Beecham and myself.'

During the immediate post-war years, the years when my own opera-going first began in London, there was a drabness and an austerity in the air which were scarcely conducive to the emergence of a new generation of prima donnas. The First Lady of the operatic stage was still the incom-parable Kirsten Flagstad, but while her artistry was based on the two unshakeable rocks of vocal magnificence and musical impeccability there was nothing glamorous or exotic about her. It was as if, in a world of clothes rationing and coal shortages, an old-style prima donna would strike a jarringly sybaritic note; but then for a few brief, glorious years the comet known as Ljuba Welitsch shot across the operatic sky. No artificial gimmicks were required to build Welitsch into a 'character', Nature had already done the job. Born on 10 July 1913 under a tree near the Bulgarian village of Slavjanovo – her mother was taken short while tilling the fields – Welitsch was blessed with a wondrous head of flaming red hair, a temperament to match, and one of those rare and marvellous voices which are so much an instrument of their own that half a bar on an old recording is enough to make anyone who ever heard her in the flesh sit up and exclaim 'Ah! that's Ljuba Welitsch!' It was a voice of extra-ordinary clarity and brightness, a voice which could take wing with a thrillingly soaring quality, but it was also a voice with an edge on it, not a harsh or grating edge, but an edge of unabashed sensuality. She worked her way upwards from the chorus of the Sofia Opera via five invaluable years in Graz; during one of them, 1938, she added fifteen roles to her repertoire ranging from First Bridesmaid in *Der Freischütz* to Manon and

Ljuba Welitsch as Donna Anna in Don Giovanni.

Butterfly. Eventually she found her way to Vienna, and it was there, in what at the time was called the Opernhaus der Stadt Wien, but is now familiar as the Volksoper, that she first tackled the role with which she became internationally identified, Richard Strauss's Salome.

I doubt whether any other voice has ever been so *right* for this basically impossible role, demanding as it does the girlishness of a teenager combined with a febrile eroticism and the muscularity to survive against one of opera's most daunting orchestral accompaniments. Welitsch had the benefit of Strauss's personal assistance in the preparation of the role – the production was mounted in the summer of 1944 in honour of the Master's eightieth birthday – and as she herself later declared 'Strauss recognized possibilities in my voice and coaxed colours from it which I myself had not yet discovered.' If one listens to certain passages from the earliest of her various *Salome* recordings one can detect the fidelity with which she assimilated Strauss's advice on how to delineate the character of the depraved young princess through his own diabolically clever setting of the text – the chilling sense of disappointment, for instance, in the words 'Ach, ich habe ihn geküsst, deinen Mund!', 'Ah, I have kissed it, your mouth!', delivered in a flat, almost factual whisper – while at the role's ferocious climax the sheer brilliance of the tone cuts through the welter of orchestral sound like a highly polished rapier. It is significant that when Strauss presented Welitsch with a photograph of himself he inscribed it with the words 'Ich wusste nicht, dass man meine Salome so schön singen kann', 'I did not know that one could sing my Salome with such beauty.'

Welitsch's knack of driving audiences wild with her Salome was, of course, only partly attributable to careful coaching by the composer; the special magic came from her. To quote Beverly Sills again, who witnessed her historic triumph at the Met in 1949, 'The inner brilliance transmitted by Welitsch was a hundred times brighter than anything which the lighting department could ever have produced. It was the first time I experienced what it means for an operatic performance to lead to pandemonium. The public went mad with enthusiasm.' In the measured phrases of Philip Hope-Wallace, reviewing Welitsch's London performance in the same year, 'she has not only the voice for one of the most exacting parts in opera, but, what is even rarer, enough temperament to cope with the role without ever appearing to be absurd, and indeed touching at some points a kind of grandeur.'

Temperament! That, apart from her extraordinary voice, was what set Welitsch apart from the many other wonderful sopranos who graced the Vienna Opera at that time. Schwarzkopf, Seefried, Jurinac, Gueden, della Casa – they were all heavenly singers, but it was Welitsch who possessed that dash of outrageousness which set her apart and which made her, as far as such a thing was possible, the natural successor to Maria Jeritza. Nevertheless, if temperament helped to make her Salome the sensation that it was, all nubile femininity, top notes soaring, flaming hair flying, it brought many a critical rap to her knuckles when she brought it to bear on certain of the other roles in her repertoire. Her anarchic flamboyance as Musetta in the Covent Garden *Bohème* of 1948 turned the last few minutes of Act II into a shambles – 'A most absurd display,' wrote Hope-Wallace – for the simple reason that the public flatly refused to stop applauding after her no-holds-barred performance of the familiar solo, 'Quando m'en vo''. Lord Harewood, who was there that evening with the distinguished British soprano Joan Cross, later wrote in his memoirs 'Ljuba as we had expected stormed onto the stage, smiling fit to bust, but we were hardly prepared for the diamond brilliance of her singing of the Waltz song; nor apparently was the audience, which went pleasurably mad. Joan and I yelled with the rest of them and we were still applauding when the act came to an end, fully four minutes after she had finished the solo proper – and we were properly castigated next morning in *The Times* . . .' When Welitsch persuaded Rudolf Bing to let her sing the same role for one evening at the Met in 1952, by which time her voice was already in decline, the result was, in Bing's own words, 'probably the best-remembered performance of the season'. 'It could', his memoirs continue, 'be said to define the difference between a mischievous courtesan and a raucous whore. She jumped on the tables and danced, forced her Marcello to carry her on his shoulders around the stage, elbowed everybody out of the way, and just misbehaved shockingly.' As the critic Howard Taubman put it in the *New York Herald Tribune*, Welitsch's display 'had to be seen to be believed', but it did fulfil one important function for Rudolf Bing. A young American soprano who enjoyed great success as a soubrette had long been pestering him to let her sing the role of Mimì – a task, in his opinion, far beyond her capabilities – and in the end he had relented. When she heard, though, on the very day of the performance, who her Musetta was to be 'she virtually fled the country' and had to be replaced by a colleague of sterner mettle.

The tragically early decline in Welitsch's vocal powers has been attributed by many different experts to many different causes. Some say that she simply sang too many Salomes, others that one performance of Donna Anna in *Don Giovanni*, sung against doctor's orders with an inflamed throat, did the damage, while others simply shrug their shoulders and mention the burning of candles at both ends. I remember the great bass-baritone Paul Schoeffler telling me many years ago of an occasion when he and Welitsch were both staying in the same hotel on some foreign tour. She rang him up the morning after a performance and asked him to come and visit her as she was feeling lonely; when he went to her room, there she was sitting up in bed with a glass of champagne in one hand and a large cigar in the other. Now, this story may be purely apocryphal, but if it is I know that Madame Welitsch will forgive me, as it is one of the privileges of the prima donna to figure in apocryphal stories; and she, blessed as she is with a robust sense of humour, would be the first person to admit that she has always had a healthy appetite for the good things of life.

At the time of writing Ljuba Welitsch has just celebrated her eighty-second birthday,* and though her operatic career may have come to an untimely end some forty years ago she has by no means lived in idleness. Switching in her late fifties to the style of operetta roles disarmingly categorized in German as 'die komische Alte', 'the funny old woman', she adorned the stage of the Volksoper for season after season, and she claims to have appeared in seventy-five movies as well as thirty-five television plays. When she returned to the Met in 1972 to appear in the speaking role of the Duchess of Crakentorp in Donizetti's *La fille du régiment* she was received, so she once assured me, with 'half an hour's applause' – and in case readers may feel that some of these figures appear to have benefited from mild inflation, one can only ask why Ljuba Welitsch should suddenly start doing things on a normal humdrum scale?

The occasion on which she presented me with these statistics was a visit which I paid her in her Vienna apartment back in 1984 to record her memories of Maria Jeritza for a radio programme which I was presenting for the BBC, and it was an unforgettable experience. She was not married at that time – her second marriage, to a young Viennese policeman named Schmalvogel, whom she first met when he stopped her for a driving offence, had come to an acrimonious end – but a young American conductor appeared to be in residence. The day before, someone had tried to break into her apartment – 'Can you imagine, someone try to burrgle Ljuba?' – and shortly before my arrival 'a lovely boy' had come to fix her lock, so there was plenty going on. Before we settled down to our interview, which in view of the broadcast had to be conducted in English – the language had several engaging embellishments bestowed upon it – she asked her American friend to bring her a glass of white wine 'with a leetle drop of cognac in the bottom'. After he had returned with a glass con-

---

*Sadly, Ljuba Welitsch died as this book was going to press.

taining a suspiciously dark-hued liquid we got down to work, and I wish the printed word could convey even a fraction of the vivacity which illuminates the resultant tape. One remarkable feature was Welitsch's generosity towards other singers. 'For me,' she told me, 'Jeritza was the greatest Tosca I ever saw. I also was a good Tosca (fruity chuckle) but in comparation (one of her favourite words) with Jeritza I was nothing' – and how often does one hear a great prima donna say a thing like that? She rounded off the reminiscences of her famous predecessor with one expression of regret: 'Jeritza always had rich men. I always had poor gentlemens as my husbands. I don't know how she did that – I was untalentiert in that position!' (extremely fruity chuckle).

Not unexpectedly, Welitsch, like Jeritza before her, was able to shed some interesting light on the business of being a prima donna. 'My dear,' she told me, 'many people say I am difficult, but any person who stands on a stage and *is* something and has some personality is not so easy. Stage is something like a warr.' Her main enemies, it appeared, had been Italian singers – 'sometimes they are not quite fair, you know?' – and I have a suspicion that at that moment the baritone Paolo Silveri may have crossed her mind. He was the unfortunate Marcello in both the Covent Garden and the Met performances of *Bohème* who had had to carry her round the stage shoulder high, and the two of them had tangled on several occasions. When they appeared together as Don Giovanni and Donna Anna at the Edinburgh Festival of 1948 she, with an assertiveness worthy of Melba herself, had had all of Silveri's costumes removed from the number one dressing-room and carried to some distant spot upstairs, claiming that as she was the prima donna of the piece the dressing-room was hers by right. Silveri somewhat naturally saw to the reversal of this procedure on the grounds that his was the title-role, and in any case he needed to be near the stage because of his many changes of costume. Within weeks they were cast together again in *Aida* at Covent Garden and the bickering continued, with the costumes featuring once again amongst the various bones of contention. It was Welitsch's wish that Silveri, who was playing her father Amonasro, should wear a red wig, thus establishing the existence of some gene in the family which would justify her in keeping her own hair, despite the fact that the story of the opera obliges them to hail from Ethiopia, where red hair is, to say the least, a rarity. Moreover, after Silveri had selected for himself a highly fetching leopard-skin costume with heavy gold bracelets on his arms and sandals on his feet, making him look, as he later wrote, 'every inch the noble savage', she did her best to persuade the wardrobe department to replace it with a long cloak and spiked helmet 'which would have been the envy of a Visigoth'. Her sole reason for doing this, she explained to the management, was that Silveri did not have shapely legs, and it would be doing him a favour. She herself was accoutred, as he put it, 'in black chiffon and elegant titian coiffure', with the result that she looked more like a Paris model than an Ethiopian slave. 'There was', Silveri summed up, 'a strong feeling of animosity between us.'

I cannot leave the subject of the glorious Ljuba – the name, by the way is Bulgarian for 'Love' – without relating the story of an incident which befell her on one of her visits to London. After lunching with that celebrated gourmet, the conductor John Pritchard, she realized that time had flown and she was late for a vital appointment. Out she rushed in search of a taxi, shouting 'Carr! I need carr!' and when she spotted a black vehicle driven by a man in a chauffeur's uniform coming slowly towards her she ran into the street, signalling to the driver to stop and calling out 'I need you, I need you!' With infinite courtesy the driver wound down the window and replied 'You do not appear to need me yet, Madam.' The vehicle was a hearse.

If we take imperiousness as one of the hallmarks of the classic prima donna then room must be found for the great Croatian soprano Zinka Milanov (1906–1989). Her dramatic post-retirement entrances into the auditorium of the Met worthily maintained the Jeritza tradition, making it perfectly evident to the audience that whoever the leading soprano of that particular evening might be the true star was sitting in the stalls. She was famous, too, for the succinctness of her one-liners. When told that the American soprano Eleanor Steber had twisted her ankle during Tosca's death-leap from the battlements of the Castel Sant'Angelo her reply was short and to the point – 'I always said the role was too heavy for her'; and asked if it was true that a certain colleague had a tendency to sing out of tune she replied, 'Not out of tune exactly, but in a different key from the pianist.' There was an occasion, too, when Milanov and several associates were having lunch during the making of a recording,

A prima donna in the grand tradition. Zinka Milanov (1906–1989).

and despite the fact that Giuseppe di Stefano was amongst those present she launched into a sweeping diatribe on the awfulness of tenors in general and Italian tenors in particular. Di Stefano tried to shrug it off by observing that she could not be referring to him as he was not Italian but Sicilian, whereupon she fixed him with a devastating glare and spat out the one word: 'Worrse!'

There are those who feel that with the disappearance from the stage of such legends as Callas, Welitsch and Milanov we have seen the last of 'the sublime species', and that the operatic profession of today has no place for the exoticism of the classic prima donna. I am not so sure. Certainly in the last few decades there has been no shortage of superb female singers, originating from every corner of the world – they are far too numerous to be listed here – and amongst them there have been several whom Jeritza herself would have been happy to salute as 'characters'; it is simply that times change and the vagaries of the prima donna's conduct change with them. On one not so distant occasion the Canadian soprano Teresa Stratas, recognizing at the first rehearsal of a new production that the director was incompetent, whipped out her mobile telephone, rang up her agent, and strode round the stage demanding in no uncertain terms that as he had got her into this mess it was up to him to get her out of it, while the hapless director, who understood no English, trotted along behind her explaining his requirements for Act I. Julia Migenes, too, has been known to make some spirited remarks – when a director objected to her and the tenor Neil Shicoff indulging in a passionate kiss in *Manon* she simply said, 'Well we're going to do it, so if it upsets you you'd better look away!' – but the palm for genuinely disruptive shenanigans by a contemporary prima donna should probably be awarded to another American soprano, the brilliantly talented Kathleen Battle. She survived a seismic fall-out with the conductor of a *Rosenkavalier* production at the Met because she had already been announced as Pavarotti's partner in *L'elisir d'amore* on a company tour to Japan, but it was another Donizetti comedy, *La fille du régiment*, which brought about her downfall. The opera contains a scene in which the soprano sings an aria accompanied at the piano by another member of the cast, the old Marquise. On this occasion the Marquise was being sung by the mezzo Rosalind Elias, but Battle objected to her piano-playing and demanded that she should be replaced. She had overplayed her hand; it was she who was given the order of the boot, and Joseph Volpe, the General Manager of the Met, made it plain that she would not be welcomed back until she had proved in some other house that she could behave like a responsible company member. Since then, sadly, she has restricted herself mainly to concert work, often involving a considerable amount of musical 'crossover', and a major talent appears to have been lost to opera. It would be a pity if, in future years, her name is principally remembered for the T-shirt issued by the company of the San Francisco Opera after she had sung some guest performances there – 'We have survived the Battle.'

Perhaps the greatest shift in the nature of prima donna-hood lies in the requirements of the current repertoire. Today it would be scarcely possible for a critic to write, as Ernest Newman did in 1919, 'My own objection to the prima donna is that, as a rule, she represents merely tone and technique without intelligence.' Many of the demands on the modern diva tend to be of a different nature from anything which her predecessors would have encountered – it is hard, for instance, to imagine Jenny Lind or Adelina Patti singing the excruciatingly difficult soprano aria from the second act of Alban Berg's *Lulu* while riding a bicycle round the stage topless, as a partner of mine in one of the German opera houses was obliged to do – but just occasionally we are still blessed with the presence of a personality willing and able to fight a rearguard action on behalf of the status quo. Some twenty years ago the Spanish soprano Montserrat Caballé, a lady whom tactful commentators have been known to describe as 'statuesque', arrived at Covent Garden to rehearse the role of Leonora in a revival of *Il trovatore*, and a young staff producer was given the task of taking her through the production. 'You make your first entrance at the head of this staircase,' he explained, 'and while you sing the opening recitative you walk slowly down it, bringing you to the centre of the stage in time for the opening of the aria.' With a charming smile Madame Caballé replied 'Darrling, let us get one thing straight – either I sing or I move!'

It would of course be a mistake to assume that prima donnas are only to be found amongst the ranks of the superstars – many an operatic chorus boasts its own resident *grande dame*. When that brilliant American soprano June Anderson came to Covent Garden a couple of years ago to sing Lucia in a production which had become a trifle haphazard – it had first been mounted as a vehicle for Joan Sutherland – she adopted a stage position at the dress rehearsal which struck her as apt and convenient for that arduous showpiece the Mad Scene. 'Hey!' came a voice from the chorus, 'you can't stand there – that's my place!' It was the spot which had been assigned to the chorister in question by Franco Zeffirelli back in 1959 and no upstart was going to wrest it from her.

Finally, a brief salute to that truly formidable representative of the 'sublime species', the *Kleinstadtdiva* or Provincial Prima Donna. One of the roles which I sang with a small company in Switzerland during my first year as a singer was that of Camille de Rossillon in Lehár's *The Merry Widow*. It involves one extremely demanding scene consisting of the aria 'Wie eine Rosenknospe', complete with top C, immediately followed by the high and taxing tessitura of the so-called Summerhouse Duet, 'Komm in den kleinen Pavilion'. Although the latter is indeed a duet the soprano's

Joan Sutherland, 'La stupenda', as Marie in La fille du régiment, *Covent Garden, 1966, with a youthful Luciano Pavarotti as Tonio and Spiro Malas as Sulpice.*

contribution is minimal, so that during the scene as a whole the tenor undertakes, let us say, four-fifths of the work. On the first night of the production in question I had one of those rare and memorable evenings when everything went right, and as my partner and I vanished on the final note into the little summerhouse the applause was as deafening as applause can be in a theatre with only three hundred seats. It soon became evident, moreover, that it was not going to stop. No provision had been made in the production for such an eventuality, and as my partner was a more experienced performer than myself I turned to her and whispered 'What do we do now?' 'You stay here,' came the reply. 'I will go out and take a bow.'

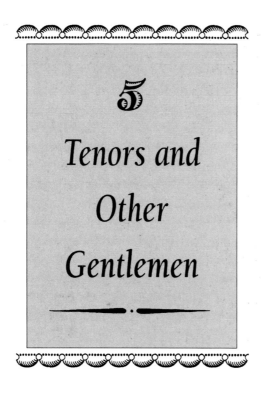

5

Tenors and
Other
Gentlemen

When the New Zealand-born prima donna Frances Alda published her memoirs she gave them the title *Men, Women and Tenors*. For many years Madame Alda had been a lady to reckon with at the Metropolitan Opera, not least because she had married the General Manager, Giulio Gatti-Casazza, and her decision to segregate tenors from the rest of the human race may well have been inspired by personal experience. We tenors, however, have long become inured to this kind of thing. Within the operatic profession we are the butt of innumerable jokes – 'Tenors have resonances where their brains should be', 'tenor is not a voice, it is a disease' and so forth – while in German a favourite translation for 'stupid, stupider, stupidest' is 'dumm, dümmer, Tenor'. Speaking without a whiff of bias I can state categorically how it is that jibes such as these have become such common currency – the others are jealous. 'The tenor always gets the best tunes', 'the tenor always gets the girl', 'the tenor always gets the most money.' Now we are at the heart of the matter.

The 1990s have been perhaps the most tenor-conscious decade in operatic history; could posters proclaiming the impending arrival of The Three Baritones or The Three Mezzo-Sopranos ever result in hundreds of thousands of people storming the box-offices of the world, and millions of dollars pouring into the pockets of all concerned? So what is it about the tenor voice? Well, scientists claim to have established that the highest tones in the normal male voice (in other words excluding the male alto, *haute-contre*, counter-tenor and so on) are the ones which most notably excite the emotional responses of the listener, and who am I to disagree with their findings? The audience, I believe, senses a greater feeling of danger with a tenor than with other male singers. Of course baritones and basses also have testing high tones to sing, but the baritone's occasional high A flat and the bass's occasional high F do not represent such an evident tight-rope act as a note like the celebrated high C in *La bohème* – will he hit it or will he tumble to his doom? The tenor voice, too, gives an impression of youthfulness. Over the years it has become almost habitual for composers to regard the romantic lead as the natural territory of the tenor, while the wicked baritone plots his downfall and the bass dons a long white beard to make weighty pronouncements as the king or the high priest; and as there are seldom more than a handful of people around at any one time who can make a convincing job of these high-C-heroes it follows as the night the day that their market value rises above that of other singers – which in turn results in certain of them developing an unrealistic view of their own importance. Every now and then, as we shall see, baritones and basses do crop up who can compete on equal terms with the most temperamental of tenors; moreover when we compare tenors with the female of the species it must signify something that while the term 'prima donna' has entered the realms of everyday parlance the term 'prim' uomo' has not, and that while everybody knows what is meant by the word 'diva', 'divo' has remained an unfamiliar expression. Not wishing to be accused of male chauvinism I shall take this particular point no further.

It is perhaps strange to note that back in the early days of operatic history the 'lover' role which we nowadays associate with the tenor was much more likely to be assigned to a castrato, and even when, as in the case of Monteverdi's *Orfeo* of 1607, the task was entrusted to a tenor, he was expected to excel not in the trumpeting of his top notes but in precisely the same virtues as characterized the castrati, namely vocal agility and flexibility. When Monteverdi's Orpheus seeks to soften the heart of Charon and persuade him to break the rules by ferrying a living man over the River Styx it is with a dazzling display of embellishments and ornamentations that he sets about his business, not with the kind of unanswerable lung power which became the *sine qua non* of the Italian tenor three hundred years on.

The more usual fate of the seventeenth-century tenor was to be given a comic role to play, often in drag, and it was really Mozart who established the tenor as the natural choice for the 'juvenile lead'. Mozart, like most composers of the time, wrote specifically for those voices which happened to be available to him. When he had the leading German tenor of his day, Valentin Adamberger, at his disposal for *Die Entführung* he cast him as the hero and wrote an extremely taxing role; when he wrote *Le nozze di Figaro* his tenor was the Irishman Michael Kelly, a natural *buffo*, to whom the two comic figures of Basilio and Curzio were assigned. Had Kelly been a performer of Adamberger's mettle it is perfectly possible that the role of Count Almaviva would have been written for a tenor. Either way, though, we would still have been treated to the delightful vignette which Kelly gives us in his memoirs of Mozart at rehearsal – 'I never shall forget his little animated countenance, when lighted up with the glowing rays of genius; it is as impossible to describe it, as it would be to paint sunbeams.'

The history of opera is dotted with singers who have influenced the composers of their day; another was the tenor Giovanni Battista Rubini (1794–1854), famous for his collaborations with Bellini and Donizetti. Rubini's special claim to fame lay in his remarkably extended upper register – Bellini even wrote an F above high C for him in *I puritani*, Rubini having already proved that he could climb that high when he hit the note by mistake in rehearsal – and many a role written for the tenor during this period has proved a difficult nut for modern singers to crack. The fact is often overlooked, however, that in those days no tenor was expected to sing any note above an A natural with what we nowadays call 'full voice';

The creator of many a bel canto *tenor role. Giovanni Battista Rubini (1794–1854).*

the sound of the castrati was still in people's ears and it was considered entirely acceptable for a tenor to take his top notes in a sort of cultivated falsetto. Rubini, indeed, in order to avoid too crass a gearchange between his different registers, used to sing whole arias in a gently cooing tone, thus making his celebrated top notes appear part of an organic whole; but things began to change when a Frenchman named Gilbert Duprez took his courage in both hands and astounded the operatic world with the first ever publicly performed high C from the chest.* He achieved this notable feat in the role of Arnold in Rossini's *Guillaume Tell*, and it caused a sensation something akin to breaking the sound barrier or the four minute

---

*Normal pitch was lower in those days than it is now. Musicologists tend to set the difference at something slightly less than a semitone, so that Duprez's C was probably nearer to what we would call a B natural.

mile. The tone was not by all accounts a pleasant one – like the old story of the dog playing the piano, it was not that he did it well but that he did it at all – and Rossini himself preferred to hear Duprez's rival Adolphe Nourrit who used to take the note in head voice. The ungrateful composer even went so far as to compare the sound of Duprez's operatic landmark with 'the squawk of a capon whose throat is being cut', but it was not long before other practitioners of the *Do di petto* ('C from the chest') began to make their presence felt, and the manly tenor tones so beloved of the modern public gradually began to replace the suaver utterances of classical *bel canto*.

One such was Enrico Tamberlik (1820–1889), a particular favourite with the London public, which was regularly driven into a state of near-frenzy by his clarion top notes. In 1850, so the *Illustrated London News* assures us, he 'electrified' Covent Garden by taking a high C sharp from the chest in the role of Rossini's Otello, and as a proof that such rare attainments have never come cheap, by 1854 he was receiving from the Royal Italian Opera the then staggering sum of £480 per month, and paid in advance too. Tamberlik's was an early example of the style of voice known as the *tenore robusto*; his natural territory was not the world of Rossini, Donizetti and Bellini, but that of the vigorous newcomer Giuseppe Verdi. Tamberlik introduced Manrico, alias Il trovatore, to London audiences in 1855, and in 1862 he created the role of Alvaro in *La forza del destino* in St Petersburg, both of them parts which call for plenty of meat in the voice. It was, however, with the role of Otello that Verdi carried his demands on the Italian tenor voice to their ultimate pitch,* and it was specifically written to match the exceptional range and resonance of the great Francesco Tamagno, a singer once described by the critic of *The Graphic* as being 'an actor and singer head and shoulders above every other artist alive'. One can only hope that that particular number of *The Graphic* did not find its way into the hands of a gentleman who had every

---

*Lest anyone should suppose that Verdi was as universally admired in his own day as he is now, it is interesting to read the following reference to *La traviata* in an *Illustrated London News* of 1878, twenty-five years after the opera's premiere: '*Traviata* is not merely a repulsive, but in many respects a disgusting opera, and no young lady can study the part of Violetta without sullying the purity of her own mind.'

Above An early exponent of the 'high C from the chest'. Enrico Tamberlik (1820–1889).

Above right Giuseppi Verdi with his first Otello, Francesco Tamagno (1850–1905).

reason to regard himself as the tenorial apple of the public's eye, the one and only Jean de Reszke. De Reszke, a Pole by birth, had had a strange career, starting as a successful baritone, restudying as a tenor, failing dismally at his second coming, withdrawing for five whole years, and finally establishing himself the third time around as *the* 'French' tenor of his day. Thanks to his technical mastery and his fine musicianship he eventually extended his range to include the heaviest of the Wagnerian roles, but it was as Gounod's Roméo that he truly captured the hearts of London's *haute volée*.

It would probably be impossible to enjoy the reputation of a Jean de Reszke without suffering from a *soupçon* of vanity, and though he was a performer of immaculate conscientiousness there was one little incident, back in 1894, when things did not quite go his way. The management decided to present Massenet's latest opera, *Werther*, and despite a starry

cast – the lovely Emma Eames as Charlotte, Sigrid Arnoldson as Sophie, and of course *le beau* Jean in the title-role – the premiere found so little favour with press or public that the manager of Covent Garden, Augustus Harris, decided to withdraw the piece forthwith. De Reszke urged him to reconsider, and was sufficiently unwise to prophesy that while the piece itself might not sell the house his presence in the cast assuredly would. As was his wont, on the day before the performance de Reszke applied to Harris for the few stall seats which might remain unsold, and which he used to distribute amongst his faithful supporters; but instead of the usual small envelope this time he received a sizeable parcel, accompanied by the following letter:

Mon cher Jean,
    Avec plaisir. Voilà quelques billets pour demain soir. Si vous auriez

Above left *The darling of Victorian High Society. Jean de Reszke (1850–1925), le beau Jean, as Raoul in* Les Huguenots.

Above *'The Giant Czech Appendix-Breaker'. Leo Slezak (1873–1946).*

besoin d'autres, écrivez un petit mot. Je vous envoie 140 Fauteuils, 150 Balcons, et soixante amphithéatres.

Augustus Harris.

Back came a telegram announcing that the tenor had been struck by a sudden *malaise* and would not be able to appear; and it was to be some thirty years before what is probably the truth about this incident was eventually revealed. The critic Herman Klein, when he came to write his memoirs, gave it as his opinion that the withdrawal of *Werther* had not been brought about by 'the menace of an empty house, but an intimation from an exalted quarter that the *grandes dames* of the grand and pit tier boxes had no wish to see their beloved Jean in costumes so drab and un-interesting as those of the Goethe period. Accustomed as they were to feasting their eyes on his superb, manly figure in the picturesque attire of one of his dazzling heroes of romance, they simply refused to put up with the repetition of the saddening display.'

Within less than a year of these strange events in London a young Neapolitan, destined to succeed de Reszke as the world's best-loved tenor, took his first bow before an operatic public. In appearance Enrico Caruso was assuredly no 'dazzling hero of romance', but such were the beauty of his voice and the all-embracing warmth of his personality that within a few years he had attained a position of eminence and popularity such as few singers have ever enjoyed, either before or since. Only once were he and de Reszke to be engaged by the same theatre at the same time, though never, of course, in the same piece. It was in Monte Carlo during the season of 1902. De Reszke was fifty-two, Caruso was twenty-nine; the one was the dignified *beau idéal* of the fashionable world, refined and aristocratic, the other was an irrepressible young parvenu whose suit of 'screaming checks' made an indelible impression on Geraldine Farrar when they met for their first rehearsal, but whose voice, when he opened the floodgates in performance, was of such indescribable richness that out of pure amazement she missed her next few cues. History sadly does not relate what de Reszke and Caruso thought of one another, but within a short time Caruso had become the unstoppable harbinger of a new style of operatic singing, one which, as far as the Italian repertoire is concerned, still holds the field today.

'Others abide our question, thou art free.' Enrico Caruso (1873–1921), king of Italian tenors, as Enzo Grimaldo in La Gioconda.

It was Caruso's good fortune that he and the gramophone arrived on the scene virtually hand in hand, and it would be hard to assess which of them was more deeply in the other's debt. When Caruso died the obituary notice in *The Times* declared 'It is quite safe to say that no tenor voice equal to his, in its combination of power and extreme beauty of quality, has been heard in this generation'; to which, thanks to Caruso's recorded legacy, it is still possible to add the words 'nor has it since'. The art of Jean de Reszke, however, is only to be sampled via a handful of Mapleson cylinders, the voice half submerged by the fog of extraneous sound; *his* reputation has to rest on hearsay. It was also Caruso's good fortune that the new wave of so-called *verismo* operas which were being written by the composers of his own generation – Puccini, Leoncavallo, Mascagni, Giordano and others – so exactly suited his voice and style. As many of his recordings reveal, he did indeed possess the technical mastery demanded by the *bel canto* operas of earlier generations – his immortal 1904 version of Donizetti's 'Una furtiva lagrima' is a perfect example – but it was the contemporary composers who gave full scope to the overwhelming emotional excitement which Caruso could unleash upon the listener apparently at will.

There are countless eye- (and ear-) witness accounts of this potency of Caruso's, one of the most vivid coming from the distinguished Italian conductor Vittorio Gui, who, during his student days in Rome, attended a rehearsal of Puccini's *Manon Lescaut*. Caruso was coasting through the role of des Grieux, using no voice, and with his hat and cane carried nonchalantly in his hand. Suddenly, at the end of Act III, something astonishing occurred:

> Caruso has thrown his hat and cane into the wings; he is no longer there, in his place the living character of des Grieux, who explodes with his cry of desperate supplication. A great wave of emotion has overcome all of us – musicians, chorus, conductor. We, the students, dry our tears in the dark. Finally the rehearsal had to be interrupted, the poor old supporting singer who was supposed to ask 'Do you want to go and populate the Americas, young man?' could not get beyond the world 'populate' before he burst into tears. The conductor Vitale took a large white handkerchief from his pocket and, pretending to mop his brow, dried his eyes.

Jean de Reszke, who retired at the age of fifty-two and settled for a life of teaching, used to tell his pupils 'Strive ever to move your hearers, not to astonish them', but it is evident that in Caruso's case moving and astonishing were inextricably linked. The ability to cast this kind of spell is given only to the fewest of the few, and when it happens it produces in the listener that frisson which, to the true aficionado, is the special preserve of opera in live performance. Not long ago I spoke about Caruso to the singer and actress Mary Ellis, the first ever Rose Marie in Friml's famous operetta of that name, and subsequently a much-loved leading lady in the works of Ivor Novello. As a young singer she had been engaged on a beginner's contract at the Met, and on the occasion at the end of Caruso's career when he suffered a haemorrhage during a performance of *L'elisir d'amore*, it was she (in the role of Giannetta) to whom he passed his handkerchief with the request that she should mop the blood from his chin while he sang on. People often ask her, she told me, how she would compare Caruso with the leading tenors of today, and her habitual answer is that if you could combine the technique of Carreras, the passion of Pavarotti and the vocal richness of Domingo you would be *beginning to approach* the experience of hearing Caruso in performance.

In Caruso's own day there was one other Italian singer of comparable vocal and emotional power, not a fellow tenor, but a baritone. Titta Ruffo, like Caruso himself, came from the humblest of backgrounds, and though he received virtually no formal education he turned himself into a cultural polymath, a passionate devotee of modern painting and a voracious reader of classical literature. His stage characterizations were arrived at by thought and observation, never more so than in the case of Tonio, the embittered clown in Leoncavallo's *Pagliacci*. He based his reading of this role on the behaviour of a mentally defective peasant whom he had encountered while on holiday in the Italian countryside, and the resultant performance was once described by Edward Moore, the leading critic in Chicago, in the following terms: 'No one else has ever done Tonio the same way. Ruffo's Tonio was mournful, tragic, imbecilic, trembling on the verge of epilepsy, a condition portrayed with almost the accuracy of a clinic. But it was a whirlwind of passion, and as far as the audience was concerned it was a riot. They said that ushers gathered up split white gloves by the basketful after the performance was over.'

Only once did Ruffo and Caruso appear together in *Pagliacci*, in Montevideo on 16 August 1915, and it must have been an occasion to treasure. Ruffo's voice – which his friendly rival Giuseppe de Luca used to describe as 'not a voice, but a miracle' – possessed, as did Caruso's, the quality known as 'chiaroscuro', a fascinating blend of dark-hued tone with a brilliant surface shine to it; and as he could carry both the weight and the brilliance right up to a stentorian high A flat the effect on an audience of his *Pagliacci* Prologue can be easily imagined. His 1912 recording of it is an elemental, titanic piece of singing, the towering personality of the man as vividly preserved as the formidable quality of the voice itself. Ruffo was known as *'Il leone'*, as much for his imperious presence, the directness of his gaze and his sweeping mane of hair as for his vocal prowess, and his unwavering opposition to Mussolini resulted in political persecution and even a brief period behind bars.

Ruffo and Caruso were true operatic giants, but they were not the only two to bestride the stages of the day; they were, by common consent, members of a trio, the third being that unpredictable genius, the Russian bass Feodor Chaliapin.* If Caruso's childhood could safely be described as impoverished and Ruffo's as rough in the extreme, Chaliapin's was downright brutal. Subjected in his early years to every imaginable hardship, ranging from endless vicious beatings to near-starvation, he soon learnt to live in a world of his own imaginings, and in time the theatre became more real to him than an actual reality which could only with difficulty be survived. Chaliapin's artistic trademark was total immersion in every role which he undertook, starting with a make-up which would so transform his physiognomy that one can study photographs of him in twenty different roles without finding a trace of similarity between any of them; while in none of them can one detect the slightest resemblance to the bland and open countenance which was his in private life.

Here again I have been treated to a fascinating personal account by Mary Ellis, who sang the role of the young Tsarevitch to Chaliapin's Boris Godunov at the Met in 1921. To be engulfed at close range in the rumblings of that mighty voice, she told me, even during the semi-whispered passages of the death scene, was an awesome experience, and backstage Chaliapin was evidently a fairly awesome proposition too. 'We girls', as Miss Ellis put it, 'were terrified of him; we used to hide if we heard him coming down the corridor', and to judge from some of the anecdotes related by Arthur Rubinstein in his book *My Young Years* concerning Chaliapin's voracious sexual appetite, 'we girls' were wise to be so cautious. One sentence of Rubinstein's sums things up with particular succinctness: 'Chaliapin exceeded all normal bounds; any female of sensual promise fell victim to his brutal frankness, and, more often than not, gladly.' Chaliapin was a man of imposing stature and a wildly explosive temperament, and of all the singers of the last hundred years only he could possibly have featured in a certain episode of which Sir Thomas

---

*Fashions in the transliteration of Russian names are subject to constant change, and Chaliapin is often to be found listed in dictionaries and record catalogues as Fyodor Shalyapin, Fedor Schaljapin and so on.

Compatriots on the croquet lawn. Anna Pavlova and Feodor Chaliapin, July 1923.

Beecham has left us a hilarious description. This occurred during a season of Russian opera in the Drury Lane Theatre shortly before the First World War, when the chorus refused to go on stage for the Coronation Scene in *Boris Godunov*, on the grounds that Chaliapin had not honoured an agreement to donate his fee to their benefit fund. An unholy row erupted during the interval and the choristers' spokesman so inflamed the star's temper that with one mighty blow Chaliapin stretched him insensible on the floor. As the Bow Street police station is only just round the corner from that particular theatre a call from the stage-door keeper rapidly brought 'a dozen familiar figures in blue' onto the scene, where they were confronted by the unlikely sight of the Tsar of All the Russias fighting off a howling mob of peasantry, armed with a businesslike variety of sticks and staves. When Chaliapin emerged from his dressing-room for Act II he took the precaution of stowing a brace of loaded

Three immortals meet in the Savoy Hotel. Beniamino Gigli, Feodor Chaliapin and Richard Tauber, London, 1931.

pistols in the pockets of his sumptuous gown, and I do not suppose that anyone doubted his willingness to use them if the need arose. The altercation continued until well after 5 a.m. but, in Sir Thomas's concluding words, 'the following morning they all turned up punctually for rehearsal, as blithe and unconcerned as if nothing unusual had happened, and as if wrath and violence had no part in the Slav temperament.'

Giants such as these cast long shadows; no subsequent interpreter of Boris has managed to throw off the Chaliapin legacy however hard he may try, and Caruso can be clearly seen as the prototype of the twentieth-century Italian tenor. Though the lighter-voiced style of singing did manage to survive the shock tactics of the *veristi*, notably in the immaculate artistry of Tito Schipa, those tenors who have become house-

Beniamino Gigli distributing the presents at a Christmas party for New York policemen's children, 1927.

hold names in the Italian repertoire can be seen as a virtual line of succession stemming from Caruso himself. The first of these was Beniamino Gigli, he of the beguilingly honeyed tone, who, like Caruso, came from the humblest of backgrounds and ended up as master of a palatial villa and a vast agricultural estate. In Gigli's case this was just outside his birthplace, the town of Recanati in the province known as Le Marche, and it was here, in his own fiefdom, that Gigli once suffered a minor dent to his pride, almost comparable with that which befell de Reszke apropos *Werther*. When the Allies were fighting their way up the 'leg' of Italy in the latter stages of the Second World War two British officers, men of military distinction but unacquainted with matters operatic, were briefly billeted in Gigli's villa. Gigli treated them as welcome guests, inviting them to join him in his elegant dining-room for as fine a meal as could be provided in the circumstances, and when it was over he paid them the ultimate compliment. 'Now', he announced, 'I shall sing for you!' – whereupon the exhausted British officers, under the impression that their host was some kind of prosperous industrialist, looked at him in horror and replied 'Oh please don't bother, we'd rather get to bed!'

Gigli was not, by his own confession, blessed with Caruso's irresistible warmth of personality, but even so I shall never forget the ease with which, even in the last years of his career, he could hold the audience of a sold-out Albert Hall in the palm of his hand by the sheer magic of his voice. His regular impresario, S. A. Gorlinsky, once told me that he was the easiest of singers to manage, and that he only had one strange little quirk of his own – he liked to be paid before a concert and in cash. When Gorlinsky asked him why this was he replied that after certain experiences in other parts of the world it was a comfort to pat his back pocket between arias and know that all was well. When I was on holiday with my family in Le Marche a couple of years ago I visited Gigli's tomb and found

*The tomb of
Beniamino Gigli in
the cemetery of
Recanati.*

that it has become virtually a place of pilgrimage. Beside the sarcophagus lay a large, lined school exercise-book which served as a register for visitors, and in the month of July alone five whole pages had been filled with names and addresses from all over the world, often with messages of personal gratitude appended to them. Gigli had at that time been dead for thirty-five years – let no one underestimate the power of song!

If Gigli was an easy man to manage the same cannot be said of that supremely gifted Swedish tenor Jussi Björling. Possessed of one of those voices which go straight to the listener's heart, Björling combined all the vocal virtues required of a truly great lyric tenor – the easy flow of tone, the brilliant top notes, the effortless breath control and so on – with an almost freakish musicianship, which enabled him to learn new roles at an astonishing speed and to keep them, once learnt, safely tucked away in some corner of his prodigious memory. It does seem to be a salutary rule of nature, though, that no one in the world of opera ever has everything handed to him on a plate, and it was Björling's misfortune to suffer from a deeply uneasy temperament. In the words of his regular London accompanist, Ivor Newton, 'Björling was a man of surprising contradictions; as an artist he was superb, with a remarkable range and an impeccable style . . . As a man he was obstinate, difficult, taciturn and unusually lazy.' It is also no secret that Björling had a serious drink problem, and to me the ultimate proof of what an astonishing physical mechanism his voice must have been lies in the fact that at the time of his death the sound he produced was even more beautiful, even more thrilling and even more moving than it had been when he was young. He was still only forty-nine when he died, but quite apart from the fact that he had already been singing professionally for thirty years he had a record of alcohol abuse which would have rendered the average tenor *hors de combat* by the age of twenty-five.

The tales of Björling's escapades are legion. I remember one soprano in the Stockholm Opera telling me of an occasion when he sang in a Royal Gala performance of *Tosca* in a state of such inebriation that she could not imagine how he would be able to remain standing. In fact, though, not only did he give a faultless performance, but after the final curtain had fallen he gathered the rest of the cast round him and told all of them where they had gone wrong. The conductor Erich Leinsdorf describes in his memoirs an occasion when he was recording *Butterfly* in Rome for RCA with a seriously miscast *tenore leggiero* as Pinkerton. Björling, who was also in Rome at the time recording *Tosca*, quite rightly believed that the record company should have taken him for both roles, and while Leinsdorf was in the control room listening to the playback of the Love Duet Björling suddenly appeared at his elbow in a very drunken state and started demonstrating into Leinsdorf's ear how the tenor line should have been sung. 'Of course', wrote Leinsdorf, 'Björling singing into one's ear carried better than other voices shouted at top strength', so that no one involved in the recording, least of all the unfortunate tenor, was left in any doubt as to the extent of Björling's sense of grievance – even discounting the spoken asides, which were 'not for public print or hearing'.

Other glimpses of Björling's peculiar temperament have been provided by his close friend and regular partner, the American baritone Robert Merrill. One of the problems involved in getting Björling home from a bar in Rome, New York or wherever they might be, lay in his formidable physical strength; he loved a scrap, and taming him was not a one-man job. Sometimes what Björling needed was simply a boost to his artistic self-confidence. When the two of them were due to make some of their classic recordings of operatic duets Merrill spent the previous night in Björling's apartment, in order to guarantee his appearance in the studio at the appointed time of 3.00 p.m. After listening to the only recording which Caruso and Ruffo made together, their spine-tingling version of the Oath Duet from *Otello*, Björling, whose voice was a lighter instrument than Caruso's, was so filled with gloom that at 2.30 Merrill had to manhandle him into a cab and then walk with him half a dozen times round the studio block before he could be persuaded to go inside. The result was a set of duets which, forty-five years later, still features high on the list of best-selling operatic recordings.

I have no doubt that one of the problems which beset Jussi Björling was his own personal brand of perfectionism. There is a hideous weight of responsibility in the knowledge that the public will be disappointed, even embittered, if any single performance that you give falls below your own best standard. This is a nagging fear which manifests itself again and again amongst the greatest of operatic artists, and to appreciate this feeling one only has to read the deeply moving letters which Caruso wrote towards the end of his career to his young American wife. 'My sweet-heart,' he wrote from Havana on 19 May 1920 after a performance of *L'elisir*, 'you cannot immagine the work which I was obliged to doo. The public here dont care if the other artists sing well or not, if the orchestra dont play well, if the corus sing half toon low, or if the stage is not well arrenged. They wait for me and pend from my lips. Fortunately I was in good voice and good spirit and I win the battle.' Again and again this is the imagery that he uses; every performance that he gives is a battle against the public's expectations. One high tone needs to crack – only one – and suddenly the thousands of people who have queued for hours to hear him, be it in the bull-ring, the open-air arena or whatever venue the impresarios can find which is large enough, will be at his throat instead of at his feet. 'I have win another victory,' he writes the following week, 'and I hope to conquist at the end all the country.' Then, almost prophetically, 'I am fighting with my work and I hope to go to the end vittoriously even dead, and come back to you with palm and laurel.' This, at the height of his fame, from the man whom the music director of Covent Garden had described early in his career as always 'larking around and playing prac-tical jokes'!

Where Caruso found refuge in ever mightier exertions Björling found his in the bottle, and neither of them lived to see fifty. Perhaps it is a more comfortable safety valve simply to establish a reputation for being diffi-cult and then live up to it. One of Caruso's more recent successors, Franco Corelli, a tremendous favourite at the Met during the Rudolf Bing regime, found a number of richly individual ways to sublimate his inse-curities. Nervousness used to result in his mouth becoming dry, and although his wife was ever present in the wings with a supply of water this did not solve the problem during those scenes when he was unable to leave the stage for half an hour at a time. The solution which he (or his wife) hit upon was to have numerous little sponges sewn into his cos-tume, which were soaked in water and on which he would suck when necessary. The first time I saw him on stage I was baffled by his habit of turning away from the audience and plucking purposefully at his apparel, but later I understood. Another strange quirk of his was his absolute refusal to travel anywhere in America without his dog, which meant that he could never use a scheduled airline, because that would have involved the dog being put in a container in the luggage compartment. This could lead to extraordinarily complicated arrangements when the company of the Met was on tour, but, as Bing expressed it, 'If I hadn't put up with this sort of thing, somebody at another opera house would have, and would have paid Corelli a higher fee, too.'

Corelli was, I would judge, the most handsome man I have ever seen on an operatic stage, tall, slender and with the face of a pre-war Hollywood star, and to cap it all his voice was one of those instruments which explained, the moment he opened his mouth, why he could get away with behaving the way he did. I, however, was never very lucky with Corelli. The first time I heard him he was singing Andrea Chénier in Vienna, and although he and the golden-throated Tebaldi made a stupendous job of raising the roof in their final ecstatic duet he spent so much of the evening at odds with the conductor that I could never really settle into the performance. His Calaf at Covent Garden, too, was only a moderately happy affair. The Welsh soprano Elizabeth Vaughan, who sang an unforgettable Liù, received more applause at the end than he did, which would in itself have been enough to persuade him (and his wife) that he was at the wrong address, but I think it was the small matter of the gong which really put his back up. In the Met production he was used to bringing the house down at the end of Act I, when he would stride across the stage and strike a huge gong three times while holding a high note on the cry of 'Turandot!' The Covent Garden production, however, a superannuated and moth-eaten affair, did not offer a real gong. Instead there was a replica of one painted on the backdrop, and Calaf was only required to mime the action while a percussionist, seated directly behind, actually did the deed. Whether Corelli had not been told about this, or whether it had momentarily slipped his mind I do not know, but in any case he struck the backdrop three mighty blows, each of them in succession tearing a slightly larger hole, until eventually the percussionist, gong in hand, became visible to one and all. Corelli never sang at Covent Garden again.

The classic casting for *Turandot* at the Met had Corelli partnered by Birgit Nilsson in the title-role, with Leontyne Price as Liù, and often with Leopold Stokowski in the pit. On one occasion Stokowski lost interest in what was happening on stage and left the soloists to fend for themselves at the end of Act II, whereupon Nilsson held on to the final high note

Franco Corelli, the tenor with the film star looks.

after Corelli had run out of breath. Corelli stalked straight off the stage and into his dressing-room, where Rudolf Bing, who had been hastily summoned to pour oil on the troubled waters, was confronted by pandemonium. Corelli, while slamming his hand onto his dressing-table, had picked up a splinter. A drop of blood had been shed, Corelli was screaming, his wife was screaming and the dog was barking. Bing somewhat mischievously suggested that Corelli should get his own back on Nilsson by biting her ear during the Act III love duet, which he did; and when the curtain fell Birgit Nilsson was heard to call for a veterinarian, on the grounds that she had probably contracted rabies.

Keeping Corelli cheerful was referred to by Rudolf Bing as one of the things he was paid for – though he did once add 'in this instance grossly *under*paid' – and it was a source of relief to him that in Richard Tucker the company of the Met possessed one tenor at least whose singing was up to the highest international standard, but who wasted none of his own or anyone else's time on pointless shenanigans. To Tucker, too, goes the credit for one of the very few instances on record of Bing being verbally worsted by a singer. It happened after a performance of *Andrea Chénier*, when the applause was so persistent that the evening was threatening to run into overtime, and Bing was becoming increasingly furious as the soloists went out for one curtain call after another. Eventually Tucker, who had been singing the title-role, came up with the perfect solution – 'You go out and take a bow, Mr Bing,' he suggested, 'that'll end the applause!' This remark, made to a figure as austere as Rudolf Bing, has gone down in the annals of the Met as the ultimate example of tenorial directness, but back in the 1920s an even more reckless piece of *lèse-majesté* was perpetrated at the Royal Opera in London. The English tenor Tom Burke, who, despite having spent much of his training and early career in Italy, remained in essence a blunt Lancastrian, was visited in his dressing-room after a performance by one of the equerries to King

The forthright Lancastrian tenor Tom Burke (1890–1969).

Nicolai Gedda in one of his finest roles, the doomed poet Lensky in Eugene Onegin.

George V; His Majesty, the equerry was empowered to inform him, had enjoyed the evening and wished to congratulate Mr Burke in person. 'Tell the old bugger he can wait,' replied Burke – a remark which is not thought to have had a beneficial effect on his subsequent career.

Lucky as we have been in recent years to have had three such outstanding tenors as Carreras, Domingo and Pavarotti all in their prime at more or less the same time, it is perhaps worth pointing out that when Corelli was at his best so also were two other unusually charismatic Italian tenors, Giuseppe di Stefano and Mario del Monaco.* Del Monaco

---

*Come to that, a few years later Carlo Bergonzi, Nicolai Gedda and Alfredo Kraus would have made a nicely marketable cosmopolitan package; and how about Gigli, Martinelli, Lauri-Volpi, Pertile and Schipa as a Five Tenor bandwagon back in the 1920s?

Possessor of 'the most glorious lyric tenor voice to have emerged from Italy since Beniamino Gigli'. Giuseppe di Stefano as Nemorino in L'elisir d'amore.

possessed a voice of great beauty and considerable power, and though any attempt to throttle it back below a *mezzo-forte* tended to result in a flattening of pitch he was an exciting singer when in full cry. As Don José in *Carmen* it was his party trick to hold the final high G of his entrance song in Act II while he walked the whole width of the stage along a ramp at the back and down a long flight of stairs. The effect of this *tour de force* was enhanced by his wearing the tightest pair of military trousers I have ever seen on anyone, and it used to be rumoured that artifice had emphasized the generous masculinity at which they hinted. Del Monaco's most stunning role was that of Otello, and it was in his Otello costume that he was buried, having sung the part, by his own calculation, 427 times.

The story of Giuseppe di Stefano, del Monaco's junior by six years, can be taken, to my mind, as the ultimate proof that a voice is only a fraction of what is needed to secure a singer's place at the top of the operatic tree.

Di Stefano's was the most glorious lyric tenor to have emerged from Italy since the heyday of Beniamino Gigli, added to which he was blessed with Sicilian good looks and a winning stage personality; all that he lacked was a sense of obligation towards his public. A happy-go-lucky character, universally known as Pipo and loved by almost all who knew him, he found it impossible to resist the lure of *la dolce vita*, as represented by fast cars, expensive restaurants and, above all, the gaming tables; as the Decca recording manager John Culshaw put it, 'the eventual, almost total breakdown of his voice was attributable to a life-style he could not abandon because it meant more to him than singing.' If Rudolf Bing had to work hard at keeping Corelli cheerful he had to work even harder in his attempts to bring home to di Stefano that a contract was not just any old piece of paper. Before he had assumed the management of the Met Bing once heard di Stefano sing a diminuendo on the high C in *Faust*, of which he was later to write 'I shall never as long as I live forget the beauty of that sound'; now Bing was planning to revolutionize production standards at the Met and he was determined that for the new *Bohème* and the new *Faust* di Stefano should be his tenor. Di Stefano, however, was not keen on wasting his time at rehearsals when he could be earning urgently needed money elsewhere. While declaring himself too sick to travel to New York on the date specified in his contract he happily appeared eight times in a fortnight at La Scala. A flurry of increasingly acid cables whizzed to and fro between Bing and his opposite number in Milan, and Bing was eventually reduced to applying for a hearing with the American Guild of Musical Artists to have di Stefano disbarred from the stages of the United States. To add to the complications di Stefano had also become involved in contractual negotiations with the Lyric Opera in Chicago, the management of which thereby acquired a strong interest in di Stefano *not* being disbarred. The relationship between the two American houses became soured – one piece of advice contained in a letter written to Bing by his lawyer on 9 February 1955 started with the words 'Since, in my opinion, Chicago is no more to be trusted than di Stefano . . .' – and all in all di Stefano's name became synonymous with trouble.

I heard di Stefano several times, but only twice did he bother to give of his best all the way through the opera, once as Edgardo in *Lucia*, with Maria Callas in the title-role and Herbert von Karajan in the pit, and once as des Grieux in *Manon Lescaut*. I heard him sing a last act of *Carmen* which was one of the most scorching performances I can ever remember, but it was no more than the audience deserved after he had eased his way through Acts I to III; and I well remember a *Bohème* when he shamelessly sang himself in throughout Act I, almost as if 'Che gelida manina' and 'O soave fanciulla' were incidental trifles, unworthy of serious attention.* Least forgivable of all, however, was a *Ballo in maschera* in the Vienna State Opera during my student days. I had queued, I remember, from the crack of dawn to be sure of a ticket, and I also parted with a hefty portion of that month's money to pay for it, as the Opera charged fancy prices on di Stefano nights. During Act I the great man wandered round the stage more or less aimlessly, and was then replaced for the rest of the evening by an understudy with a score in his hand – none of which would have been held against di Stefano had he been genuinely sick. In the early hours of the morning, however, he rang his agent to say that he needed bailing out of a casino some miles outside Vienna, where he had spent the intervening hours and where he had lost all his money. When Culshaw wrote 'at the mere mention of his name stage and recording producers had been known to turn white and run as fast as possible in the opposite direction' he knew whereof he spoke – di Stefano once walked out on an almost completed recording of Boito's *Mefistofele* because of forty bars which he did not know, and the entire piece had to be re-recorded with del Monaco in the tenor role. If Nature had been just a little less prodigal with her gifts perhaps di Stefano would have learnt to treat them with greater respect. As Jean de Reszke was fond of saying, 'The voice is an elegance – it cannot be treated like old shoes'; but if Pipo had been *le beau* Jean he would not have been Pipo, and I cannot help wondering if de Reszke's last act of *Carmen* was ever *quite* as spine-tingling as di Stefano's?

Another singer who fell victim to the temptations of a luxurious lifestyle, though not as prematurely as di Stefano, was that king amongst baritones, Lawrence Tibbett. For a number of years his was a classic

---

*In fairness to di Stefano perhaps I should mention that when Jean de Reszke sang the role of Radamès he used occasionally to omit the aria 'Celeste Aida' altogether on the grounds that it came too early in the piece for vocal comfort.

Lawrence Tibbett leaves Mitchell Field, Long Island, to fulfil an engagement in Chicago.

American success story. Born in 1896, the son of a Californian sheriff who was gunned down by an outlaw in 1903, Tibbett grew up to be the first male American singer to make a front-rank career without the backing of European training and stage experience. The story of how he drove the Met audience wild with his Ford in *Falstaff* while he was still in his twenties has been told often enough, and one only has to listen to his early recordings to see that it could hardly have happened otherwise – the virility of timbre, the brilliant top notes, the passionate delivery and the immaculate stylishness instantly proclaim an artist of rare attainment. He was also another splendid-looking man, six-foot-one in height, a non-smoking teetotaller who built up his physical strength by exercising with weights and medicine balls, and a committed, convincing actor. In his mid-thirties, though, he divorced his wife of eleven years and married a banker's daughter, and gradually New York's party circuit claimed more and more of his time. Robert Merrill, in many ways Tibbett's natural successor, provides in his memoirs a tragic picture of the end result – Tibbett chain-smoking in his dressing-room before a performance of *Pagliacci*, going on stage for the Prologue with shaking hands and sweating with fear, clutching the curtain for support, and producing nothing but a tortured scream instead of the climactic high A flat. 'I was so appalled', wrote Merrill, 'at the deterioration of this gifted, genial man that I ran out of the theater.'*

Tibbett's heyday lasted from the mid-1920s to the early '40s, and it was a period of great male stars at the Metropolitan Opera. Prominent amongst them was the glamorous Italian *basso cantante* Ezio Pinza (1892–1957), as famous a Don Giovanni off the stage as he was on it. On the occasion of his centenary I presented a radio programme about him for the BBC, to which several of his erstwhile lady colleagues from the Met, amongst them Risë Stevens, Patrice Munsel and Licia Albanese, were kind enough to contribute interviews, and from the terms in which they described him it was easy enough to judge how powerful a spell he had exercised over the fair sex. Miss Munsel in particular delighted radio listeners with a description of how, when she had been engaged by the Met at the unprecedentedly early age of seventeen and was cast alongside Pinza in *The Tales of Hoffmann*, he offered to save her some wearisome

---

*One of the saddest stories of a singer being floored by the bottle concerns a Wagnerian baritone named Randolph Simonette, because he was, or so it seems to me, more sinned against than sinning. A newcomer to the Met, with only five performances under his belt, he was sitting at home having just finished a large dinner, washed down by generous quantities of liquor, when he was suddenly called upon to take over the role of Wotan in the last act of *Die Walküre* because Otto Edelmann had fallen ill during the performance. 'Wotan tritt in höchster zorniger Aufgeregtheit auf', reads Wagner's stage direction – 'Wotan enters in an extreme state of wrathful excitement' – but the state in which poor Simonette was bundled onto the stage had less to do with wrathful excitement than with advanced intoxication. Instead of the terrible cry 'Wo ist Brünnhild', wo die Verbrecherin?' – 'Where is Brünnhilde, where is the criminal?' – the best Simonette could manage was to peer unsteadily into the prompt box asking 'What did you say?' One of the eight Valkyries was reported to have let fly with the line 'Unser Vater ist gepflastert!', which, with a stretch of the imagination, could be said to mean 'Our father is plastered', but Simonette had not actually managed to sing a single note before the curtain came down again and Edelmann was cajoled into carrying on. No more was ever heard of Randolph Simonette.

Ezio Pinza re-establishes his status as a faithful nephew to Uncle Sam. New York, 1942.

running around on the huge stage of the old theatre by picking her up and carrying her. 'Well, my dear,' Miss Munsel said, her voice still vibrant with the recollection, 'to be picked up in the arms of that *glorious* man! I just wished always that it had been a little longer, and that I had been a little older and not quite so naive, because I didn't realize how flirtatious he was and what it could all lead to . . . which could have been quite marvellous!' Ah! Yes, indeed.

As in the case of Chaliapin, there were some of the younger ladies at the Met who used to find it advisable to avoid Pinza's company backstage – one of them, the soprano Nanette Guilford, told me in her old age 'I guess my upbringing had been too sheltered' – and the American press used to take a considerable interest in the great *basso* and his various amours. My favourite description of him is one penned by the American journalist Winthrop Sargeant – 'When Pinza is seated at a restaurant the entrance of a good-looking girl will throw him into a trancelike condition like that of a well-bred hunting dog that has scented quail' – and in readership polls he was awarded such titles as 'One of the ten best-dressed men in the United States' and 'One of the fourteen most glamorous men in the world'. There was, however, one occasion when Pinza hit the headlines in a much less desirable fashion. In March 1942 the FBI, tipped off, or so it was widely assumed, by a jealous colleague, arrested Pinza on grounds of pro-fascist sympathies and incarcerated him on Ellis Island for eleven extremely uncomfortable weeks. After his release he did everything imaginable to re-establish his status as a patriotic American, singing for the Treasury Department to promote the sale of war bonds, posing in pictures for the blood donor service, and joining in a campaign to urge motorists not to park in city streets. I am also happy to report that the jealous colleague in question signally failed to topple Pinza's popularity with the public.

Towering above most of his contemporaries at the Met, in the physical sense at least, was the Great Dane, Lauritz Melchior, a man whose status as *the* Wagnerian tenor of the century still remains unchallenged. In the words of Francis Robinson, the company's assistant manager, 'Melchior was a natural phenomenon, something on the order of Niagara Falls', and though his appetite for party life was unrivalled even by Lawrence Tibbett – Melchior's idea of a good time was to have several dozen people in his apartment eating Danish sausages and drinking aquavit until the small hours of the morning – his gigantic frame seemed able simply to shrug off such mundane influences as over-indulgence and lack of sleep. One of his most resplendent recordings, the 1939 version of the Love Duet from *Tristan und Isolde* with Kirsten Flagstad, was made in circumstances which to any normal tenor would have been unthinkable. Melchior arrived in the studio at the very last moment, straight from an all-night duck shooting expedition, unshaven, unwarmed-up and smoking a malodorous black cigar, none of which had the slightest ill effect on his voice, though it did not please Mme Flagstad.

Melchior prided himself on being the last of the international Wagnerians to have learnt the Bayreuth style under the Master's redoubtable widow Cosima, a fact which made him something of a problem figure during his final years at the Met.* On the one hand he was vocally irreplaceable, on the other it was pointless to suggest to him that

---

*If some mischievous fairy wished to create the operatic explosion of the century I suggest that she should wave her magic wand and cast Lauritz Melchior in a Richard Jones *Ring* cycle or a new production of *Tristan* directed by Peter Sellars.

he might rethink any aspect of his work. He was growing lazy, too. Early in his career he had explained in an interview with the paper *Musical America* why he regarded Parsifal as his favourite role. 'You must act every minute of the time,' he said, 'even during the long scene where Parsifal has to stand motionless with his back to the audience for three-quarters of an hour.' During his latter years, however, far from standing motionless he used to work his way towards a shadowy spot at the side of the stage, vanish into the wings and head off to his dressing-room. His excuse for this unconventional interpretation was that the spot he was supposed to occupy on stage was dangerously draughty, though cynics felt that the draught he had in mind was one of nice cold beer.

It is doubtless no coincidence that dramatic tenors of gigantic size seem to possess a greater knack than most other singers of becoming publicly recognized 'characters', rather than merely respected figures in operatic circles. When one of Melchior's predecessors, the six-foot-four-inch Czech tenor Leo Slezak (1873–1946), first visited the United States for a concert tour, it was explained to him by his manager that in order to build up advance publicity for various of the more obscure cities on his itinerary it would be *de rigueur* to invent some tantalizingly *outré* personal characteristic. Accordingly Slezak was filmed on board his transatlantic liner accompanied by a goat on a lead. He was virtually unable to perform, so the press was told, unless accompanied by this devoted pet – in fact it had been borrowed from a Pole who was travelling steerage – and although it was a matter of disappointment in every city Slezak visited that the goat had apparently been mislaid at the last stopping-off place, audiences were alerted to the fact that a most unusual tenor had come amongst them. It was, however, a performance of *Otello* with the company of the Metropolitan Opera in the Brooklyn Academy of Music which earned Slezak his most unlikely headline. His Desdemona, Frances Alda, had been complaining of stomach-ache, and no sooner had the curtain come down than she had to have her appendix removed. Slezak, who would normally have been called upon to fling her to the floor in Act III, not to mention the small matter of throttling her in Act IV, had been at pains to treat her with a gentleness quite inappropriate to the dramatic situation, but in the morning there was the newspaper report for all to see – 'Rough Russian Tenor Breaks Madame Alda's Appendix!' Slezak, so the readers were informed, had been so carried away during his bestial imper-sonation of the jealous Moor that, using the full strength of his gigantic physique, he had hurled his luckless partner with such violence to the ground 'that the cracking of her appendix could be distinctly heard in the back row of the stalls'. Some weeks later another American paper at least put matters straight on the question of Slezak's nationality when a favourable concert notice appeared under the headline 'Giant Czech Appendix-Breaker Wins Audience'.

Though in this particular instance press reports may have been wildly far from the mark it does occasionally happen that singers become carried away by the excitement of events on stage. The most powerfully built tenor to undertake the role of Otello in recent years has probably been the American Richard Cassilly. In private life as jovial and friendly a col-league as one could hope to meet, Dick, an even bigger man than Melchior or Slezak, is one of those singers whose acting is so intense that they sometimes appear to have lost themselves in their role. There is a scene in which the Moor, half out of his mind with fury, rounds on Iago, flings him to the ground and threatens to kill him should his allegations against Desdemona prove to be false; and I remember the Finnish bari-tone Tom Krause telling me that whenever he was cast as Iago to Cassilly's Otello his terror during this episode was entirely genuine. On the only occasion when I personally have felt in danger from a fellow singer the circumstances were rather different. As Luigi in Puccini's *Il tabarro* I was being strangled by the cuckolded husband Michele, sung by one of those people who always need to be beating time with some part or other of their anatomy. In this particular passage he chose to do it with his thumbs, which were firmly locked on either side of my larynx, and the hoarseness of my request, made at the end of the dress rehearsal, that he should refrain from doing so filled the poor fellow with remorse – he was, after all, a baritone, and had no vested interest in the premature termination of my career.

Neither Richard Cassilly nor my Michele would ever knowingly do anything to upset a colleague's performance, but it is possible to meet singers so wilful that they brook no competition on the stage. I once asked a famous mezzo-soprano whether she would describe a certain tenor with whom she had frequently appeared (and whose name I shall not divulge for fear of hideous retribution), whether it would be fair to describe him as a perfectionist. 'If by that', she replied, 'you mean that everything had to be perfect for him, yes he was'; and that kind of singer can be awkward to have around. One such was the great Bulgarian bass Boris Christoff, who, like Chaliapin, assumed the right to interfere in all aspects of any production in which he was appearing. During the interval of a Covent Garden *Boris* in 1950 he caused general alarm by seizing Adèle Leigh, the young and exceptionally pretty soprano who was singing the role of the Tsarevitch, hauling her into her dressing-room and locking the door. Fearing the worst, several colleagues gathered outside ready to force their way in at the first cry for help, but it turned out that the object of Christoff's attention was not Miss Leigh herself but merely her stage make-up. It was, in his opinion, wrong; so he sat her down, removed it and replaced it with a creation of his own. Rehearsals, to Christoff, were mainly opportunities for telling the director what he, Christoff, would be doing, how he would be doing it, and where he wished the other singers to be at the time. He once came to blows on stage during a performance of *Don Carlos* with the tenor who was singing the title-role, and an off-stage feud between Christoff and his brother-in-law, the great baritone Tito Gobbi, caused considerable awkwardness for managements, who were unable for several years to cast the two of them together. The quarrel was said to have started in Chicago, when an unflattering remark of Gobbi's was reported to Christoff and Christoff responded by punching Gobbi on the nose. Peace was not restored until the death of their mutual father-in-law, the distinguished Italian musicologist Raffaello de Rensis, reunited the two families; and in his memoirs Gobbi was sufficiently forgiving to write 'if I am cooking lunch (which I enjoy doing) there is no one I would rather have with me in the kitchen as critic and appraiser than my brother-in-law.'

Perhaps this was Gobbi's diplomatic way of indicating that as far as Christoff was concerned he would rather be in a kitchen with him than on an operatic stage – I do not know. What I do know, though, is that without those singers who are in some way larger than life and who have the knack of generating electricity the moment they step on stage, the world of opera would be a poorer place. As the critic of one American magazine wrote back in 1956, 'Though opera impresarios, including Mr

Bing, find prima donnas pretty exhausting and issue statements about wanting ensembles instead of stars, there is no question that audiences want headliners.' It so happens that in recent years the drawing power of even the most prominent prima donnas has been eclipsed by that of the Three Tenors, but the principle remains the same. Much of today's repertoire, extending as it does from Monteverdi to Stockhausen, demands singers of great sophistication. Such singers will always be prized, respected and admired; but if an opera manager wants to see all-night queues winding round the block what he needs, like it or not, is still an old-style headline star, preferably singing Verdi or Puccini. And let us make no mistake – here again, of course, I speak without a whiff of bias – the most important people in any operatic performance are the singers; however wonderful the director, the conductor or the designer it is the singers who deliver the goods on the night. I have encountered operatic performances without a conductor, without an orchestra, without a set and without a director; not once have I encountered an operatic performance without singers. Some of them, sometimes, can be rather trying people, but the pressures on them can be enormous. After all, despite the common parlance, the operatic stage is not populated by gods and goddesses, *divi* and *dive*, it is populated by ordinary people who happen to possess extraordinary voices; or in other words, by men, women – and tenors.

6

Words and

Music

In Richard Strauss's *Capriccio*, his final work for the stage, we meet a poet, Olivier, and a composer, Flamand, who engage in a passionate altercation over the relative importance in opera of words and music. To which should precedence be given? Is it a case of 'Prima la musica, dopo le parole', 'First the music and then the words', as Flamand maintains, or of 'Prima le parole, dopo la musica', as Olivier insists? The question takes on a more than merely aesthetic importance for them both, because they are rival suitors for the love of the beautiful Countess Madeleine, a dedicated lover of the arts, and if in their intellectual debate she casts her vote for words or for music she will also, in a personal sense, have declared her preference for the poet or the composer. When Olivier writes her a sonnet Flamand promptly sets it to music, an act which Olivier regards as little less than the rape of his cherished brainchild. 'I knew it,' he sings, 'he is destroying my verses. Their symmetry is gone, the rhymes are obliterated, the sentences are mashed into little pieces and reduced to an arbitrary series of short and long notes!' The Countess, however, finds

An early photograph of Richard Strauss. For his final opera, Capriccio, *he and the conductor Clemens Krauss collaborated as librettists.*

that the words now shine with a new light, and she asks herself what can have been the source from which the music sprang. Was it the text which set the melody singing in the composer's imagination, or was the music somehow already there, dormant and waiting for words which it could lovingly embrace? Finally, in the last of the shimmering, moonlit closing scenes of which Strauss was such a masterly exponent, Madeleine strives to achieve a choice. Hers, however, is a dilemma without a solution. Words and music are no longer divisible; inextricably interwoven they have combined to form a new whole. As to their creators, if she chooses the one she loses the other – does the act of winning, she asks herself, not always involve some form of loss?

The relationship of words and music was something which exercised

Strauss's mind throughout his career. He regarded *Capriccio* as his artistic testament,* and as far as the piece can be said to reach a conclusion it is that Words v. Music is a drawn match. In this, though, it seems to me that a deeper layer of irony lies concealed. Even as this burning question is being debated in the opera house and the equal significance of words and music is being established, by which I mean whenever *Capriccio* is being performed, one glaring inconsistency becomes apparent – everyone in the audience can hear the notes which the singers are singing, but how many of them can hear or understand enough of the words to be able to follow the argument? Therein lie two of opera's age-old bones of contention, or perhaps I should say potential sources of discontent on the part of the public – why is it frequently so hard to hear the words, and should opera be performed in the original language or in that of the audience? To these there has recently been added a third – are surtitles a blessing or an abomination?

If one were to ask that elusive character 'the average opera-goer' whether he or she considers the words or the music to be the more significant component I have no doubt that a virtually unanimous vote would be cast for the music. After all, with the exception of Gilbert and Sullivan the author is seldom even referred to when an opera (or operetta) is mentioned. We talk about 'Mozart's *Don Giovanni*', not 'the Mozart/Da Ponte *Don Giovanni*', or 'Rossini's *Barber of Seville*', not 'the Rossini/Sterbini *Barber of Seville*', and many more people leave performances of these operas able to whistle the tunes than to recite the words. It is the melody, not the poetry, which has the audience sitting up in joyful recognition as Don Giovanni whispers (or bellows, as the case may be) 'La ci darem la mano' into the ear of the saucy Zerlina; and though there will be plenty of people present at any performance of *The Barber* who can mentally hum along with every note of Rosina's famous aria, how many of them could quote the text beyond the opening words 'Una voce poco fa'?

This leads, I think, towards a general tendency to underestimate the contribution of the librettist. The first stage in the creation of most operas

---

*In this instance he was, in tandem with the celebrated conductor Clemens Krauss, his own librettist.

is the preparation of the text, and it is the composer's response to the written word which produces the music – the exact functioning of that process being as much a mystery to me as it is to the Countess Madeleine. In that sense it is definitely a case of 'Prima le parole',* even though, in the majority of operas, the music may ultimately be deemed to aspire to a higher artistic level than the text. The qualifications for a good librettist are not, after all, that he or she should be a great poet or dramatist in his or her own right; more important is the ability to identify the special requirements of opera and cater to them. There are effects which opera can more easily achieve than straight drama (as well, naturally, as vice versa) and the skilled librettist will provide the composer with situations which exploit them. Extremes of emotion, for instance, can be more convincingly expressed with the help of music than by the spoken word alone, and a sudden, total switch of atmosphere – something which is not easy to create on the dramatic stage – can be brought about in an instant by one chord from the orchestra. Elements of the eerie, the exotic or the magical can be more grippingly conjured up with the help of music, and the orchestra can even make words superfluous by acting as a commentator on the innermost thoughts of the characters on stage. If the leading lady enters in Act II to the strains of the Act I love duet, but transposed this time into a mournful minor key, she has no need to tell us that the course of true love is failing to run smooth; and if, while the baritone offers her a friendly greeting, the orchestra indulges in nasty discordant mutterings we know that he is not the open-hearted fellow she takes him for. These are but an obvious few of the myriad effects available to the theatrically skilled composer, but it is the librettist who must provide him with the necessary framework to deploy his skills. It is tempting, certainly, to dismiss a piece like *Il trovatore* as a farrago of preposterous rubbish which only retains its place in the repertoire thanks to the genius of its composer, but it is worth remembering that it was Verdi who settled upon the vast, rambling play on which it is based, and it was his long-suffering writer friend Salvatore Cammarano who was left with the task

---

*One composer who did frequently oblige his librettist to provide words to a ready-made melody was Johann Strauss, and the result often strengthened the argument of those who felt that he should have stuck to writing orchestral music.

of hammering it into some sort of usable shape.* What he came up with may not be a classic of lucidly constructed drama, but it provided the Maestro with exactly what he needed for the igniting of his musical passion.

It is easy enough to see why few literary figures of the first rank should have been attracted to a task which consists basically of feeding another artist's creative imagination. There have, as always, been exceptions; such eighteenth-century figures as Metastasio and Goldoni come to mind, and more recently writers of the stature of Hugo von Hofmannsthal, E. M. Forster and W. H. Auden, but the yoke of the librettist is likely to weigh heavily on any writer who is accustomed to creative independence. He will inevitably be required by the composer to prune or even jettison many of his most valued lines; vocally comfortable syllables will have to be incorporated at points where the composer happens to have conjured up a challenging high note; melodies which have started off as a perfect marriage with the first few lines of an inspired passage of verse will display the nasty habit of acquiring a life of their own, whereupon it is the poem which has to be rewritten; and however much midnight oil the librettist may have expended on texts for the duets, trios and quartets in which so many scores abound, or the massive choral scenes with which opera unleashes the full panoply of its dramatic might, he must patiently accept the fact that when two or three are gathered together singing different words at the same time nobody is going to understand any of them. If, let us say, the tenor singing the role of Arturo in the famous sextet from *Lucia di Lammermoor†* were to forget his words and fill in with some such substitute as 'Baa baa black sheep', as long as he kept to the notes which Donizetti wrote he would be unlikely to draw attention to himself.

---

*Cammarano in fact died before the libretto was finished and it was typical of Verdi, as Dyneley Hussey relates in his biography of the composer (see bibliography), that when he was told of the desperate circumstances in which Cammarano's widow and family found themselves he promptly sent them the full fee that had been agreed upon, plus another hundred ducats as a gift. As Hussey puts it, Verdi 'was as generous to anyone in misfortune as he was "close" in his dealings with publishers and operatic impresarios'.
†Also by Cammarano.

Predictably, the relationship between composer and librettist can be an uneasy one, especially if the composer in question is himself gifted with a strong theatrical instinct. Puccini, who knew as well as any dramatist what would and would not work on stage, ran through no less than five writers before he was satisfied with the text for his first operatic triumph, *Manon Lescaut* – or seven if one includes the various lines contributed by his publisher, Giulio Ricordi, and himself. The best results are usually achieved in cases where composer and writer have been able to pool their ideas throughout the creative process, and surviving correspondences such as those between Verdi and his various librettists, or Hofmannsthal and Strauss, whose list of joint creations includes *Elektra*, *Der Rosenkavalier* and *Arabella*, invariably cast fascinating lights on the minutiae of characterization, verbal expression, musical form and general dramatic structure which together comprise an operatic masterpiece. Verdi is often absolutely precise in his requirements – 'There should be two stanzas of ten lines each,' he wrote to Antonio Ghislanzoni, his librettist for *Aida*, 'the first strophe of four lines warlike, the second amorous and then two voluptuous lines for Amneris'; and though he was prepared, when need be, to indulge in such outspoken criticism as 'The characters do not express themselves as they should and the priests are not sufficiently priestly', he made a habit of sugaring his less palatable pills by stepping up the degree of respect expressed in his form of address at the beginning of the letter in question. 'Caro Signor Ghislanzoni' usually introduces a letter of general approbation; 'Egregio Signor Ghislanzoni' tends to precede requests for fairly extensive rewriting; and 'Gentilissimo Signor Ghislanzoni' can be taken as meaning 'This one is going to hurt.' Arrigo Boito, whose libretto for *Falstaff* was accepted by Verdi without a single drastic alteration, had a rougher ride with its predecessor *Otello*, but although he was himself a composer of some distinction he knew just where he stood in the pecking order. 'Simply take your pen', he wrote to Verdi, 'and write to me "Dear Boito, please change such and such verses etc", and I will gladly alter them at once' – an attitude which reminds me of a letter in *The Times* a few years ago in which a nonagenarian wrote that whenever people asked him the secret of his sixty years of happily married life he would reveal that it lay in the two words 'Yes, dear'. On the subject of pecking order it is also amusing to

Arrigo Boito's libretto for Verdi's Falstaff, *issued at the time of the first production in 1893.*

note that throughout the voluminous correspondence between Richard Strauss and Clemens Krauss during the writing of *Capriccio* Strauss invariably starts his letters with the greeting 'Lieber Freund', 'Dear Friend', whereas Krauss habitually addresses the composer as 'Lieber, hochverehrter Herr Doktor', 'Dear, highly honoured Doctor . . .'

The most harmonious relationship of all between librettist and composer is naturally to be found when the composer writes his own text – a convenient arrangement if he happens to be as adept with words as he is with music, which is by no means always the case, but one which, by obviating the necessity for lengthy correspondence, robs us of insights such as those quoted above. The foremost figure amongst operatic sole-progenitors is indubitably Richard Wagner, a dramatist of undeniable grandeur even if his actual poetry can occasionally grate on the nerves; and it is perhaps owing to his example that the undertaking of this dual role has found special favour amongst composers of the twentieth century. Names such as Hindemith, Krenek, Egk, Orff, Berio, Ligeti, Tippett and Dallapiccola provide obvious examples; and two who made a conspicuously good fist of it were Alban Berg, whose adaptations of plays by Georg Büchner and Frank Wedekind produced two librettos, *Wozzeck* and *Lulu*, of startling theatrical potency, and Leoš Janáček, whose highly personal choice of dramatic subjects would have been hard for any single librettist to cater to, stretching as they do from tales of passion amongst the Moravian peasantry, via tangled lawsuits in aristocratic Prague and animal high jinks in the depths of the forest, to the searing experiences of a group of desperate criminals in a Russian prison camp.*

Whether or not I am right in feeling that the contribution of the librettist in the creation of an opera is often much more important than he (or she) is given credit for, I have to admit that in performance it is immaterial to most of the public whether the words are by Metastasio, Janáček or the Man in the Moon; they simply want to understand enough of them to be able to follow the story, and when they are unable to do so, which is far too often the case, they have a legitimate grievance. This can frequently, though by no means always, be attributed to poor articulation on the part of the singers, and something which has constantly surprised me during my many years in the operatic profession is how seldom singers are picked up on this point by directors or conductors.† It is an obvious fact that if you yourself are familiar with the words of an aria you will understand them even if they are not being clearly enunciated, and therein, I believe, lies the problem; directors and conductors, thoroughly versed in the piece they are rehearsing, underestimate how difficult it will be for members of the public who are hearing it for the first time. Singers

---

*Strange as the comparison may seem, the only other composer I can think of with as successful a track record as Janáček in making unlikely subjects work for him on stage is Andrew Lloyd Webber. Although he does not write his own librettos he does choose his own material, and the chances of anyone making money out of musicals on such disparate themes as the Bible, railway engines, cats and South American politicians would, thirty years ago, have struck me as being slender.

†It was a maxim of the great Polish tenor and teacher Jean de Reszke that 'the singer who does not articulate clearly shows that he distrusts himself'.

Pietro Metastasio (1698–1782). Over 3,000 composers availed themselves of his twenty-seven opera seria *librettos.*

do not hear themselves as other people hear them, and they often find it hard to believe that their words are not clear; they may feel that they are articulating with immense conscientiousness, and remain blissfully unaware that for the last seven pages not a single consonant has found its way over the orchestra.

In any case, mere intelligibility should be the humblest of a singer's ambitions. Incisive and imaginative delivery of the words will give the vocal line a purpose and a delineation which it otherwise does not possess; it will bring the role to life for the listener. It has been my experience that almost every singer with a reputation as a great operatic actor is a singer who really *uses* the text; this is what transforms a vocalist into a communicator. It was the secret of Maria Callas at her best; every musical phrase that she uttered had a meaning because the notes that she sang served, *via the words*, a distinct dramatic purpose. How often does one

Two supreme users of the text: Tito Gobbi and Maria Callas in Act II of Tosca, Covent Garden, 1964.

hear an aria such as 'Qui la voce' from Bellini's *I puritani* presented as little more than a vocal exercise, a titbit for the canary fancier, whereas in Callas's hands it became a riveting theatrical experience.* One of her regular stage partners, the great baritone Tito Gobbi, was another masterly user of text. His well-deserved reputation as one of the great operatic actors of his day was founded as much on verbal characterization as it was on physical gesture;† and looking much further back in time it is not merely the glorious flood of tone which enables Enrico Caruso still to

---

*Her 1949 recording of this aria, now reissued on CD (Nimbus *NI7864*) is an example of her interpretative artistry at its best.

†In Gobbi's case I would recommend anyone to listen to the infinite nuances which he achieves in Renato's great solo scene from Verdi's *Un ballo in maschera*, now to be heard on EMI *CDM 7 63109 2*.

leap from an ancient recording as a vital, vibrant personality. It is the fact that with every phrase he sings he is *telling* us something; the text, even in the humblest Neapolitan song, is always the launching pad from which that incomparable voice takes wing towards its twin targets, the listener's ear and, through it, the listener's heart.

Sometimes, if the singers are not managing to put their message across, the blame is not to be laid at their door but at that of the conductor. By and large, in any opera written before the mid-nineteenth century singers are not likely to be faced with a problem of audibility, but as composers gradually developed the orchestra's potential as an entity in the drama rather than merely as a means of accompanying the singers, so too did they increase its size and the scope of tone colours which they required it to produce. I have experienced performances of twentieth-century operas when the conductor has become so carried away by the glory of the sounds welling up around him that he appears to have become oblivious to the fact that there is also something going on on stage. The singers may cast piteous glances in his direction, but he goes thrashing majestically onwards; and the moment singers are brought face to face with the fact that nothing but the deployment of herculean lung-power will secure their survival the finer points of enunciation somewhat naturally fly out of the window. Furthermore, orchestral musicians, when let off the leash in this way, cannot be blamed if they get their own back for being per-manently penned in the crepuscular anonymity of the pit, while the singers bask on the limelit uplands of the stage. I remember one occasion when I was singing the role of Captain Vere in Benjamin Britten's *Billy Budd*, and as the conductor mounted his rostrum to start the second act he was greeted by a voice from the auditorium calling out 'Keep it down, Maestro, we can't hear a thing!' – though to be fair to the conductor in that instance I believe that the lack of balance was due as much to the acoustical peculiarities of the theatre as to any lack of sensitivity on his part. On a more recent occasion, however, when I was playing the role of the Haushofmeister (Majordomo) in Strauss's *Ariadne* in the Teatro Colón, Buenos Aires (a character who never has to compete with the orchestra as it is a purely speaking part and there is an obliging silence from the pit every time he opens his mouth), the conductor, a man of international repute, appeared to have declared war on the talented young

mezzo who was singing the role of the Composer. Despite the fact that in *Ariadne* Strauss settled for a chamber orchestra rather than his customary big battalions the conductor succeeded in whipping up such an astonishing racket that we might have been listening to the *1812* Overture with full symphony orchestra, the band of the Scots Guards and special effects on the cannon.

Apart from sloppy diction by the singers, inconsiderate scoring by the composer or the occasional Napoleon complex exhibited by the conductor, the most obvious barrier which stands between operatic audiences and their chance of appreciating the minutiae of the action is the fact that it so often unfolds in a language which few if any of the listeners understand. Of all performing artists in the classical field opera singers are the only ones to be regularly confronted by this problem. Straight actors and actresses rarely make careers in tongues other than their own – a fact which, while simplifying their lives in one way, greatly limits their sphere of action in comparison with a singer's – and both dancers and instrumentalists naturally dispense with language altogether. It is likely, however, that the repertoires of most sizeable opera houses in Europe or the Americas will include operas that were written in French, German, Italian, English, Czech or Russian and the question to which I have referred above – should they be performed in the original language or in that of the audience? – is one which arouses constant controversy. On the one hand there is the argument that no opera in translation sounds as the composer intended; he shaped his melodies to the contours and the spirit of one certain tongue, and his inspiration can only emerge in a disfigured form if it is forcibly harnessed to alien vowels and consonants. On the other hand he wrote his music in order to emphasize the story's inherent drama, romance, comedy, or whatever the case may be, with the greatest possible immediacy, and how can this be achieved if nobody knows what the characters are saying to each other? The best of all possible situations is, I think, quite evident; operas should be performed in the original language by a cast, and to an audience, all of whom are genuinely conversant with that language. The moment that that ideal stipulation ceases to apply, any solution can only be a compromise.

Looking at the problem for a moment from the singer's point of view it is extraordinarily frustrating to have devoted a lot of time and effort to the preparation of a part, working out to your own satisfaction just what the composer was driving at with this, that or the other little detail, and how best to give maximum expression to all the nuances of characterization which are hidden in the intricate tapestry of the musical score, only to find, when the performance takes place, that you might just as well be reciting the London telephone book for all the chance there is that any of these finer points will have registered with the audience. To quote one brief instance from my own recent experience, I was singing the part of Herod in Richard Strauss's *Salome* in German to a British audience. The real kernel of the role lies in the scene in which Herod begs Salome to back down from her demand for the head of John the Baptist. With increasing urgency he offers her one inducement after another to change her mind; first the most beautiful emerald in the world; then his fabled white peacocks which wander amongst the myrtles in the royal garden, peacocks such as no other king possesses; then a dazzling assortment of the rarest imaginable precious stones, treasures of whose existence even

Opposite Benjamin Britten and Peter Pears at work on early sketches for Billy Budd, *attended by Ronald Duncan, Britten's librettist for* The Rape of Lucretia, *and one of Britten's pupils, the composer and chorus master Arthur Oldham. Few composers have paid more meticulous attention than Britten to the art of word setting.*

the queen has no notion. Finally, in a paroxysm of desperation, and to the horror of the assembled company, he offers her the High Priest's mantle and the veil of the Holiest of Holies – anything Salome covets if she will only desist from her hideous demand. It is a wonderfully written scene, emotionally and physically exhausting to perform, the sort of scene which, on a good evening, makes you feel that every member of the audience must surely be thinking 'How can she resist such a flood of powerfully presented rhetoric?' It was therefore with a slight sense of disillusionment that I found myself after the performance in question being asked by a very charming lady, 'Do tell me, Mr Douglas, when Salome is sitting on that big rock and you spend a long time singing at her, am I right in thinking that you are angry because she won't let you kiss her?'

For reasons such as this I personally prefer, whenever it is in my power to do so, to perform in the language of the audience. It can sometimes be a nuisance when it involves relearning roles such as Herod in English, or Peter Grimes and Albert Herring in German, all of which have fallen to my lot, but the enhanced contact which one establishes with the audience amply repays the effort. This is particularly the case when the work in question is a comedy, be it an opera buffa containing a mass of rapid recitative, or an operetta with most of the jokes contained in the spoken dialogue. My memory has seldom been more mercilessly tested than when I had to learn not one English version of Eisenstein in *Die Fledermaus* but two different ones in the same year, despite the German original being ineradicably etched on my subconscious mind; but the effort was essential, because there are few more deflating experiences than delivering a line which you know should raise the loudest laugh of the evening, only to have it pass by without a titter for the very good reason that nobody has understood it. Even in more sophisticated comedies, such as Mozart's *The Marriage of Figaro*, much is lost if the public cannot follow the words. During the early post-war years at Covent Garden, a period during which almost everything was sung in English, there was, for instance, invariably a gale of laughter when, after the Count has discovered Cherubino hiding under a sheet, the oleaginous Don Basilio repeats a certain phrase which he had used a couple of minutes before – 'If I mentioned Cherubino, all I said, sir, was mere conjecture.' It is a piece of gloriously sly mischief-making, and Mozart has given the phrase, both times it occurs, particular prominence in the score; but the words 'Ah, del paggio, quel che ho detto, era solo un mio sospetto' will not produce the same response from an English-speaking audience.

There is without doubt some strength in the argument that the importance of intelligibility varies from piece to piece. During a romantic tragedy by Donizetti or Bellini, for instance, as the orchestra sighs along with the vocal line, or strums beneath it like a giant guitar, many members of the audience are likely to think 'I really don't need to follow the words – I have taken it in that the heroine has gone off her head, so I'll just sit back and let the tunes wash over me'; whereas in theatrically and psychologically more starkly conceived works, such as some of the twentieth-century pieces mentioned above, the audience is lost if it cannot follow the argument. Characters such as the Doctor and the Captain in *Wozzeck* do not sing the kind of tunes in which many members of the public will be content to wallow – if you cannot understand what they are saying they have little purpose on the stage. I am, of course, aware that many people deeply disagree with me about all this, and I remember one old gentleman telling me years ago that the reason why he preferred opera in any language other than his own was precisely because it prevented him from understanding the words, which were 'a load of rubbish anyway'. He had been driven to this conclusion by attending a performance of *Madam Butterfly* in English, when he felt affronted that the tenor should have offered the baritone a glass of whisky. 'I don't need to spend a fortune', he explained, 'just to listen to that sort of thing.'* It would clearly have been pointless to expand on the subject of how much the listener misses even in operas as familiar as *Madam Butterfly* or *La bohème* by having a general rather than a detailed idea of what the characters are saying to each other. Such heart-rending moments as Musetta's eager 'Yes' when the dying Mimì asks if it was Rodolfo who had bought the muff for her freezing hands, or Butterfly's last agonized words to her little son, will pass as if they had never been spoken.

---

*He would have sympathized, I feel sure, with the American writer H. L. Mencken who was of the opinion that 'Opera in English is, in the main, just about as sensible as baseball in Italian.'

There is naturally a halfway house between the two alternatives of singing in a language with which the audience is familiar or being met with blank incomprehension, and that lies in the hands of audiences themselves – perhaps it could best be summarized as 'homework'. Even if it is too expensive or too troublesome to acquire and listen to a full recording of a piece which one is about to hear for the first time most opera houses which pursue an original language policy do offer copies of the libretto translated into the language of the country in question, and to read the average operatic text from cover to cover is seldom the work of more than half an hour.* I am often amazed by people's willingness to spend a large sum of money to attend an entertainment of which, unless they have done at least a modicum of preparation, they can only possibly be expected lightly to scratch the surface. There is, after all, a huge amount to take in during the performance of an opera. To delight (or occasionally repel) the eye there are the sets, the costumes and the lighting; to provide a feast for the ear there are an orchestra, probably a dozen or so solo voices and a chorus as numerous as the opera house in question can afford, frequently singing music of considerable complexity; and to stretch the concentration still further there is the small matter of the plot. A hasty dip into the programme to check up on the synopsis before each act begins is scarcely preparation enough for the enjoyment of an artform in which the combined talents of so many creative artists have been deployed, not to mention those of the performers.

As far as operatic managements are concerned one argument in the language debate nowadays outweighs all others – any house which aims to secure the services of the world's leading singers is virtually obliged to pursue an original language policy. It is interesting to note that during the

---

*The word 'libretto' simply means 'little book' in Italian, and originally referred to the copies of the text which were brought out, usually at the expense of the ruling personage who was putting on the entertainment in question, to assist the audience in following the action during operas of the seventeenth and eighteenth centuries, when candlelight necessitated the auditorium remaining lit throughout the performance. The practice died out in the early nineteenth century when gas lighting was introduced, which could be dimmed at will. The word 'libretto' gradually extended its meaning to refer to the actual text itself, and the word 'librettist' was coined to refer to the author.

post-war period at Covent Garden, to which I have referred above, artists of the calibre of Kirsten Flagstad and Hans Hotter were prepared to relearn such massive roles as Brünnhilde, Isolde, and Wotan in English; and that when the company of the Vienna State Opera came over to London for a triumphant season in 1947 they opened their account before 'the most brilliant audience to have assembled in the auditorium since before the war'* with a performance of *Don Giovanni* in German. The singers on that occasion – Elisabeth Schwarzkopf, Maria Cebotari, Hilde Gueden, Erich Kunz, Anton Dermota, Ludwig Weber and Paul Schoeffler – were undeniable stars, but they were resident company members of a house which performed, as did Covent Garden, in the language of the local public.† Circumstances change, and it is clearly out of the question to expect the jet-setting stars of today to do the same thing. I can scarcely imagine Kiri te Kanawa learning Desdemona in German for the privilege of singing it in Vienna, or Luciano Pavarotti learning Cavaradossi in English to sing it in London, nor would today's audiences accept a situation which used to be commonplace, when the visiting star would perform in a different language from the rest of the company. When the great tenor Jussi Björling made his debut in the Vienna State Opera in 1936 as Radamès in *Aida* he used the only language in which he knew the role, which was Swedish. When Victoria de los Angeles made her Covent Garden debut in 1950 as Mimì she sang in Italian while the rest of the cast sang in English, and later that same year the London public was invited to suspend its disbelief yet further when the soprano Margherita Grandi and the tenor Libero de Luca appeared together in *Il trovatore*, he singing Manrico in Italian, and she singing most of Leonora in English but reverting to Italian whenever they sang together. Nowadays this kind of thing normally only occurs in the case of an emergency, but polyglot performances do have an honourable place in the glorious illogicality of operatic life. The most exotic combination I have ever experienced was, I think, a performance of *Madam Butterfly* which I attended in Tel-Aviv in 1963. The Japanese Butterfly sang in her native

---

*Harold Rosenthal's *Two Centuries of Opera at Covent Garden*.
†The first time I heard Schwarzkopf was in 1949 at Covent Garden, singing *La traviata* in English.

tongue, a Spanish tenor sang Pinkerton in Italian, and the Israeli Sharpless sang, as did the rest of the company, in Hebrew. I wish I could pretend that I left the theatre predicting a great future for the Spanish tenor, an unknown beginner named Placido Domingo.

Nowadays the usual policy is for international houses and festivals to retain the original language, whatever that may be, while smaller companies vary their policy from opera to opera. In Britain, for instance, our principal touring companies such as the Welsh National Opera, Scottish Opera and Opera North may well perform familiar French or Italian operas in the original but are likely to use English translations for tougher nuts such as *Wozzeck*, *Der Ring*, or operas from the Czech and Russian repertoires; while in London the English National Opera pursues a fixed policy of singing everything in English and the Royal Opera House virtually everything in the original language. This is probably as logical a situation as any which can be achieved in the complex world of opera, but it does still lead to undeniable anomalies. When, for instance, a Janáček opera is performed at Glyndebourne, or *Boris Godunov* at Covent Garden, with most of the company having learnt their Czech or their Russian parrot-wise, and without having any genuine feel for the language in which they are performing, is it likely that they will bring much subtlety to their delivery of the text? I am in no position to judge, as I, along with 99 per cent of any British audience, do not speak either of those languages; but I do know that almost always when I hear singers performing in a language with which I happen to be familiar and they are not I feel the lack of that extra layer of insight which any intelligent artist will bring to a performance in his or her own native tongue. Language coaches can ensure that a singer's actual pronunciation will leave little or nothing to be desired, but there remains a tendency for the sound simply to come rolling out; it may be gorgeous in quality, but if while you are singing in one language you are thinking in another there is bound to be something missing.

It is, to my mind at least, one of the many attractions of the operatic profession that it brings together all sorts and conditions of people, often in the oddest situations, and it is frequently to this question of language that the oddity can be ascribed. My last foray as Herod was with the company of the Opéra-Bastille in 1994, and though we rehearsed in Paris, for

Richard Wagner sets about splitting the ear-drum of the world.
A caricature from L'Eclipse *by André Gill (1840-1885).*

One of the last of the 115 or so stage works which flowed from the pen of Jacques Offenbach, Madame Favart *first saw the light of day in 1878.*

Lehár's 'Ballsirenen' at the Act 1 Embassy Ball. An illustration by Talbot Hughes from a souvenir programme of The Merry Widow, *the Gaiety Theatre, London, 1907.*

The personification of operetta, as seen by the French caricaturist Moloch in 1882. Zola would have approved.

Johann Strauss II conducts his orchestra at a court ball. From a painting by Theodor Zasche.

Th. Zasche. Johann Strauß' Kapelle beim Hofball.

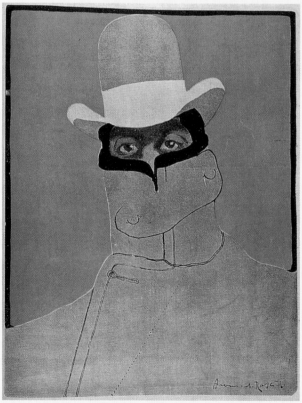

Puccini with his librettists Luigi Illica (standing, right) and Giuseppe Giacosa (seated), and his publisher Giulio Ricordi, in the wings of the Teatro Regio, Turin during the final scene of the premiere of La bohème, *1 February 1896.*

The eyes have it. Giacomo Puccini as seen by L'Assiette au beurre, *1902.*

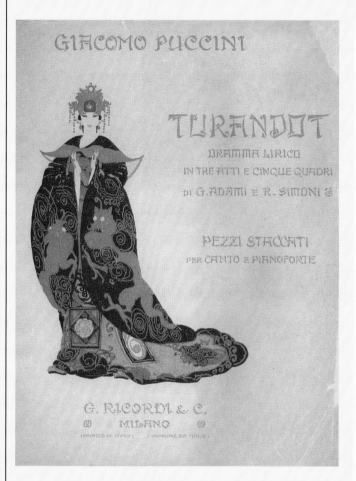

Above *Puccini's final masterpiece was first
performed in its unfinished state at La Scala,
Milan on 25 April 1926, a year and a half after
the composer's death.*

Right *An opera which has been the vehicle for
many a seductive prima donna. Poster for
Massenet's Thaïs by Manuel Orazi, 1894.*

'La Baignoire', or 'The Box in the Pit', by Jean Beraud, c. 1883. Not many eyes are directed towards the stage.

Opera as a social function. Osbert Lancaster's view of the audience at Glyndebourne, 1969. (copyright © Osbert Lancaster)

Top *Stage set and costumes by Ludovico Burnacini (1636-1707), the leading designer of his day in Vienna, for the opera* Il fuoco eterno custodito dalle Vestali *by Antonio Draghi, produced at the Hoftheater auf der Cortina, 30 October 1674.*

Bottom *Set model by Maria Björnson for Janáček's* From the House of the Dead *in a co-production by the Welsh National Opera and Scottish Opera, director David Pountney, 1982.*

Octavian in the opening scene of Der Rosenkavalier. *Alfred Roller's design for the premiere in 1911 reflects the local predilection for feminine posteriors in skintight breeches*

the performances we flew out to Seoul. The Salome was American, the Herodias and the Jokanaan were both Welsh, the Narraboth was South African and the rest of the company French, and there we all were singing a German opera to an audience of South Koreans, with half the cast singing a version of the German language so heavily gallicized – the company appeared not to believe in language coaches – that no German could possibly have understood it; a fact which clearly worried nobody, as it was a fine production and all five performances were greeted with unrestrained enthusiasm. A less enjoyable experience for me was rehearsing Loge in *Das Rheingold* in a German-language production with the Opéra de Nice under a French director who understood no German and could not follow a vocal score. He directed from a French translation of the libretto, so that whenever he interrupted to make a correction, saying (in French) something on the lines of 'Let's start again where Loge says "What are you grumbling about?"', it would take five minutes of heated debate before singers, stage management and rehearsal pianist had all agreed that this must be the line 'Was Wunder wimmerst du hier?' on page 150 of the score.

Another production in which I participated and which set me wondering whether all the right decisions had been made was an original-language *Capriccio* in the magnificent Teatro Massimo Bellini in Catania in 1993. The cast was a strong one, several of them from the Bavarian State Opera in Munich, but an opera which consists almost entirely of an intellectual conversation in German is not guaranteed to bring an audience of Sicilians cheering to its feet, and by the end of the piece even those hardy members of the public who had determined to sit it out had an undeniable air of somnolence about them. I was reminded of the opera's first performance at Covent Garden when the company of the Bavarian State Opera came over to London in 1953. On that occasion no English translations of the libretto had been made available and the synopsis in the programme was woefully inadequate. It was the only occasion I can think of at the Royal Opera when people all around me were standing up and walking out, angered by the work's incomprehensibility.

It was precisely to combat the risk of incomprehensibility that surtitles (or supertitles, as they are generally known in the United States) were introduced, and apart from the vexed question of over-the-top 'concept

Will she choose words or music? Elisabeth Söderström as the Countess Madeleine in Capriccio *(Glyndebourne, 1973, dir. John Cox), with Richard Stillwell as the poet.*

productions' I can think of no other element in contemporary operatic life which has created such radical rifts of opinion. On one side of the argument we tend to find the genuine operatic expert who has no need of assistance in understanding the piece, and on the other our old friend the average opera-goer who is heartily thankful for it. In an informative article in *The New Grove Dictionary of Opera* Roger Pines has set out the history of this new development – how the Iranian-born opera director Lotfi Mansouri conceived the idea when he was in charge of the Canadian Opera Company in Toronto in 1983, and how, with significant rapidity, it has now spread to virtually every opera house in the world which performs opera in the original language.* Those who object to surtitles have

---

*In the United States surtitles are nowadays used with increasing frequency even for performances in English. The Royal Opera House used them for Birtwistle's opera *Gawain* (in English) in 1991, and at the time of writing there are rumours that they are to be introduced by the English National Opera.

some powerful arguments on their side, but, weighing the pros and cons in the balance, I am definitely one of those who approve. I remember one distinguished British critic and music lecturer with whom I discussed the subject a couple of years ago expressing astonishment that I, as a performer, should not resent the fact that every few seconds the audience's attention was being deflected from me up to a screen way above my head, but this strikes me as being a distinctly preferable alternative to the knowledge that most of what you are trying to express will be falling on deaf ears.* To give a specific example, the performance of *Salome* which led to the charming lady's erroneous supposition was one in which surtitles were not used, while for the performances of the same opera which so delighted the audiences in Seoul they were.

One point which should not be overlooked is that the satisfactory presentation of surtitles is a skilful and tricky business. Enough of the text must be translated to ensure that no cardinal points of the plot go unremarked, but there must not be so many messages flashed onto the screen that the audience's concentration on the stage is seriously disrupted. The timing, particularly in a comedy, has to have the precision of an expensive Swiss watch – nothing is more puzzling to a singer than a hearty laugh from the audience just before the joke has been delivered. It is hard, too, to hit upon the right style of translation. In an historical opera a mass of 'thee's and 'thou's would be irritating to read, but anything smacking of modern colloquialism would be even more so. The higher the literary level of the original text the harder it is to do it justice, and in a *Times* review of *Der Rosenkavalier* at Covent Garden in February 1995 Rodney Milnes was moved to write: 'The surtitles are unacceptable. Quite apart from the omission of key lines, the wit, colour and irony of Hofmannsthal's text are ironed out into bland anonymity, almost a case for action under the Trades Description Act.' Quite so, but, to be honest, how many peole in the average Covent Garden or Metropolitan audience have ever appreciated the wit, colour and irony of Hofmannsthal's text in any case? At least, thanks to surtitles, they will have come away from the performance with some idea of what Baron Ochs goes on about at such

---

*I would, however, feel very affronted if anyone suggested that surtitles were necessary when I was singing in the audience's own language!

length in Act I, and how shamelessly the Marschallin manages to pull rank on him in Act III.*

It could be argued, no doubt, that the advent of surtitles is a green light for just those indolent opera-goers whose knuckles I rapped a couple of pages back, but on the other hand the overwhelming enthusiasm with which the innovation has been welcomed by the public must surely indicate that many people who used to feel at a disadvantage when listening to opera in a foreign language will now be more likely to take their courage in both hands and give it a try. Perhaps those captions flashing on and off do momentarily distract attention from the music – I certainly find them hard to ignore even in an opera in which I have no need of them.† I believe, though, that many opera-goers are assisted by surtitles to a greater insight into the emotional situation of the characters on stage, and that their own emotions are thus more fully engaged by the complex experience of watching and hearing an opera. Something may perhaps be lost, but something else is won. 'Does the act of winning not always involve some form of loss?' Prima la musica or prima le parole? I imagine that the debate will last as long as opera itself.

*　*　*

When advocating the practice of singing certain types of opera in the language of the audience I was making one crucial assumption – the translation has to be a good one. Translating an opera is far from simple, and

---

*I have long felt that Baron Ochs is the only honest, straightforward character in *Der Rosenkavalier*.

†Since this chapter was written I have experienced what seems to me to be the perfect, the ultimate solution. The new surtitle system installed by the Metropolitan Opera, New York, at a price, so I have been credibly informed, of $2.7 million, is a veritable miracle of modern technology. Fitted to the back of every seat is a small screen which you can switch on or off as you will, and it is so constructed that not the slightest glimmer from your screen will distract either of your neighbours. The last time I was at the Met I occupied one of the dozen or so cheapest seats in the house, which are individual free-standing chairs at the sides of the uppermost balcony, but even these are provided with screens attached on swinging brackets to the balustrade at your side – truly a fabulous innovation.

every bad translation puts a powerful weapon into the hands of lobbyists for 'the original language at all costs'. Nowadays quite eminent literary figures appear happy to try their hands as operatic translators, but unless they are both linguists and musicians the results can leave a great deal to be desired.

The translator must be constantly conscious of several basic requirements; the sense of the original text must be retained, words must be found which fit as naturally as possible to the pulse of the music, in many instances rhyming patterns must be adhered to, sounds which will be hard for a singer to articulate must be avoided, and a style must be established which is suitable for the opera in question as performed in the present day. This last requirement is particularly tricky, because one inconvenient feature of translations is the speed with which they date. An opera's original text is sanctified by usage; if the language is archaic, well and good, that was the language of the day and no one questions it. A translation which adheres to the verbiage of that period, on the other hand, creaks and groans a generation later. Back in the days when the celebrated critic Ernest Newman wrote his translation of Wagner's *Der Ring* it may have been acceptable for the goddess Fricka to say such things to her husband Wotan as 'I see thy valiant maid, shouting hither she hastes', or 'I shudder at heart, my reason doth reel: took for his bride the brother the sister', but they would fall strangely on modern ears. On the other hand, though, how far can you go in introducing contemporary language without imposing a style anachronistic to that of the music? As an instance of changing fashions, when the drunken gardener Antonio bursts in during the glorious Act II finale of *The Marriage of Figaro*, complaining that someone has trampled on his precious carnations and exclaiming 'Che insolenza! ch'il fece? chi fu?' (literally 'What insolence! Who did it? Who was it?'), the version by Professor Edward J. Dent, written around the time of the First World War and still in standard use fifty years later, offered 'Oh, my lord, oh, my lady, look here!' – short on inspiration, one might say, and a long way from da Ponte's original, but singable and inoffensive. The translation by Jeremy Sams, however, which is used by the English National Opera today, has a very different ring to it; his version of the line reads 'Bloody man, bloody nerve, bloody cheek!', a rendering which I feel sure Mozart would have appreciated, but which, until very recently, would have been totally unthinkable in public performance. I well remember that when I directed a number of Viennese operettas in my own English versions at Sadler's Wells in the mid-1980s I received several letters of protest because that same word 'bloody' occurred once in the dialogue. One gentleman even wrote, more in sorrow than in anger, that although he regarded the performance as 'the finest he had ever seen' he would never again be able to attend one of my productions as I had 'traduced the nature of family entertainment'.

To illustrate in greater detail some of the commonest problems confronting the translator I would like to take a random phrase from one of the most familiar of all operas and put it briefly under the microscope. In the first act of *La bohème* the painter Marcello offers to keep the stove alight by sacrificing his current masterpiece, *The Crossing of the Red Sea*, but his friend Rodolfo objects that canvas with paint on it will make a filthy smell – 'No!' he sings. 'Puzza la tela dipinta':

Now, taken word for word 'puzza la tela dipinta' means 'stinks the canvas painted', and the original English translation by William Grist and Percy Pinkerton had Rodolfo singing 'No, think what a stench 'twould occasion!' – perfectly acceptable in 1896 but it would sound antediluvian to an audience of today. The modern version (Jeremy Sams again) is 'No, canvas on fire smells ghastly', which fits perfectly well into the jocular style of the scene in question but which, even so, can scarcely be called ideal. As Puccini has placed 'Puzza' at the beginning of the bar the heaviest emphasis falls on the first syllable of that word, making the element of stink the mainspring of Rodolfo's announcement. The word itself is also something of an onomatapoeia, the hard 'p' and 'ts' sound of the Italian double 'z' making it a word which the singer can spit out with relish. In the Sams version, though, the vital word 'smells' is on the weakest beat of the whole phrase and needs to be artificially stressed if it is not to pass unnoticed. The old version does at least place the keyword 'stench' on the second-strongest beat of the bar, but here another problem arises. The

Italian word 'tela' trips off the tongue, its two vowels assisted rather than hindered by a couple of very accommodating consonants, and that can certainly not be said of the Grist/Pinkerton setting. Their two vowel sounds are fenced in by no less than eight consonants (not counting the l of 'would'), and any tenor who can throw off the syllables 'stench 'twould' in a lively tempo with the same insouciance as 'tela' has my admiration. Looking once again at the phrase as a whole, the second strong beat falls on 'dipinta', emphasizing that canvas only achieves its ultimate malodorous potential when paint has been slapped onto it, yet neither Sams nor Grist/Pinkerton give the paint a mention. The reason is clear enough – in Italian eight syllables are all that is needed for Rodolfo to make his point, but in English we need more; and in an opera, as opposed to a play, the constraints of the music prevent you from simply adding syllables as you feel inclined.

Very occasionally a line of translation manages to become as firmly enshrined in the public's consciousness as anything in the original text, and one such occurs in this same Grist/Pinkerton rendering of *La bohème*. Anyone writing a new version naturally eschews the option of simply copying out the old one, but when Jeremy Sams was commissioned to take a fresh look at this particular opera and reached the opening phrase of Rodolfo's aria 'Che gelida manina' he must have felt that to rewrite the words 'Your tiny hand is frozen' would be a blasphemy almost on the scale of rewriting 'To be or not to be'. To change or not to change, that must have been the question, and I feel that his final solution must be saluted as a prime example of the classic British compromise. Turn to page 64 of the score and there you will find 'Your tiny hand*s* *are* frozen'.

Different languages naturally present different problems, and certain of them translate in and out of each other more easily than others. German and English do not, on the whole, present too much of a problem, but one of the hardest marriages to bring off is Italian into German. In the opera school of the Vienna Music Academy and in the small provincial opera houses of Switzerland and Germany, in which I started my career, we used to sing everything in German, including the operas of Rossini, Verdi and Puccini, and one particular phrase sticks in my memory as a nut which I never managed to crack. In the last act of *Tosca* the painter

Cavaradossi, believing that he has been saved from the threat of execution, tells his beloved Tosca that it was only because of her that he felt bitterness at the prospect of death. 'Amaro sol per te m'era il morire,' he sings, and Puccini has set these mellifluous words to a melody of elegance and charm. How, though, can one reproduce an easy flow of sound when faced with 'Nur deinetwegen wollt' ich noch nicht sterben'? Confronted by consonants which bristled like a barbed-wire fence my attempts to maintain an italianate legato were doomed to failure; the result invariably sounded more like Wagner than Puccini.* Italian into English is not so problematic. The English National Opera's current version of this particular phrase is 'That death would part us was my only sorrow'; no problem there with consonants, but nonetheless a somewhat unhappy solution as the full weight of the phrase, which in Italian falls on the essential word 'te', 'you', is now thrust firmly onto the word 'was', where it absolutely does not belong.

Every now and then one encounters a piece of translation which is so inept that it etches itself ineradicably on the memory, and to this day I am unable to hear the stately, dignified aria in which Prince Gremin speaks of his devotion to his wife Tatiana in the last act of Tchaikovsky's *Eugene Onegin* without my mind turning to the version in use at Sadler's Wells during my youth – 'Onegin, I would not be human/If I did not adore that wooman.' There was another passage, too, in the same opera which typifies the degree to which language is in a constant state of flux. During the rustic festivities chez Madame Larina the chorus used to come out with a line which did not, presumably, give rise to any unseemly laughter in the days when the version was first written, but which stood no chance of survival once the world had become, let us say, a more scurrilous place – 'Balls in the country are quite a sensation!' the guests used joyfully to exclaim. In due course this gave way to the demure emendation of 'Here in the country we live in seclusion.'

In my youth there used also to be another inexhaustible source of

---

*Amongst the comparatively few singers who have proved that it is actually possible to maintain an immaculate legato when singing Italian opera in well-enunciated German I would give pride of place to Richard Tauber. His recording of the duet 'Solenne in quest'ora' (or 'In dieser feierlichen Stunde') from Verdi's *La forza del destino* on Pearl CD 9327 is a splendid example of this exacting art.

translational gaffes, namely the operatic synopses in the programmes of foreign festivals. Nowadays when an English translation is required most of the international festivals have an Englishman or an American within reach to handle the matter. In the immediate post-war years, however, the task would usually fall to a local figure with a reputation as a linguist, and I remember one delightful sentence in the programme of *La Valkyria* (*Die Walküre*) at the Verona Festival of 1951. Describing the outcome of the long scene in Act II in which Wotan comes under fire from Fricka for supporting the adulterous and incestuous Wälsung twins the synopsis used the phrase 'All' istante Wotan si rivolge', meaning 'Wotan immediately changes his mind.' The translation, however, put it much more dramatically – 'Wotan instantly revolts himself', a phrase which fairly set my imagination racing. We know that both in his business dealings and in his sexual conduct Wotan cared little for moral scruples. When he hired two giants to build his fortress home he offered them a lissom young goddess in lieu of a wage – there are words nowadays for that kind of thing – and if we look at the dramatis personae of *Die Walküre* we see that he himself had adulterously fathered virtually the entire supporting cast. I have no doubt at all that he revolted Fricka on frequent occasions; not for nothing is she moved to complain (as Ernest Newman puts it) 'Thy own true wife thou oft hast betrayed; never a deep and never a height but there wandered thy wantoning glance.' Now, however, according to the programme in Verona, he has come up with something so appalling that he has even managed to revolt himself, and instantly too. What a shame that we shall never know what it was.

The Lightly
Clad Muse

The Muse of Operetta is known in German as 'die leichtgeschürzte'; compared with her more serious-minded sisters she is 'lightly clad'. Her penchant for frivolity has for some hundred and fifty years brought joy to the hearts of millions, fame and fortune to the select band of composers upon whom she has smiled most sweetly, and grief and pain to certain figures of loftier purpose who have been compelled to witness her heedless triumphs. 'The Operetta', wrote Emile Zola, 'is a public menace. It should be throttled like a dangerous animal!' It promoted depravity, he complained, conferred a halo on stupidity and distracted the public in criminal fashion from the serious things of life. I remember a prominent Austrian critic in more recent days announcing with relish that the time had come when references to operetta would no longer be hymns of praise, but funeral addresses. Both of these gentlemen, however, were neatly refuted – Zola by his compatriot Camille Saint-Saëns who remarked that though Operetta may indeed be Opera's daughter gone astray, going astray does not automatically rob a lady of her charm; and the Austrian critic by unanswerable statistics. The year after he had delivered his dictum the five pieces which achieved the greatest number of performances on the lyric stages of the German-language countries were *The Magic Flute*, *The Marriage of Figaro*, *Die Fledermaus*, *The Merry Widow* and *My Fair Lady*.

The explanation for this state of affairs is plain enough – however often the sterner style of judge may pass a death sentence on operetta the general public demands a reprieve. There are, after all, operas enough to harrow us, to thrill us, to shock us, to inspire us and in true Aristotelian style to purge us of pity and fear. Operetta, on the other hand, exists on a humbler plane; all it sets out to offer is old-fashioned escapist entertainment. A good operetta performance should be a feast of melody, glamour, comedy and romance. Its objective is to send people out of the theatre feeling happier than they did when they came in, and if that is regarded as a trivial ambition, then so be it. Having myself had the pleasure of appearing in dozens of operetta productions (varying in quality from the glorious to the extremely ordinary), and in more recent years of directing quite a number, I may perhaps be regarded as prejudiced in operetta's favour. It has, however, often been my experience that those who profess to despise operetta turn out to have very little acquaintance with it and very little understanding of how rewarding a component of the repertoire it can be, both for audiences and performers. The leading British opera companies tend only to recognize the existence of three operettas* outside the Gilbert and Sullivan canon, and when they produce them they have a nasty habit of being 'clever' at the works' expense. The lightly clad Muse can never be wooed and won by people who wish her to be other than she is. She yields up her delights to those who treat her with proper respect, and as far as I am concerned long, long may she thrive.

For the purposes of this chapter it is pointless to become involved in an attempt to define operetta, or to lay down the law about what should strictly be labelled as an operetta, a light opera, an opera buffa, a Singspiel, an opéra comique, a musical comedy or a musical. To say, for instance, that operetta is opera with spoken dialogue between the musical numbers takes us a little way down this tortuous road, but it also makes *The Magic*

---

* *Orpheus in the Underworld*, *Die Fledermaus* and *The Merry Widow*.

Flute an operetta. As far as certain passages in *The Magic Flute* are concerned this is not quite as absurd as it may seem because the comic scenes did have their roots in the same fertile soil from which Viennese operetta was destined to sprout, but when we find that we have also labelled *Fidelio* and *Der Freischütz* as operettas it is evident that we have lost our way. Suffice it to say that when we talk about operetta we know what we mean, whether it be an 'opéra-bouffe' by Offenbach, a 'Savoy opera' by Gilbert and Sullivan or a 'musikalische Komödie' by Franz Lehár.

Of the various national styles of operetta it is the Viennese variety which is my own special passion and which will feature most prominently in this chapter, but Vienna was not the birthplace of operetta – that distinction must be accorded to Paris. Even there it did not spring Minerva-like, fully armed and ready for action, from the head of any one composer; it was more a process of stitching the general ragbag of popular musical entertainment into a reasonably formal garment, and the credit for having done so goes principally to a Monsieur Florimond Ronger and to his contemporary Jacques Offenbach. Ronger, under his professional name of Hervé, was a jack of all theatrical trades, author, composer, singer, conductor, actor, producer and theatre director. The neatest description of him might lie in the generic term 'entertainer', and one of his most famous numbers was the Air du Jambon, or Ham Song, which he used to sing on horseback in the first act of a piece called *Chilpéric*, during a scene set in a forest glade. When the Prince of Wales (later King Edward VII) saw Hervé in the London production he was so taken with this rendering that he sent a message backstage expressing the wish to hear the number again. Hervé obliged by inserting it into the third act as well, and he sang it as always on horseback, undeterred by the fact that Act III is set in the royal bedchamber.

Where Hervé's operettas were often unashamedly vulgar in tone, Offenbach, a German who adopted the city of Paris as his home, aimed higher. A deluge of one-act entertainments flowed from his pen during the mid-1850s, in which he displayed an extraordinary facility as a musical wit and parodist, until in 1858 he set the pattern for all future full-length operettas with his two-acter *Orpheus in the Underworld*. His fame by then had spread far beyond the boundaries of France, and when he brought his company to London's St James's Theatre in 1857 he was honoured by a visit from Queen Victoria (the offerings of Hervé, I feel, might have amused her less than they did her son). When Arthur Sullivan began to turn his hand to the writing of music for the theatre his familiarity with Offenbach became very evident, and it was Offenbach who lit the fuse for the veritable explosion of operetta in the Vienna of the 1860s, '70s and '80s.

For Vienna the mid-nineteenth century was a period of change. A generation earlier, during the so-called Biedermeyer epoch, social evolution had largely stagnated under Prince Metternich's police-state methods, and the head of steam which they built up led to the outbreak of revolution in 1848. This brought the young Emperor Franz Joseph to the throne, and with him a more progressive outlook. In 1857 he decreed that the fortifications encircling the inner city should be torn down and replaced by the magnificent Ringstrasse, thus opening it out to combine with the more

Opposite left *Paris and Vienna unite. Johann Strauss, after attending a performance of* Orpheus in the Underworld *in March 1860, paid Offenbach the compliment of arranging his melodies as the* Orpheus-Quadrille, *op. 236.*

Opposite right *Offenbach, the caricaturist's dream, as seen by Nadar.*

modern suburbs and to form a capital worthy of so extensive an empire. Vienna now invited comparison with Paris; the homespun traditions of popular Viennese theatre began to smack of the provincial, and Offenbach's style of sophisticated big-city entertainment was just what the newly emancipated Viennese were looking for. During the late 1850s Vienna's Carl-Theater was virtually taken over by pirated versions of the Offenbach operettas – there were no copyright laws in those days – and when eventually Offenbach himself was invited to come and conduct there he received a hero's welcome.

It was only natural that in due course Vienna's own musicians should try their hands at the writing of operettas. Offenbach remained for several years a figure of immense popularity, but the Viennese were ripe for a home-grown alternative as well. Despite the infectious high spirits of much of Offenbach's music, especially his celebrated can-cans, the Viennese were less attracted by the element of political satire which so endeared Offenbach to the Parisians; they wanted something rooted in the same familiar experiences as themselves, and aimed more at the heart than at the head. It had also become evident to librettists, composers and theatre managers that there was money in this operetta business, and if one were to seek an honest definition of the essential difference between opera and operetta I think it would be that whereas most operas have been written in the conscious attempt to create a lasting work of art, operettas have always been written with the purely commercial aim of filling a certain theatre at a certain time. The great opera composers of the mid-nineteenth century would not, I believe, be altogether surprised to know that their works are still being performed all these years later. The operetta composers would be astonished.

The real father of Viennese operetta was not, as many people suppose, Johann Strauss II, but Franz von Suppé. Suppé (or, to address him correctly, Francesco Ezechiele Ermenegildo Cavaliere di Suppé-Demelli) was born in the sunny south of the Habsburg Empire, on the coast of Dalmatia, and his early musical education, entirely Italian, combined the sobering influence of a thorough grounding in church music with the headier fare of regular visits to La Scala, Milan. He moved at the age of sixteen to his mother's native Vienna, where he became equally well grounded in the Viennese classics, and in due course he was appointed staff conductor to various different theatres, his duties including the provision of music for popular plays and farces.* In 1860 he began to try his hand with one-act operettas and his first great success came with *Die schöne Galathee* in 1865, the piece which really established the genre of Viennese operetta. By poking irreverent fun at the classical Greek legend of the sculptor Pygmalion, who has created a statue so beautiful that he begs Venus to bring it to life, Suppé was sticking close to Offenbachian example – no sooner is the virginal nymph Galatea transformed into a living, breathing creature than she demands an enormous meal, washes it down with an excessive quantity of wine and falls into the arms of Pygmalion's manservant – but the music is already unmistakably Viennese.

With Suppé enjoying the success that he did it was inevitable that sooner or later the more brilliant Johann Strauss should follow in his footsteps. Unlike Suppé (and the third of Viennese operetta's original 'Big Three', Karl Millöcker of *Der Bettelstudent* fame) Strauss was not a man of the theatre, but of the ballroom, a fact of which he himself was very conscious and which probably explains why he hesitated so long before turning his attention to works for the stage. The moment he did so, though (firmly pushed by his wife), with a piece entitled *Indigo und die vierzig Räuber*, the musical potency of operetta was transformed by the introduction of a new and irresistible force, that of the Straussian waltz. The premiere of *Indigo* took place in the Theater an der Wien on 10 February 1871, ticket prices were pushed to the maximum, and the packed house, including a starry collection of prominent names from every branch of the Viennese intelligentsia, was abuzz with expectation. A journalist named Josef Wimmer was amongst those present and he has left us a vivid description of how the evening began: 'When Johann Strauss appeared in the orchestra pit he was greeted with a storm of applause. As was his habit in the dance hall, so also in the theatre, he leapt with a spirited bound onto the conductor's rostrum; as was his habit he flashed a fiery glance to the left, then flashed a fiery glance to the right, and now comes the signal to begin.'

---

*One such was a piece called *Dichter und Bauer* or *Poet and Peasant*, his overture to which has never lost its place in the repertoire.

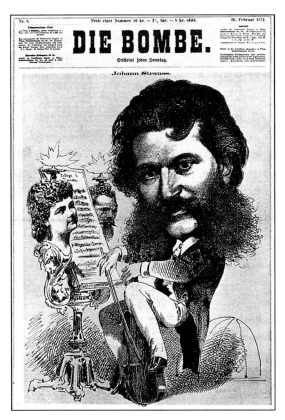

Johann Strauss II at the time of the Indigo *premiere. The figurines depict Marie Geistinger, soprano lead and directrice of the Theater an der Wien, and her fellow director, Maximilian Steiner.*

At the sound of the first waltz melody in the overture the music was interrupted by applause* and when it returned as the first act trio 'Ja, so singt man in der Stadt wo ich geboren' the occupants of the boxes and stalls could no longer remain still. They were up on their feet, taking their partners in their arms, and to quote Josef Wimmer once again, 'One had the feeling that at any moment Strauss would have to snatch the fiddle from the hands of the nearest first violin, whip it under his chin and . . . lead us in the dance.'

The critical reception for *Indigo* was as one would expect, and as

---

*As Dr Marcel Prawy has pointed out in his book *Johann Strauss – Weltgeschichte im Walzertakt* it was a normal habit up till the middle of the nineteenth century, even in symphony concerts, to greet favourite melodies in this way.

*Marie Geistinger as
Fantasca in the first
production of* Indigo und
die vierzig Räuber *at the
Theater an der Wien, 1871.*

indeed it remained for most of Strauss's operettas. To quote the authoritative Eduard Hanslick in the *Neue Freie Presse*:

> It is Straussian dance music with words underneath and roles handed
> round. Strauss cannot imagine any high-spirited or even good-
> tempered passage of text in any other form than that of the waltz or
> polka ... Whenever an allegro or allegretto crops up the Waltz King
> pushes the Opera Composer out of the way without a second
> thought; though one has to say that he does his job well – so well that
> the ladies and gentlemen listening in the stalls start going mad.

There, I believe, lies in a nutshell the eternal appeal of the best of Viennese
operetta – when it is done as it should be there is such a lilt to it that it is

A scene from the Australian Opera's production of Kálmán's Die Csárdásfürstin, directed in 1990 by the author. Boni (Roger Lemke) expounds his philosophy of life to the Young Ladies of the Budapest Orpheum.

hard to sit in the audience and remain physically uninvolved. A typical example of this in my own experience was the first time I heard Emmerich Kálmán's *Die Csárdásfürstin.** It was in the Zürich Opera House and I happened to be sitting in the middle seat of the front row of the stalls, immediately behind the conductor. As the flood of rhythm and melody which comprises that particular score washed over me – now a bouncing csardas, now a thumping waltz, now a jaunty two-step – I found it increasingly difficult to keep still. I did not, like so many of the audience at the first night of *Indigo*, actually stand up and start to dance, but the degree to which I was carried along by the music evidently transmitted itself to the conductor, who gave me a long and penetrating stare when he turned to the audience and took his bow at the beginning of the

*This is the piece which is misleadingly known in English as *The Gypsy Princess*.

last act. A couple of years later I found myself working with him, and when I introduced myself at our first rehearsal his immediate response was: 'But I know you already. You once sat behind me in the *Csárdásfürstin*.'

It is this prevalence of exhilarating dance rhythms, most notably that of the waltz, which has earned for the best of the Viennese pieces the nickname of 'champagne operettas'. Dancing had for generations been an absolute passion amongst the Viennese; Michael Kelly, the Irish tenor who worked with Mozart and sang in the first performance of *The Marriage of Figaro* in 1786, describes the Viennese in his memoirs as 'dancing mad'. In 1809, during the worst of the Napoleonic wars, the number of Viennese out dancing on any given night was reckoned to represent a quarter of the total population, and one dance-hall was even thoughtful enough to provide a 'delivery room' for expectant mothers

Caricature from Der Floh, *Vienna 1883, depicting the effect of Johann Strauss's music even on a coldly critical theatre audience in Berlin.*

taken by surprise. When the basic country dances, known as Ländler, in which the waltz had its origins, first reached Vienna's suburbs, attempts were made by various public authorities to have them suppressed on the grounds that the hectic whirling and the flying skirts encouraged immorality in the masses,* but within a few years it was the vitality of the popular element which had won the battle. Elegant society was lured

---

*The social confrontation between the new dances and the old is memorably depicted in Mozart's *Don Giovanni* during the scene in which Leporello and the peasantry lurch around in a Ländler while their aristocratic betters perform the stately minuet.

from the ballrooms of the inner city to the giddier ambience of the suburban dance-halls, social barriers were relaxed, and with a slight quickening of tempo and an almost imperceptible shift of rhythmic impulse the peasant dances were transformed from their crude, stamping patterns and refined into the elegant but intoxicating dance which has remained ever since the symbol of nineteenth-century Vienna. It has been claimed that the waltz achieved for Vienna what in France cost rivers of blood – an exaggeration, no doubt, but one with more than a grain of truth in it.

The two great figures in the early evolution of the waltz were the bandleaders Josef Lanner and Johann Strauss I, and the essence of its peculiar spell is neatly captured by a contemporary description of Lanner as 'the man who sets your feet flying while a tender tear steals into your eye'. Lanner's music acted like a magnet which drew people onto the dance floor, while Strauss's was a frontal assault which drove them onto it. The nineteen-year-old Richard Wagner described Strauss as 'a raven-haired Pied Piper' and was deeply impressed by the demonic power which enabled him to fill a dance-hall to bursting point and to set the people alight with his music even though cholera was raging through the city at the time. It then fell to Strauss's son Johann II to hone the Viennese waltz to that pitch of perfection in which the contrasting elements of energy and elegance, gaiety and melancholy blend to form one intoxicating whole. It was as if he had set out to distil into musical terms the whole spirit of the Vienna of his day, and the greatest mistake one can make in assessing that spirit is to see it as one of perpetual buoyancy.

It is true that the myth of Vienna as a city without cares has been generously nurtured by the superficial jocularity of nineteenth-century operetta, but beneath the surface other strains can be easily enough detected. The city in fact had more than its fair share of trouble. The Emperor's pride, and the showplace of the aristocracy's ambitions, was the army. For any young man with claims to social prominence a commission in one of the smarter regiments was virtually *de rigueur*, but when this splendid force went into action its effectiveness did not match its elegance or its courage, and it was decimated in the two fearful carnages of Solferino (1859) and Königgrätz (1866), the former costing Austria many of its richest Italian possessions and the latter putting the country at the mercy of Bismarck and the new Greater Germany. The illogical multinational agglomeration of the Habsburg Empire was beginning to show its cracks and the Imperial family itself was rocked by one private tragedy after another. The Viennese affected a sort of wistful flippancy with which to shrug it all off, reversing the classic military dispatch of 'Situation serious but not desperate' to produce the everyday catchword 'Situation desperate – but not serious', and nothing, to my mind, encapsulates this mood more comprehensively than a certain phrase from the first act of *Die Fledermaus*. The interloper Alfred, intent upon seducing the lovely Rosalinde during her husband's absence, urges her to drink up her champagne and forget her scruples and her inhibitions. 'Glücklich ist, wer vergisst was doch nicht zu ändern ist,' he sings – when confronted with a situation which cannot be changed the secret of happiness lies in dismissing it from your mind. This convenient philosophy was set by Strauss to a melody which exudes an utterly Viennese flavour of bittersweetness. It caresses the ear, it delights the senses, it brings a smile to the lips – and behind it it leaves a lingering aftertaste of despair.

I do not, of course, wish to suggest that in order to enjoy a modern production of *Die Fledermaus* (or even, indeed, to direct one), one must be steeped in the history of Vienna, but I do believe that one reason why the best of the Viennese operettas have shown the strength to endure as long as they have lies in the firmness with which they were originally rooted in their Zeitgeist and their Ortgeist – the spirit of their time and place. If we move on to Kálmán's *Die Csárdásfürstin*, to which I have already alluded, the same point can be made. It is set just before the First World War in the milieu of the Stage-Door Johnnies of Vienna and Budapest, the aristocratic *jeunesse dorée* who turned night into day as they paid court to their latest flames in the various cabaret clubs. The plot revolves around a young Viennese prince who causes family ructions by his determination to marry one of these glamorous creatures, and as such could perhaps be dismissed as just another frothy piece of operetta nonsense. Yet it is more than that. Despite its generous (and hilarious) element of farcical comedy it holds up a surprisingly accurate mirror to the morals and ethics of its time. Such problems did loom large in the lives of the great and the good in pre-1914 Vienna, just as they did in Edwardian London – I have no doubt that plenty of eyebrows were raised when a social figure as exalted as the Marquis of Headfort chose as his bride a

Gaiety Girl by the name of Rosie Boote.* We may take a scornful attitude today towards a society in which young men had nothing better to do with their time and money than to squander both on showgirls and race-horses; but it is worth remembering that by the time *Die Csárdásfürstin* opened in Vienna those same young men were laying down their lives in their thousands in the 'war to end all wars'. The people who packed the Johann-Strauss-Theater night after night and month after month were beginning to realize that the world they saw depicted on the stage, the world they had grown up in, was vanishing never to return. The day before yesterday had suddenly become the good old days, and there was a more than superficial message in the words sung by the elderly roué, Feri von Kerekes, 'Weisst du wie lange noch der Globus sich dreht/ob es morgen nicht schon zu spät' – or, as I rendered it in the English version which I wrote for Sadler's Wells some years ago, 'Who knows how long this sad old world will survive/and at least we are still alive.' I well remember meeting an old gentleman during my days as a student in Vienna, back in the late 1950s, who told me 'If anyone wants to know what life was like when I was young he'll find it in a good production of *Die Csárdásfürstin*.'

Kálmán's masterpiece was one of the most brilliant successes of the so-called Silver Age of Viennese operetta; during the 1890s the Golden Age had faded to a close. Suppé died in 1895, Strauss four years later, and Karl Millöcker, as if he could not quite bring himself to face the twentieth century, breathed his last shortly before midnight on 31 December 1899. There were of course other talents at work during this time, and they came from a variety of musical backgrounds. In Carl Michael Ziehrer, composer of *Die Landstreicher* and *Der Fremdenführer*, the two most vigorous sources of Viennese light music were combined, because as well as being Director of Dance Music to the Imperial Court he was also the military bandmaster par excellence. Austrian military bands were of such remarkable quality that they were in regular demand for foreign tours, and Ziehrer led many such expeditions, notably to the Chicago World Fair of 1893. In the words of Eduard Hanslick 'The peaceful conquests

---

*The marriage was a great success and by all accounts the British aristocracy made a glittering acquisition.

which our army makes with the clarinet rather than the bayonet are by no means its least significant.'

Carl Zeller, whose *Der Vogelhändler* remains one of the classics of the genre, was not a professional musician at all, but a civil servant who attained the rank of Sektionschef in the Ministry of Arts and Education, and whose contact with the world of popular entertainment was only tolerated by his Minister on the written understanding that he was never to jeopardize the dignity of his position by actually setting foot on stage. Another interesting figure amongst the operetta composers of the *fin de siècle* was Richard Heuberger, a man whose musical pedigree could not have been more impeccably classical. Apart from being the composer of several semi-successful operas (it was he who coined the 'mot', 'How sad that premieres are so rapidly followed by dernieres'), a professor at the Konservatorium and the chorus master of the prestigious Männer-gesangsverein he became Hanslick's successor as critic on the *Neue Freie Presse* and he wrote the first truly perceptive biography of Franz Schubert.

It may seem strange that such a man as Heuberger should have been the composer of *Der Opernball* (*The Opera Ball*), which contains the im-mortal duet 'Gehen wir ins Chambre séparée', surely one of the most per-fect scenes in the whole of operetta, but the division between the 'serious' and the 'popular' has never been as strict in Vienna as in certain other places. At the end of the eighteenth century operas by Gluck and Mozart would share the bill in suburban theatres with pantomimes and farces, and men like Emanuel Schikaneder, the librettist of *The Magic Flute* and creator of the role of Papageno, were active in both camps. Franz Schubert used to sit in a popular dance-hall improvising waltz tunes on the piano, Johann Strauss would conduct excerpts by the controversial Richard Wagner between his own waltzes and polkas, and the eminent conductor Hans Richter used to include Johann Strauss in the same con-cert programmes as Mozart and Beethoven. Richter also used to enjoy taking the world's most celebrated musicians to hear the Schrammel brothers playing their Heuriger music in the wine-gardens of Grinzing; the Schrammels, in turn, had studied with the great classical violinist Georg Hellmesberger – and so the cross-fertilization went on.

By the end of the nineteenth century Viennese operetta, ironically

Die lustige
Witwe,
Mörbisch, 1964.
The author as
Danilo and Sari
Barabas as
Hanna.

through its own astonishing popularity, was beginning to do itself to death. Writing operettas had become a craze for anyone with the slightest pretensions to musicianship; voice teachers, instrumentalists, critics, stockbrokers, lawyers and industrialists, they were all at it – anyone in fact who could afford the expense of hiring a theatre. Faced with this sea of mediocrity the public started to stay away, and the age of operetta seemed to be moving gently to its close. Come the hour, though, come the man. In 1905 the Theater an der Wien took the risk of putting on a piece entitled *Die lustige Witwe* (*The Merry Widow*), by a composer with a short and not very impressive track record, Franz Lehár. After a shaky start the piece established itself not only in Vienna but throughout the world as the greatest box-office hit ever written for the musical stage, and perhaps it can be taken as an indication of its unique appeal that on a certain Saturday night in the year 1907 in the city of Buenos Aires it was being performed in five different theatres at the same time and in five different languages.

At this distance in time it may be hard for us to appreciate quite what a revolutionary piece *The Merry Widow* was, but its 'newness' lay chiefly in a change of emphasis from the jocular to the romantic, and in the introduction of a 'modern' element of realism. Just as Puccini and his fellow *verismo* opera composers were aiming to present their publics with flesh and blood characters such as Mimì and Rodolfo in *La bohème*, rather than figures with whom nobody could be expected to identify such as Leonora and Manrico in *Il trovatore*, so Lehár, albeit within the more flippant parameters of operetta, created musical characters whom audiences could take to their hearts. When you play the role of Eisenstein in *Die Fledermaus* (to take an instance from my own repertoire) you can have tremendous fun, singing a stream of marvellous numbers, cracking some venerable jokes and capering your way through waltzes and polkas galore, but it is never on the agenda to make the audience *believe* in what

The irresistible Lily Elsie, London's first Merry Widow and Dollar Princess.

you are up to. When you fail to recognize your own wife at a fancy dress ball because she has donned a mask and a phoney Hungarian accent you and your public are simply surrendering to one of those conventions which flourish so delightfully in theatre's enchanted never-never land. When, as Danilo in *The Merry Widow*, on the other hand, you launch into the deceptively simple-sounding but deeply evocative final duet it is part of your task to ensure that there are not too many dry eyes in the house by the time you have finished. Danilo and Hanna are human beings with human sorrows and human joys, and you *must* make the audience care what happens to them. The point can perhaps be reinforced by citing the fact that in certain quarters attempts were made to ban performances of *The Merry Widow* as being too shocking a piece for decent society. The reason for this lay largely in the scene in which Camille de Rossillon, an amorous bachelor, lures Valencienne, a married lady, into the 'kleiner Pavilion', the little summerhouse. Aided and abetted by probably the most seductive melody ever written even by Franz Lehár it is a blatantly erotic scene and it is evident that the two of them do not vanish into the summerhouse merely for the goodbye kiss to which they both refer. Adultery is in the air, and that is, or was, strong stuff to put on stage in a piece of family entertainment. Yet in *Die Fledermaus* there is scarcely a participant whose mind is not brimming with visions of adultery from the beginning of the piece to the end, but they are presented in a fashion so far removed from real life that no offence can be taken.

The success of *The Merry Widow* acted as a green light to a whole new group of Lehár's contemporary composers, Oscar Straus, Leo Fall and Emmerich Kálmán being the most gifted amongst them. They were all impeccably trained musicians* and they were all richly individual in style, but there was one invaluable characteristic which they possessed in common – an apparently inexhaustible ability to write attractive tunes. It is this above all else which explains the lasting popularity of Viennese operetta and it is this, too, which makes it such a joy to sing. I have

---

*Straus had studied with Max Bruch in Berlin, Fall had been accepted by the Vienna Conservatory at the age of fourteen, and Kálmán, whose fellow students at the Royal Academy in Budapest had included Bartók and Kodály, won the Franz-Joseph Prize of the City of Budapest in 1907 for his serious compositions.

seldom met a soprano or tenor who does not adore singing operetta music,* and it is no coincidence that over the years so many great artists have contributed to the treasury of recorded operetta – besides the towering figure of Richard Tauber such names as Elisabeth Schumann, Lotte Lehmann, Elisabeth Schwarzkopf, Anneliese Rothenberger, Lucia Popp, Nicolai Gedda, Rudolf Schock, Fritz Wunderlich and even Placido Domingo come to mind. Wunderlich summed up the appeal of singing operetta when he said 'you do not have to worry about being clever, you can just let go with the voice', and I can think of few more gleaming examples of a great singer revelling in the joy of singing than the various operetta excerpts which Wunderlich recorded, especially those from Leo Fall's *Die Rose von Stambul*.† I have occasionally played some of these recordings when giving lectures on operatic matters, and it is always amusing to observe the effect that they have on the audience – faces which may have been creased in concentration (or even blank with boredom) become suddenly suffused with happy smiles.

The fact that operetta is so rewarding to sing does not mean that singing it is easy. I remember Nicolai Gedda, of all the great tenors of the post-war generation surely the most consummate technician, telling me how taxing he found the title-role in Lehár's *Der Graf von Luxemburg* when he made a complete recording for EMI, though to hear the results you would certainly not be aware of it.†† Emmerich Kálmán wrote melodies for his leading tenors which take them through two octaves in a single page, something which Puccini never did; furthermore he enjoyed compounding the felony by doubling the melody in the brass, and whereas in many an opera you can legitimately be seen to put your full

---

*Mezzos, baritones and basses get a much fairer crack of the whip in the French operettas than in the Viennese, and in concentrating so exclusively on the Viennese repertoire I mean no disrespect to such delightful scores as those of Planquette's *Les Cloches de Corneville*, Lecocq's *La Fille de Madame Angot*, Audran's *La Mascotte*, Chabrier's *L'Étoile*, or Messager's *Véronique*, to name but a few.

†They are available as part of a 3 CD set on EMI CZS 7 62993 2.

††Gedda participated in many outstanding full recordings of operettas, both Viennese and French, and the *Luxemburg* 2 CD set, EMI *CMS 5 65375 2*, offers the added attraction of an exquisite performance by Lucia Popp as the operatic diva Angèle Didier.

Richard Tauber as Paganini, the first of six roles tailor-made for him by Franz Lehár.

force into your work, operetta loses its charm if it is delivered with too evident a sense of effort. The tenor role in *Giuditta*, one of several which Lehár wrote specially for Tauber, *starts* on a high A – even Verdi's Otello does not do that – and in the operettas of Johann Strauss one regularly becomes aware that the melody one is singing would lie much more comfortably for Strauss's own instrument, the violin, than it does for the human voice.

The demands of merely *singing* operetta, though, in a recording or a concert are as nothing compared with those of performing it on stage. In operas, with the exception of the comparatively few which include spoken dialogue, the composer is always there to help you – try to sing what he has written to the best of your ability and you will not go far wrong. If you are blessed with acting talent it is a bonus, but, as many an opera star has proved, it is not a *sine qua non*. In operetta, however, the music has an inconvenient habit of stopping at regular intervals and it is then up to you to hold the audience's attention through the spoken word alone, a task which many opera singers find highly uncongenial. Nor is that all – you must be able to dance, in many instances you must cut a visually credible figure as a personable young prince or princess, in comic dialogue you must know how to time your laughs and you must have the knack of projecting your personality over the footlights. During the course of a long and varied career I have had a number of tough operatic nuts to crack – roles such as Alwa in *Lulu*, or the title-role in *Peter Grimes* cannot be described as easy – but I have never been made to work harder during any rehearsal period than when I was first cast in an operetta. This is what makes the operettas such marvellous training grounds for young singers, compelling them to master a far wider variety of theatrical skills than are called for in the average opera. Nowadays whenever I find myself directing an operetta* I am amused to observe how certain singers, often those fresh from opera school, arrive at the first rehearsal with an air of 'this'll be a pushover' – only to discover that there is much more to it than has ever met their eye or indeed ear. It is also gratifying to notice how they relish the task once they have got to grips with it.

One particularly attractive feature of operetta from the performers' point of view is that the rapport between stage and auditorium is far more direct than it tends to be in serious operas – in many of the dialogue scenes you are basically chatting with the public, and whereas in many operas the audience's active participation will be limited to applause at the ends of the acts, in operetta one hopes that each joke and each musical number will provoke its own reaction. In a good performance of a well-written operetta the audience's enjoyment can become almost tangible on stage, never more so than in those special moments when the action

---

*The temptation to hang on too long as a singer in this seductive repertoire has been the undoing of several distinguished performers, though I applaud the panache of the popular Dutch star Johannes Heesters, who celebrated his eightieth birthday by performing the role of Danilo in the Vienna Volksoper.

builds up towards the launching of a favourite number. When you are left alone on stage as Prince Sou-Chong in the second act of Lehár's *Das Land des Lächelns* (*The Land of Smiles*), and after two sentences of spoken monologue the orchestra comes crashing in with the introductory bars to 'Dein ist mein ganzes Herz', you can sense a feeling of 'Ah, here it comes!' in every corner of the house; and I swear that in the penultimate scene of *The Merry Widow*, when the solo violin joins in under the last lines of the Hanna/Danilo dialogue, and the audience recognizes that at last the famous duet is about to begin, I have often been aware on stage of an audible sigh of contentment from 'out front'.

These can be moments of musical and theatrical magic, indeed I have often felt what a privilege it is to be the person into whose hands they have been temporarily entrusted. Many of the happiest memories of my early stage career (as well as one or two of the harshest) are connected with operetta – my debut in the Zürich Opera House, for instance, in 1964, when I sang the role of Graf Zedlau in Johann Strauss's *Wiener Blut.** A cold had rendered me almost voiceless at the final dress rehearsal, an announcement had to be made before the premiere that I was unwell, and as I waited in the wings for my first entrance I was as nervous as I ever remember being. Halfway through my opening number, however, I was interrupted by the audience with a burst of spontaneous applause; suddenly all memory of my indisposition vanished from my mind and thus from my throat, and at the end of the performance I had not had time to leave the stage before I was cornered by the Assistant-Director of the Opera House, brandishing a lucrative contract for the following year. It has often been my experience that the most effective treatment for a sick singer is the sight of an eager understudy in the wings, but a timely burst of applause can also work miracles.

At the risk of sounding mercenary I must also mention one other aspect of operetta which can make it remarkably attractive to a young singer. Whereas contracted members of opera companies are normally

---

*Wiener Blut was in fact concocted out of existing Strauss music at the end of his life, and although Richard Traubner, in his splendidly comprehensive book *Operetta – A Theatrical History* (see bibliography), cannot find a good word to say about it it is a favourite piece of mine.

paid a monthly salary, once you have made enough of a name for your-self to be able to operate as a freelance you are paid by the performance, and while there have been numerous occasions when I have slaved away for months learnii.g some complex modern role, only to perform it three or four times before the opera in question is consigned to oblivion, the standard operettas, which are musically seldom hard to learn, turn up with heartening regularity. During one period of my career I often used to appear in two different operettas on the same day, because the Zürich Opera usually scheduled an operetta for the Sunday matinée, which left me time to take the train to Basle, where I also had a guest contract, and where they frequently scheduled their current operetta production on a Sunday evening. There was nothing very confusing in combining, say, the role of Edwin in *Die Csárdásfürstin* with that of Georges in *Der Opernball*, but I did have to keep my wits about me whenever I sang Eisenstein in *Die Fledermaus* twice in one day in different productions, with different dialogue and different choreography. Indeed, Eisenstein was a role which I once contrived to sing three times in two days by fol-lowing one of these 'Swiss Sunday Doubles' with a guest performance in Antwerp on the Monday – an event made especially memorable by the fact that while I performed in German the rest of the cast performed in Flemish, so that throughout the extensive dialogue scenes not a word that anybody said was remotely comprehensible to me. By stretching a point I can even claim to have been seen in three different operettas in one day, because on a certain Sunday when I was appearing in Zürich and in Basle, back in the United Kingdom the BBC transmitted their television pro-duction of *The Count of Luxemburg*, in which I sang the title-role – definitely the closest I shall ever come to a place in *The Guinness Book of Records*.

As I look back now on those hectic days my advice to anyone wishing to try his or her hand at operetta in the German-language houses would be 'Don't do it unless you can improvise in German.' So often you arrive in the opera house to be told that such-and-such a colleague is ill, so-and-so has flown in from somewhere-or-other to take over the role, and there has not been time for him or her to rehearse. So onto the stage you go for a dialogue scene with somebody you have never set eyes on in your life and who comes from a theatre where they use different cuts, or even in some circumstances a totally different text. Then there is the ever-present menace of the resident comedian, a long-established favourite with the local public, who plays some such role as the dotty old servant in Act III. He loves to insert local jokes which mean nothing to you at all, and if he can make the guest star look an idiot while bringing the house down with his unrehearsed wisecracks he is not about to turn down the opportunity. Sometimes these little difficulties arise without any malice aforethought, and the operetta character who must, I believe, have involved me in more quick thinking than any other is Baron Zeta, the Pontevedrian ambassador in *The Merry Widow*. As the role involves very little singing it is often given to a company member in the late evening of his career, and I have encountered one or two whose memories were beginning to play tricks on them. Now it so happens that one vital thread of the plot, concerning a fan with the compromising words 'I love you' written on it, involves Zeta in several confusingly similar passages of dialogue, during the first of which he simply has to hand the fan to Danilo with the words 'Vielleicht führt Sie dieses auf die richtige Spur', 'Perhaps this will put you on the right track.' Without the fan Danilo is stranded helplessly for the next half dozen scenes, and on several occasions I have found myself involved in dialogue which has run something like this:

ZETA: My dear Count, there you are. Yes, yes, yes.
DANILO: Yes, indeed, Excellency, just as you say, here I am.
ZETA: I have something important to say to you. Er, er . . .
DANILO: Did you perhaps want to tell me that you have found some vital object?
ZETA: That's it, yes, absolutely!
DANILO: And that you want to take it out of your pocket and give it to me?
ZETA: How on earth did you guess?
DANILO: Could it be a fan, perhaps?
ZETA: Precisely, my boy, well done, well done!

By this time Zeta has generally positioned himself for safety's sake directly in front of the prompt box, from which the prompter as likely as not is still hissing what he should have said about six lines back; but on one particular occasion, during a performance in English with the Sadler's Wells Opera in the London Coliseum, I became aware that the distinguished old gentleman playing Zeta seemed anxious to work his way towards the side of the stage. Standing with his back to the wings and with one hand outstretched behind him he started a discussion about the weather, until a quick-witted member of the stage management raced to his dressing-room, picked up the fan which was still lying on his table, raced back to the wings and placed it in his hand. With an expression of triumph on his face the Baron continued 'Well, my dear Count, we can't stand here all evening discussing the weather', handed me the fan, and at last came out with the longed-for words 'Perhaps this will put you on the right track!'

This was not, however, the most accident-prone of the many *Merry Widow* productions in which I have appeared – that distinction goes without doubt to the 1964 Burgenland Festival in Mörbisch. This is a town (famous for its excellent white wines and the storks which nest in its chimney-tops) on the Neusiedlersee, the vast lake which forms part of

Set for Die lustige Witwe, *Mörbisch, 1964.*

the border between Austria and Hungary. Every year an operetta is produced there on an enormous stage built over the water, with the public sitting in a specially constructed auditorium on the shore, and as the productions are designed to make the best possible use of the unusual setting it was decreed that I should make my first entrance, accompanied by six dancing-girls from Maxim's, in a motor-boat. There was a little island some quarter of a mile from the stage and shortly before the beginning of the performance we were concealed behind it, waiting for a cue on our walkie-talkie which would give us just enough time to chug forth and disembark onto the main stage as the orchestra struck up with the introduction to my entrance song. Now, one strange characteristic of the Neusiedlersee is that although it occupies an area of some 135 square miles it never reaches a depth of more than a few feet. On the night of the premiere a stiff breeze was blowing from the Austrian shore towards the Hungarian and it had taken some of the water with it, so that long before we became visible to the public we went aground in the mud. The boatmen, one at each end of the boat, tried to push us off with a pole apiece, and when they failed to do so began to berate each other in sturdy Burgenland dialect. As it seemed highly likely that all of us would be pitched into the muddy water one or two of the grisettes began to scream, and as I was aware that at any moment my throat microphone would be switched on from the central control board the thought did cross my mind that screaming girls and swearing boatmen would soon become all too audible over the loudspeakers in the auditorium. My attempts to quieten everyone down only added to the general racket, but at last we got under way and peace was restored. In the dim distance I heard my entrance music and there was nothing for it but to start singing. We reached the stage soon after the song was over, and I was later told that the sound of an invisible Danilo coming to them from the loudspeakers above their heads had resulted in most of the audience gazing towards the sky in the expectation of my arrival by parachute.

Open-air performances in vast auditoria do bring their own hazards with them, and I well remember a certain impromptu addition to the dialogue during one of my rare excursions into the Gilbert and Sullivan repertoire. I was singing the role of Colonel Fairfax in *The Yeomen of the Guard*, staged on the ramparts of the Tower of London and conducted by

Sir Charles Mackerras. The police had evidently not quite fulfilled their regular task of clearing the adjoining streets, because as I went down on one knee before the soprano Catherine Wilson and, in the stentorian tones required for intimate dialogue when many of your audience are sitting out of normal earshot, bellowed 'Fly with me, Elsie, we will be married in the morning', back came the equally well projected reply from somewhere in the distance 'Why can't you bloody well belt up?' My favourite open-air extempore, however, was provided by the immortal Erich Kunz, when playing the role of Colonel Frank in *Die Fledermaus* on another Austrian aquatic stage, that of Bregenz. It was a tempestuously windy night, the scenery seemed likely to take off at any moment, and as Kunz made his first entrance, coming to arrest the character he supposes to be Eisenstein, he turned to Gerda Scheyrer in the role of Rosalinde, and using both hands to keep his hat on his head, said 'Before I tell you who I am, Madame, could I ask you to shut the window – there's a terrible draught in here!'

Such flippancy may perhaps confirm the views of Zola and his adherents that the Lightly Clad Muse has nothing to offer the serious-minded. It has, however, often been my experience that operetta is a powerful builder of bridges, and that many people who might well be alarmed by opera's 'élitist' image will be prepared to try their luck in an opera house if there is a popular operetta on the bill, and then, having found that the place is not so daunting after all, may well risk another visit on a more demanding evening. Certainly those Sunday matinées in Zürich used to bring the schoolchildren in in droves – there were seldom less than a couple of dozen autograph hunters at the stage door on the way out – and to them the Opera House had become a friendly place, a place that you visited in order to enjoy yourself.

I have also known one other significant bridge to be built by operetta. Back in January 1963 the Grand Old Man of Viennese light music, the conductor and composer Robert Stolz, then a frisky eighty-two,*

---

*He remained in harness until the time of his death, shortly before his ninety-fifth birthday. It was a fascinating experience for a young singer to work with, and enjoy the friendship of, a man who as a child had played the piano to Brahms and had heard Johann Strauss conduct.

accepted an invitation from the Israel Philharmonic Orchestra to conduct three concerts of Viennese operetta in the Frederick Mann Auditorium in Tel-Aviv, and the soprano Adèle Leigh and myself were engaged as soloists. It was the first time that music of this kind had featured in the orchestra's concert programmes, and in those days, when recollections of past horrors were still so fresh, it was feared in some quarters that people might not want their memories of pre-war Vienna to be stirred back into life. Stolz, though an Austrian and an Aryan, had an aggressively anti-Nazi background, and it was a convenient coincidence that there happened to be two singers available who were both familiar with the Viennese repertoire, but who, being British, could obviously not be suspected of a pro-Hitler past. There remained, however, the question of language. German was quite simply not acceptable in the State of Israel, and yet a programme of operetta sung in English to an audience, so many of whom had grown up to this music in some part or other of Mitteleuropa, seemed an absurdity. We were warned that if we did settle for the original language there might be trouble, but Stolz himself was very keen that we should risk it, and we did. When Stolz appeared on the platform he was greeted with great enthusiasm and the programme began with the *Fledermaus* overture. Then it was my turn, my first number being Barinkay's Entrance Song from Johann Strauss's *Der Zigeunerbaron*. There was an air of tension as I sang the opening lines 'Als flotter Geist, doch früh verwaist, hab' ich die ganze Welt durchreist', but not a voice was raised in protest. By the end of the song it was evident that there were to be no violent demonstrations after all, and when Stolz reached the last orchestral number on the programme, a pot-pourri of his own most famous melodies, there was an atmosphere in the hall such as I have never experienced before or since. As several members of the audience told us later, this was the music to which so many of them had first fallen in love, but which they had not heard for a quarter of a century, tunes such as 'Zwei Herzen im Dreivierteltakt', the title number from the first ever German musical film, or 'Frag' nicht warum ich gehe', immortalized by Richard Tauber.* As for melodies like 'Im Prater blüh'n wieder

---

*Under its English title of 'Don't ask me why I'm leaving' this was also a great favourite of Marlene Dietrich's.

die Bäume' and 'Das ist der Frühling in Wien', composed by Stolz back in the days of his youth, they had long been regarded as part of Viennese folk music. It seemed as if, for many listeners in the hall that evening, the music had stripped away some of the pain and revived some of the happiness embedded in their memories of the past, and when, at the end of the concert, a mass of people surged to the front of the auditorium and stood just below the stage applauding and calling out to Stolz, two things left an indelible impression on my mind. One was to see how many of the ladies, decked out in their smartest evening dresses, carried the tell-tale mark of a branded number on their arms; and the other was to hear how the words which they called out to Robert Stolz were not words of congratulation, but words of gratitude. It was not the music of Mozart, Beethoven or Schubert, and certainly not the music of Richard Wagner, which had made the German language once again acceptable in public performance – it was the magic of that much maligned lady, the Lightly Clad Muse.

8

The Recording Angel

I doubt if any single event has ever contributed more to the popularizing of opera than the invention of the gramophone. Had Mozart never been born (hideous thought!) opera would have found its way somehow out of the eighteenth century into the nineteenth, and had Verdi or Wagner never seen the light of day it would have stumbled into the twentieth by some precarious means or other. Had the gramophone never been invented, however, opera would have remained an entertainment for the few instead of becoming a presence in millions of homes throughout the world.

Perhaps it is misleading to refer to the invention of the gramophone as 'an event' – like most other innovations of such far-reaching significance the gramophone evolved over a period of time. The scientist usually credited with having first experimented in the field of recorded sound was a Frenchman with the unlikely name of Léon Scott, who did not in fact busy himself with the function of playing the sounds back once they had been recorded, but merely with the measurement and analysis of sound

'Mary had a little lamb.' Thomas Edison records on his phonograph, 1899.

waves converted into visible lines. Others dabbled in the same field but it was not until twenty years later that the American Thomas Edison came up with the first practical machine for the reproduction of sound, a feat which he achieved by means of the famous Edison cylinder, christened by its inventor 'the phonograph'. As far as anyone knows the first recorded words ever to have fallen upon human ears consisted of the stirring announcement 'Mary had a little lamb', spoken by Edison himself and played back with remarkable fidelity to the astonishment of himself and his assistants.

Should any of my readers be interested in gaining a first-hand impression of those early days of the recording industry I would strongly recommend them to seek out a book entitled *Music on Record* by one of the pioneers in the field, Fred W. Gaisberg.* Gaisberg touchingly recreates the world of eccentric inventors with their weird Heath Robinson-style gadgets, and he provides hilarious accounts of the various purposes to which their brainchildren were put. Although as early as 1888 a cylinder

---

*See bibliography.

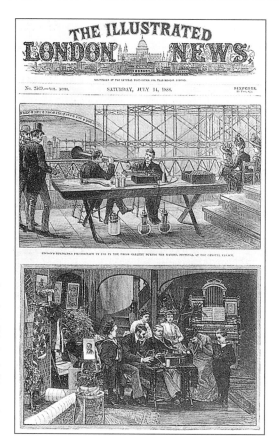

The front cover of the Illustrated London News *devoted to two astounding technical achievements, the live recording of Handel's* Israel in Egypt *and the transmission of a message from across the Atlantic.*

recording was made of Handel's *Israel in Egypt* during a live performance at the Crystal Palace the new machines were not generally considered suitable for anything more elevated than the cruder forms of popular entertainment, and Gaisberg attributes the survival of the Columbia Phonograph Company, licensees of the Edison Phonograph, to the fact that the invention was taken up as an attraction at fairground sideshows. The main problem facing the purveyors of such machines was that initially nobody had worked out how to make copies from a master cylinder. Gaisberg was employed at one point by an entrepreneur who had obtained a concession for coin-operated talking machines at the Chicago World's Fair and had installed in his studio a battery of twenty recording heads which worked as one single unit. In this way he managed to produce twenty cylinders from a single performance of a song, but twenty cylinders did not go very far and Gaisberg, who doubled as laboratory assistant and piano accompanist, ruefully observes that it was a not uncommon event for himself and some iron-lunged vocalist to record 'After the Ball Was Over' seventy times in a single day.

The man who solved this problem was a German immigrant to the United States named Emile Berliner. By the mid-1890s he had developed a machine, the first to be given the actual name of 'gramophone', which cut its recordings onto a flat zinc disc. He, like Edison, was given to using nursery rhymes for his experiments, his favourite being 'Tvinkle, tvinkle, little star, how I vonder vot you are', but he was a clever enough scientist to have made one appreciable fortune already from his pioneering work on telephones, and it was not long before he hit upon a material which could be used to take pressings from the original master disc. This was, as Gaisberg puts it, 'a mixture of shellac and byritis, bound with cotton flock and coloured with lamp-black', the invention of a company which manufactured buttons in Newark, New Jersey; and it was this, with various refinements, which became the standard material for the manufacture of gramophone records over a period of more than fifty years.

The original gramophones had to be turned by hand, rendering a steady playback speed virtually impossible, but the next great breakthrough came with the introduction of a clockwork motor. A method was discovered, too, of taking shellac pressings from Edison cylinders – for many years cylinders and discs were destined to remain in competition – but at the turn of the century recording machines of whatever variety were still regarded more as amusing playthings than as articles which could ever find a role in the world of serious music. Early on it had become evident that of all musical instruments the one which was most faithfully reproduced was the human voice, and most of the early recording artists were comedians and vocalists of a distinctly popular hue. The process involved in recording them was a purely mechanical one. The performer was obliged to sing or recite straight into a large horn which concentrated the vocal sound waves (and to a much lesser extent those created by the accompaniment) and transferred them to a diaphragm covering the narrow throat of the horn. The vibrations of the diaphragm were in turn transferred to a stylus which cut its waveforms into a master disc made of wax* (in the case of cylinders, *mutatis mutandis*, the same principle applied); from that a metal matrix would be made, and from the matrix the shellac copies would be pressed.

The first operatic artist ever to be recorded was an Italian tenor named Ferruccio Giannini,† who was talked into trying out the apparatus after Gaisberg had heard him perform with a touring company in Atlantic City. This was in or around 1896, and it was to be several more years before the event occurred which really provided the gramophone with its breakthrough into artistic respectability. In the early spring of 1902 Gaisberg was sent to Milan by the Gramophone and Typewriter Company of London to seek out some established star from La Scala who would be willing to collaborate. The operatic talk of the town at that time was the Neapolitan tenor Enrico Caruso, currently in his second season at La Scala, and, having heard him give a sensational performance in an opera called *Germania* by a composer named Alberto Franchetti, Gaisberg was determined to secure his services. He ascertained that Caruso would only be able to spare him one afternoon, but that he was willing to sing ten arias for Gaisberg at a fee of £100. This was a sum far in excess of anything ever paid before – it would need to be multiplied by over forty to reach the equivalent sum at the time of writing – so Gaisberg cabled to London to clear the matter with his head office. Back came the reply 'Fee exorbitant. Forbid you to record', but Gaisberg courageously ignored it and went ahead. Thus it came about that on the sunny afternoon of 11 April 1902 Caruso, jaunty and debonair as was his wont, presented himself at the Grand Hotel Spatz where Gaisberg had converted his room into a primitive studio. To the piano accompaniment of Maestro Salvatore Cottone the young tenor sang ten arias in two hours, pocketed his £100, then took his hat, his cane and his leave. Gaisberg's principal reaction to all this was a feeling of awe that anyone could earn so much money in so short a time.

So much money! How could Gaisberg, Caruso or anyone else have

---

*A morass of conflicting patents had to be cleared up before this part of the process became legally permissible.
†His daughter, Dusolina, became one of the outstanding sopranos of her generation.

In the opinion of Fred Gaisberg, Caruso 'made the gramophone'. This is the great tenor's own impression of how it was done.

realized what artistic and financial floodgates had been opened that afternoon? All ten of the recordings were issued by the Gramophone and Typewriter Company, and Gaisberg heard £15,000 mentioned as the immediate net profit on the venture. That sum, though, scarcely scratches the surface of the session's true significance. Caruso's subsequent recording career was reckoned to have earned him some $2 million during his own lifetime and the recording industry at least twice that much; what kind of turnover it has generated since his death would, I imagine, be incalculable.

One aspect of this story which, with hindsight, always strikes me as particularly touching is how unaware the participants were that they had created a milestone in musical history. The quality of Caruso's vocalization through ten arias of widely contrasting styles is truly remarkable – not many tenors today would include 'Celeste Aida' and 'Una furtiva lagrima' in the same session and none of them would dream of recording ten arias in less than two days – but the recordings include several glaring imperfections which would assuredly not have been allowed to slip through had anyone realized that they were setting up a monument. Caruso audibly clears his throat between the two verses of 'Quest' o quella' from *Rigoletto*, he tries to come in a beat early in 'Dai campi' from

Mefistofele, and in the *Tosca* aria, 'E lucevan le stelle', he sings the whole of the opening phrase on the wrong note – details which did not prevent the recordings from causing an international sensation.

Within a short time every leading singer was anxious to find his or her way to a recording studio and important companies were set up in Russia, France, Germany and Italy as well as in Britain and the United States. As the acoustic process continued for some years to capture the human voice noticeably better than any other instrument it was the singers who dominated the catalogues, and despite the undeniable technical limitations of those pioneering days one can still gain a fascinating impression of how the leading personalities of that particularly starry era set about their business. To take Caruso as the most obvious example, although I have often been told by those who heard him, and even by one old lady who sang with him, that his recordings give only a partial impression of the glorious richness of his voice and of the extraordinary excitement which he generated in live performance, they do nevertheless preserve enough of Caruso the artist *and* the man – his fabled generosity of spirit leaps from almost every disc he made – for his influence still to be present in the modern world of opera. Every famous tenor I have ever encountered during the course of my own singing career has made a point of listening with great care to Caruso's recordings; several admit to having learnt from them, but none has claimed to be Caruso's equal.

Does the chief value of these old recordings, then, lie in the fact that they provide evidence to the professional singer and to the musicologist of how vocal styles and techniques have evolved, or can the layman actually play them for enjoyment? There is no denying that until a few years ago historic recordings had become a specialist area, one of their trickiest aspects being the question of the speed at which they should be played. Quite early on record companies started to indicate the standardized speed of 78 revolutions per minute on their labels although the actual speed of recording had often lain anywhere between 73 and 83 r.p.m. An error of a few revolutions is enough to put the pitch of an aria up or down by a whole tone, and the most brilliant tenor voice reproduced at too slow a speed often sounds like a baritone with a cold, while a coloratura soprano played only a little too fast can assume the characteristics of a hysterical hen. Indeed, I have often wondered how that first batch of

Confidently presented as the ultimate peak of sonic fidelity - the Graphophone Grand.

Caruso's recordings could have made the impact that it did; the speed at which they were made has been scientifically established as 71.29 r.p.m., and played back at 78 they make the king of tenors sound like a frantic schoolboy in danger of missing his morning bus.

To give these so-called 78s a proper chance, then, the listener needed to possess equipment with a variable-speed turntable and to know exactly how each individual voice should sound or in what key the singer was likely to have made the recording – not always a simple task, as singers do from time to time transpose their music. Harsh words have been known to pass between rival experts on such questions as whether or not Madame X capped her 'Sempre libera' from *La traviata* with a high E flat ('Everyone knows she couldn't get above D by 1909'), or was the Victor Company's apparatus running at two revolutions a minute slower that morning than it had the previous week, when Signor Y hit his famous high C in the 'Di quella pira' from *Il trovatore*? Despite these knotty problems, however, there used in my young days to be many opera enthusiasts who were dedicated collectors of acoustic 78s and I, as far as my pocket would allow, was of their number. To the uninitiated the hiss and crackle were intolerable, while to the aficionado there was a special enchantment about the fact that the recording appeared to have been made while someone rode a motor cycle round the studio frying an egg as he went; one's ear developed a sort of in-built filter and these extraneous noises, especially those emitted by the introductory grooves, were less of a deterrent than a promise of exquisite vocalism to come.

Now that the advent of CD has eliminated so many of the technical problems facing the non-specialist listener the degree to which that vocalism still holds the power to enchant a modern ear is proved, I think, by today's remarkable sales figures for historic opera recordings. Apart from the major labels to which the artists were originally under contract – EMI, RCA Victor and so on – smaller companies have popped up like mushrooms, specializing in the transfer onto CD of recordings old enough to have outlived their fifty-year copyright. The degree of care taken by these companies to make their dubbings from mint-condition 78s and to reproduce them at the right speed can still vary, as can the extent to which they prefer either to 'improve' the tone quality of the originals or to present them warts and all. Processes used to eliminate surface hiss can also take the top layer of shine off the voice, and tastes differ – indeed the contrasting techniques used in the recreation of historic recordings is another area in which rival experts have been known to become very hot under the collar. By now, however, a high standard of reliability is generally achieved, and where in any session of listening to old records at least half of one's time used to be spent on fiddling with the machinery, it is now possible to sit back and enjoy a seventy-minute recital by the legendary voices of the past without the necessity of twiddling a single knob.

In the gramophone's earliest days many stars of the previous generation emerged from retirement, lured by this newly created prospect of immortality, and though most of them were audibly past their best it remains an enthralling experience to hear the voice of someone such as Adelina Patti,

who had dominated the operatic scene way back in the 1860s, of a figure as Olympian as Lilli Lehmann, who took part in the first complete *Ring Cycle* at Bayreuth in 1876, or of artists such as Francesco Tamagno and Victor Maurel, the creators respectively of Verdi's Otello and Falstaff. Of these four legends rescued from the mists of the past it is perhaps Tamagno who emerges with the greatest immediacy. On the early acoustics the tenor voice is frequently the best served and Tamagno was in any case only in his early fifties, an age at which he would doubtless still have been much in demand by the opera houses of the world had he not retired prematurely owing to heart trouble. Patti, of all the nineteenth-century sopranos perhaps the most adored by the public, bestowed a signal honour on the infant recording industry when, in June 1906, she allowed Gaisberg to bring one of his weird machines into her private home, Craig-y-nos Castle in South Wales. Well into her sixties,

One of the first stars of operatic recording. Francesco Tamagno (1850–1905), with an entry in the autograph book of Lady Campbell Clarke, wife of the British Ambassador in Paris.

Adelina Patti (1843–1919), perhaps the most adored of all nineteenth-century sopranos, as the serving girl Ninetta in Rossini's La gazza ladra.

she was no longer the irresistible canary whose teenage Lucia di Lammermoor or Amina in *La sonnambula* had smitten thousands of Victorian hearts; but nevertheless recordings such as her version of Amina's aria 'Ah, non credea mirarti' still give us some idea of the limpid purity of her tone as well as demonstrating a trill which many sopranos of my acquaintance would be extremely happy to have in their vocal armoury. Patti, by then a very *grande dame*, was initially somewhat ruffled when Gaisberg laid his hands upon her and drew her backwards from the horn as she approached her top notes, but upon ascertaining that this was technically necessary for the avoidance of 'blasting' she gave in graciously to the physical inconveniences of the unfamiliar medium. As to the mighty Madame Lehmann, though she too was self-evidently no spring chicken, and though she had apparently parted company with the bottom of her voice somewhere along the way, she still managed to stamp her recordings with the imprint of a redoubtable musical and dramatic personality. While one listens, for instance, to her version of Donna Anna's 'Or sai chi l'onore', one can but marvel at its vim and vigour – indeed it becomes impossible not to admire the courage of any Don Giovanni who could even contemplate the idea of having his wicked way with her.

In the dawn of the recording industry singers were invariably accompanied by the clattering of a distant piano, an effect which perhaps reaches its lowest ebb in what should be the orchestral maelstrom preceding Tamagno's titanic rendering of Otello's 'Esultate' – helter-skelter, tinkle tinkle, and our hero's ship has landed. All the time, though, the acoustic process was being refined, and by 1904 certain singers such as the eminent Polish coloratura soprano Marcella Sembrich and the imperious Australian Nellie Melba were being provided with an orchestral accompaniment; Caruso, remarkably, had to wait until February 1906 before the Victor Company in New York paid him the same compliment. Lest anyone should suppose, however, that we are moving in one bound from the kitten on the keys to the lavish textures of the modern operatic orchestra it should be emphasized that the marking 'orch. acc.' in CD leaflets does not indicate anything at work which a modern listener would recognize. Because stringed instruments (unless played solo, straight into the horn) did not produce the type of resonance to which the recording process responded, something known as the Stroh violin, or phonofiddle, was developed, with its strings stretched over a resonator and with a horn of its own on the end, something like that of a saxophone. Bassoons would be substituted for cellos, tubas for double basses, and so on, so that the general effect, though an undeniable improvement on the sadly inadequate piano, adds to the note of exoticism with which these old recordings sometimes fall on uninitiated ears.

As far as the voices themselves were concerned, though, by about 1906 many truly remarkable recordings were being achieved, and despite the 78 format's obvious limitation of being restricted to less than five minutes of music at a time, virtually all the great singers who were in their prime during the acoustic era were able to record an invaluable legacy of the individual numbers central to their repertoires. It is not merely for their curiosity value that we listen to such singers as the dazzling coloratura sopranos Tetrazzini, Galli-Curci or Selma Kurz; to the vocal gold of the young Rosa Ponselle; to Claudia Muzio, most moving of divas, with 'that unique voice of hers made of tears and sighs and restrained inner fire', as the tenor Giacomo Lauri-Volpi so memorably described it; to the glamorous Geraldine Farrar, whose Madam Butterfly can still wring the stoniest heart; to that stupendous contralto Ernestine Schumann-Heink, whose noble tones conjure up the majesty of a galleon in full sail, but whose dexterity in florid passages makes many a light soprano sound clumsy and inept; to the exquisite refinement of Fernando de Lucia; to the two starriest of Russian tenors, Leonid Sobinoff and Dmitri Smirnoff; to the easy charm of John McCormack, who of all the tenors of the era did the most after Caruso himself to promote the popularity of the gramophone; to the seigneurial elegance of Mattia Battistini, prince of baritones, and to the elemental power of his young compatriot Titta Ruffo, 'the voice of the lion'; or to the hypnotic vocal wizardry of that wayward genius, the great Russian bass Feodor Chaliapin. All of these, and many others too, can be listened to with genuine enjoyment by anyone who appreciates great singing. I am not one of those people who believe that to be a great singer you must have been dead for fifty years, but in every generation fabulous artists do arise, and thanks to the pioneers of the recording industry the gramophone arrived just in time to capture the brightest stars of an era in which singers still ruled the operatic roost. No longer were they condemned to become, as all their predecessors had, mere names from a silent past.

One of the principal problems facing recording engineers in those distant days was how to accommodate more than one singer at a time in front of the horn, something which called for diplomatic tact during the recording of duets and other ensemble numbers. As the famous accompanist Gerald Moore recalled in his memoirs, 'It often developed into a free-for-all between the tenor and bass, or the soprano and baritone protagonists. Each wanted to shine, each wanted to hog the trumpet, and the charging and pushing that went on made me marvel that they had any breath left for singing.' It is perhaps remarkable that a veritable treasury of ensemble numbers did nevertheless find its way onto disc, and one occasion when I would dearly love to have been a fly on the wall, able to monitor the charging and pushing, would have been that of Caruso's sole

Luisa Tetrazzini, the Florentine Nightingale, in somewhat puzzling studio conditions.

Claudia Muzio listens with understandable gratification to her celebrated 1934 recording of Buzzi-Peccia's song 'Colombetta'.

recording session with the formidable Melba. The result was a version of the Act 1 duet from *La bohème* which magically evokes the atmosphere of many a diamond-encrusted evening at Covent Garden. As Sir Osbert Sitwell puts it in his autobiography, these two singers summed up the age 'when, fat as two elderly thrushes, they trilled at each other over the hedges of tiaras'; while for sheer white-hot vocal drama I cannot think of any recording made in the intervening years which outstrips that of 'Si, pel ciel', the Oath Duet from *Otello*, made during the one session which Caruso shared with Titta Ruffo, the only other male singer of the day whose tonal magnificence could be compared with Caruso's own.

This astonishing record was made in the Victor studios as long ago as January 1914 and bears remarkable testimony to the technical strides which acoustic recording had made and would continue to make, but even so with the introduction of the electrical microphone in 1925 the mechanical method was suddenly swept aside. No longer was the Sextet from *Lucia* the largest-scale piece which could be undertaken with any ease; huge choruses could be recorded, the singers no longer had to sing at a more or less standardized volume, and, almost the most significant improvement of all, a proper orchestra could be employed. Happily these innovations coincided with a glorious era of Wagner singing and conducting, with soloists such as the German sopranos Lotte Lehmann and Frida Leider, the Danish tenor Lauritz Melchior, the Hungarian baritone Friedrich Schorr and the Russian bass Alexander Kipnis at the peak of their powers, and with conductors of the calibre of Bruno Walter, Wilhelm Furtwängler, Sir Thomas Beecham and Arturo Toscanini often to be found at the helm. Complete recordings of Wagner operas were still things of the future, but the 'bleeding chunks' became a great deal more extensive, and a full recording of Act I of *Die Walküre*, made in Vienna in 1935 with the Vienna Philharmonic Orchestra under Bruno Walter, and with Lehmann, Melchior and the bass Emanuel List as the three soloists, was the kind of venture which would have been unthinkable in the pre-electric days. Listening to it today in its CD form one can still thrill to the vibrant femininity of Lehmann, to the clarion call of Melchior's 'Wälse, Wälse', and to the headlong theatricality with which Walter sweeps the orchestra to its inspirational conclusion.

Two years earlier Vienna had also been the venue for another precious memento, an extensive set of excerpts from Richard Strauss's *Der Rosenkavalier* with the classic cast of Lehmann, Elisabeth Schumann, Maria Olczewska and Richard Mayr, technically less comfortable than the *Walküre* set, but enough to convince opera-goers of my generation that our seniors were not merely donning their rose-coloured spectacles when they reminisced in a tone of awe about the Covent Garden *Rosenkavaliers* of the inter-war years. Nor was the German repertoire the only area in which such ambitious schemes were afoot. The mantle of the world's best-selling tenor had been assumed by Beniamino Gigli, and in the mid-'30s he embarked on a series of complete recordings which was eventually to embrace no less than eight popular operas as well as the Verdi *Requiem*.*

It was principally on certain of the electrical recordings of the inter-war era that I and, I imagine, most other enthusiasts of my generation first cut our operatic teeth. I have known many people to be converted to opera by the sound of one specific voice on the gramophone; Richard Tauber was responsible for 'hooking' several opera-lovers of my acquaintance, and Jussi Björling takes the credit for certain others, but in my own case it was a bass who sowed the seed. In a singing competition at school I had heard a boy tackling Sarastro's aria 'In diesen heil'gen Hallen' from *The Magic Flute*, and though I was so ignorant of opera that I did not even know what an aria was, I was bowled over by the music and enquired in the local music shop if it was obtainable on a gramophone record. It was, sung by someone whose name meant as little to me as that of Sarastro himself, a certain Alexander Kipnis; and it was my good fortune that I had stumbled upon one of the most sublime pieces of music ever written, sung by one of the greatest vocal artists of the twentieth century. My next piece of luck was to find that friends of my parents possessed the entire opera from which this song was taken – this was the celebrated Beecham recording made in Berlin in 1937 – and they lent it to me. The set consisted, if my memory serves me aright, of some fifteen 78s, which I proceeded to play on our ancient wind-up gramophone, failing to notice that record 1 did not consist of sides 1 and 2, but of sides 1 and 30, record 2

---

*The concept of the full recording was in fact no novelty in Italy because as long ago as 1903 Leoncavallo had conducted a complete set of *Pagliacci*.

consisted of sides 2 and 29 and so on. Thus in blissful ignorance I played the first half of the overture followed by the finale to the whole opera, then the second half of the overture followed by the penultimate scene and so forth. What did it matter? I did not understand a word of German, so had no idea what on earth the piece was about – the booklet issued with the set had gone missing – but I was totally in thrall to the spell of Mozart's tunes, to the sound of all those marvellous voices, and to the tinkling of Papageno's magic bells.

After that I made it my business to acquire the current catalogues from His Master's Voice, Columbia and Parlophone, the only companies offering operatic recordings in Britain during the Second World War, and whenever my pocket money had mounted to the necessary sum, or whenever Christmas or a birthday came around, I dipped into them and made my next choice. Thus I gradually became acquainted with most of the great names of the inter-war years. In order to savour two voices for the price of one I was especially partial to duets, and particular favourites amongst my slowly growing collection were 'Un di felice' and 'Parigi o cara' from *La traviata*, sung by Amelita Galli-Curci and Tito Schipa, she so wistful and girlish, and he evoking with his characteristic delicacy of touch an atmosphere which was exclusively his to command. That led me on to the great scene from the second act, in which Galli-Curci was joined by that most lovable of baritones, Giuseppe de Luca, whose effortless phrasing and breath control I later came to recognize as hallmarks of the classic *bel canto* style. De Luca featured again, contentedly playing second string while Beniamino Gigli let loose a honeyed stream of scarcely containable emotion in duets from *La bohème* and *La forza del destino*, and to provide the steelier, more martial side of the Italian repertoire there was Giovanni Martinelli as Manrico, apparently untroubled by the singer's customary need to take an occasional breath, and partnered by a strangely dyspeptic-sounding Louise Homer in two scenes from *Il trovatore*. I had another Manrico to call on, too – Jussi Björling, whose dazzling 'Di quella pira' provided me with the first high C of my acquaintance; little did I realize that he was only in his twenties when he recorded it, and that he, unlike most of my other stars, would still be at his peak when the war was eventually over. There was one other tenor on my shelf, though, with whom neither Björling, Gigli, Schipa nor Martinelli could compete. Caruso was still in the catalogue and I bought his 'La donna è mobile' of 1908 and his 'O sole mio' of 1916 coupled on one ten-inch disc. Never was money better spent.

Mozart was well represented. As well as Alexander Kipnis – by now *both* Sarastro arias had been secured – there was Ezio Pinza's gloriously swaggering Don Giovanni, Tiana Lemnitz as an infinitely touching Countess with 'Porgi amor' and 'Dove sono' from *The Marriage of Figaro*,* Feodor Chaliapin as a highly individual Leporello, Richard Tauber weaving his customary spell with the two Don Ottavio arias, and Elisabeth Schumann charming the birds from the trees as Cherubino and Zerlina.

My first hesitant steps towards the daunting world of Richard Wagner were taken via two HMV 12-inch scarlet labels which must, I imagine, have been the best-selling German-language 78s in the catalogues – Kirsten Flagstad in sovereign flow with Isolde's 'Liebestod', and Lauritz Melchior exultant and unstoppable in the *Meistersinger* Prize Song. So great was my devotion to the latter that it led me on to a purchase which I still regard as a high-water mark amongst Wagnerian recordings, but which had in fact been the product of a remarkably uneasy birth. On 16 May 1931 Elisabeth Schumann, Lauritz Melchior and Friedrich Schorr, all at the peak of their international fame, were joined in the HMV studios in London by two Covent Garden soloists, Ben Williams and Gladys Parr, and by the London Symphony Orchestra under John Barbirolli, to record the *Meistersinger* Quintet, one of those operatic passages which reaches such a pitch of musical perfection that only an inspired perform-ance can do it justice. It opens with an extended solo for the young heroine of the piece, her melodic line a floating, ecstatic hymn to happi-ness as she contemplates the prospect of her beloved Walther winning the prize in the forthcoming singing contest, and with it her hand in marriage. Seldom has any soprano voice been more convincingly imbued with the knack of the ecstatic float than that of Elisabeth Schumann, and after the

---

*I remember a friend of mine telling me that he had once asked for this record in vain in a public library where he knew it to be in stock, and when he himself even-tually found it on the shelves he was firmly put in his place by the librarian with the immortal words 'If you wanted the Dove Song you should have asked for it.'

brief orchestral introduction she sailed into that opening phrase with her customary, almost disembodied, ease. Unfortunately, however, when it was time for the others to join in, instead of continuing her lark-like flight up into the realms of ecstasy she was brought abruptly back to earth – Lauritz Melchior, who had always avoided the role of Walther on stage, fluffed his cue and Barbirolli had to call a halt. Once again Schumann's seraphic tones saluted 'die Sonne meines Glückes', 'the sunshine of my happiness', but once again the Great Dane came in in the wrong place. The third time around Schumann was finding it a little harder to sustain the requisite note of angelic radiance – which turned out not to matter, as Melchior, entirely unruffled by it all, made the same mistake yet again. By now Schumann was seeing the funny side of it – Eva's 'Morgen voller

The century's most celebrated Wälsung twins. Lauritz Melchior and Lotte Lehmann off duty.

Wonne', her 'Morning full of joy', was not quite working out as she had expected – but after the fourth mistake Barbirolli decided to conduct the orchestra with his right hand alone, placing his left hand over his mouth and expressly forbidding Melchior to break into song until he had removed it. This did the trick; take five was the one which found its way onto the shelves of countless Wagner-lovers throughout the world, and I can think of no greater tribute to the power of professionalism than the apparent spontaneity with which Schumann was still managing to greet the golden promise of a sunlit summer day. Twenty years later she was invited to be the castaway on the evergreen BBC radio programme 'Desert Island Discs', and this was one of the eight records which she chose to brighten her solitude. I am not surprised that she should have regarded it as one of her personal triumphs. Slightly more surprising is the fact that Melchior was subsequently known to express great pride in *his* contribution; the first four takes conveniently forgotten, he was fond of commenting on the technical mastery with which he had steered his heavy dramatic voice along a high and taxing mezza voce line. What the other three soloists thought about it all, history does not relate.

With the introduction of the electric recording technique one other exciting possibility had become available, namely the recording of live performances, and several fascinating pieces of documentary evidence were gathered in that way. One such was the occasion of Dame Nellie Melba's final performance at Covent Garden in 1926, culminating in her touchingly theatrical farewell speech, and two years later the microphones were installed again in the Royal Opera House to capture a stunning performance by Chaliapin as Boris Godunov. Indeed, another remarkable treasure has come to light during the last few years – a full set of *Tristan und Isolde*, starring Flagstad and Melchior (Tristan was a role which he *had* put under his rather extensive belt), cunningly cobbled together by EMI from two performances at Covent Garden in 1936 and 1937 under the batons of Fritz Reiner and Sir Thomas Beecham respectively. It is a set which enshrines that rarest of operatic coincidences, a tireless Tristan and a radiant Isolde both at the peak of their powers at the same time and in the same place.

During the Second World War the international recording industry found itself in a state of semi-suspended animation, the United States even going so far as to impose a two-year ban on the use of shellac for non-military purposes. A further blow to the industry was an embargo placed on all recordings by the American Federation of Musicians in August 1942, on the grounds that recorded music on jukeboxes reduced musical employment. Initially the Federation's demands for royalties were refused by the recording companies, until Decca came to a settlement in September 1943, with RCA and Columbia following suit a year later. Once hostilities were over, the floodgates opened. In London Decca, never a member of the big league in pre-war days, came up with a process known as 'full frequency range recording' ('ffrr'), a system devised during the war for detecting the different sounds emitted by British and German submarines, and which now, devoted to the reproduction of classical music, resulted in recordings of an unprecedented dynamic range. Then came the Long Playing Record, an invention launched by Columbia in New York,* which miraculously enabled the listener to play sixty minutes of music on an unbreakable disc instead of only nine and a half on an exceedingly brittle one, and the introduction of tape, which, from the engineers' point of view, revolutionized the process of recording. No longer did the music need to be divided into short chunks with the sound waves cut into a wax disc, meaning that every time anyone made a mistake a new disc had to be installed and the chunk in question had to be taken again from the beginning. Now the music could be allowed to run for as long as anyone wanted, passages with imperfections in them could be re-recorded and spliced, and the lives of everybody involved in the recording process became a great deal less fraught than they had been before.

For the opera-lover the results of all this were sensational. The major companies hastened to put leading artists under contract and one full set after another came tumbling onto the market. Decca cornered the Vienna Philharmonic Orchestra as well as conductors such as Knappertsbusch and Erich Kleiber, whose complete *Rosenkavalier* was greeted as a tech-

---

*Strangely enough, a prototype LP recording had been demonstrated by RCA in the Savoy Plaza Hotel, New York, on 17 September 1931, but the process presumably became a victim of the Depression which had a sadly limiting effect on recordings in general.

nical and musical revelation – I can still remember my incredulity as the great waltz tune came soaring out from the full orchestra at the end of Act II, engulfing the listener in a sound such as no one had ever dared to expect from a mere recording. The same company also secured the exclusive services of two of the finest voices to have emerged from post-war Italy, Renata Tebaldi and Mario del Monaco, while RCA Victor gathered a series of star casts around the glorious Jussi Björling – who could ever forget the impact of his *Trovatore* with Zinka Milanov and Leonard Warren, shortly followed by his incomparable des Grieux in Puccini's *Manon Lescaut*? EMI, under the direct control of the formidable Walter Legge, was not, however, to be outdone. Legge could boast such stars in his stable as Maria Callas, Elisabeth Schwarzkopf, Victoria de los Angeles, Giuseppe di Stefano, Tito Gobbi and Boris Christoff, with men like Klemperer, Karajan and de Sabata to conduct them; soon there was another name to be added to this list, the young Swedish tenor Nicolai Gedda, destined to make more recordings than any other singer in the whole history of the gramophone, in a repertoire ranging from French, Russian, Italian and German opera via Viennese operetta to Neapolitan songs and English oratorio. Complete sets of Wagner operas became regular features, recorded from the Bayreuth Festival; and operas which would never previously have stood a chance of being recorded in their entirety at last found their way into the catalogues, even such 'problematic' pieces as *Wozzeck*, *Capriccio* and *Peter Grimes*.

It was indeed a dazzling period for the operatically minded record collector, but those who were beginning to feel that their cup was almost full were in for yet another surprise – the advent of stereo, which had an even more dramatic effect on the recording of opera than it did on that of orchestral music. In one sense history began to repeat itself, because to capitalize on the new sense of space which stereo provided singers were obliged to move from one microphone to another at the behest of the recording producer, a process which often involved them in being physically manoeuvred round the stage. John Culshaw, the head of the Decca team at that time, tells one delightful story in his memoirs,* which carries

*His *Putting the Record Straight* (see bibliography) is as enlightening a chronicle of the tangled politics of the recording industry in the 1950s and '60s as Gaisberg's classic is of the pioneering days.

us straight back to Gaisberg's memories of Patti and to Gerald Moore's of his various battling soloists. Culshaw's first stereo assignment, in Vienna in 1957, was Richard Strauss's *Arabella*, an opera which features two leading roles for sopranos, taken in this instance by rival divas from the Vienna State Opera, Lisa della Casa and Hilde Gueden. 'The ladies', Culshaw writes, 'took advantage of the need for movement to jostle for position. There was the afternoon when della Casa came rushing into the control room complaining that "She *pooshed* me!", which Gueden, hot in pursuit, denied. Eventually they were reconciled and collapsed into each other's arms, swearing love and devotion, although as they made their way back from the control room to the platform della Casa turned back to me and said "But she still *pooshed* me!"'

On certain other occasions exactly the reverse would occur – instead of hustling each other from one position to another singers would adopt a policy of 'J'y suis, j'y reste' and flatly refuse to back one inch away from what they erroneously felt to be the most advantageous microphone. One such was the redoubtable Croatian diva Zinka Milanov. When she recorded the role of Leonora in Verdi's *La forza del destino* for RCA Victor one of the stereophonic effects which the producer had plotted was to have the battling tenor and baritone audibly rush off from one side of the acoustic spectrum so that Milanov could make a dramatic entrance from the other side at the moment when Leonora emerges from her hermit's cave to sing the great aria 'Pace, pace'. The request that Madame Milanov should occupy a microphone at the side of the stage fell, however, on deaf ears. 'But I am in the centre', she stoutly declared, 'because I have the tune.' To make her meaning doubly clear she turned to the technician whose task it was to shepherd her around with the ominous words 'If you make me move once more I cut your beard.'

It was in the first of Decca's so-called Sonic Stage productions that I had my own first experience of recording, and it was an occasion not to be forgotten in a hurry. After only two years in the singing profession I was engaged to sing the tiny role of the Second Nazarene in *Salome* and, accustomed as I was to small orchestras in provincial opera houses, it was something of a shock to find myself on the spacious stage of Vienna's Sofiensaal with the vast panoply of the Vienna Philharmonic Orchestra at my feet and with the mighty Birgit Nilsson at the neighbouring micro-

phone. Somewhere in the distance stood a demonic figure in a black roll-neck jersey waving a baton in his right hand – Georg Solti, no less – and when his left hand stabbed in my direction it was my business to start singing. There is lasting evidence that I somehow succeeded in doing so, because while almost every other recording in which I have subsequently partaken has come and gone that one has remained in the catalogues for ever – a fact which can perhaps be more accurately attributed to the contributions of Nilsson and Solti than to any epoch-making qualities in the interpretation of the Second Nazarene.

I am happy to say, however, that my own sense of awe is not my only memory of that particular recording – it also had its humorous side. One of my dearest friends, the Viennese baritone Eberhard Waechter, was cast as Jokanaan (John the Baptist), some of whose role is sung from the cistern in which he is incarcerated. In many opera houses this causes problems – the voice must sound subterranean while at the same time hitting

Discussions in the control room. Eberhard Waechter (Jokanaan), Waldemar Kmentt (Narraboth), Georg Solti, Birgit Nilsson (Salome). In the background, the Decca team.

The Decca Salome, Vienna 1961. Georg Solti and the Vienna Philharmonic Orchestra in the Sofiensaal.

the audience with an arresting impact – but with the immense amount of sophisticated equipment available to the Decca engineers it was to be expected that for the purposes of the recording all such difficulties would be easily overcome. Not a bit of it; Eberhard sang his heart out surrounded by one piece of technical wizardry after another but nothing produced the desired effect. Eventually someone mentioned that he had been impressed by the acoustics of the backstage lavatory while warming up there with a scale or two, and so thither John the Baptist repaired to try his luck. The result was exactly what Culshaw had been searching for. A microphone was installed, as well as a television set to give Eberhard the conductor's beat, and never had the words 'Nach mir wird Einer kommen, der ist stärker als ich', 'After me will come Another who is greater than I', rung out to more riveting effect than they did from that fine old-fashioned W.C.

During my student days in Vienna it had been my good fortune occasionally to be smuggled into recording sessions by friends in the Decca team, and they provided me with a variety of vivid memories. To this day I can see Kirsten Flagstad, lured from retirement to sing Fricka in *Das Rheingold*, sitting placidly at the back of the stage, like anybody's favourite granny, doing her knitting in between her 'bits'. Then there was Jussi Björling recording the tenor solo, 'Ingemisco', from the Verdi *Requiem*, only a year before his regrettably early death. I do not think I have ever witnessed a more *efficient* piece of singing than that. Physically his was the perfect tenor build. He was short, stocky and exceptionally strong, with a remarkably large collar size, a man for whom singing was the most natural of functions. He stood on stage, score in hand, wearing a rather formal brown suit; he had come to do a job and intended to complete it with the minimum of fuss. The conductor, Fritz Reiner, took the passage through once for the benefit of the orchestra and the engineers, and Björling marked his way through the vocal line in rehearsal voice. The sound which emerged was the most heavenly mezza voce it is possible to imagine, soft, lustrous and totally even, right up to the high B flats. It appeared to cost him nothing, and it seemed to me a crime that such a masterly example of vocal art should be allowed to vanish into thin air. When Reiner announced that the engineers were ready for a take Björling seemed simply to go through the same routine again, just opening his mouth a little wider this time and bringing in the full quality of his voice. He only needed to sing the piece once; he was as incapable of making a musical mistake as he was of producing an ugly sound.

One less agreeable experience was to witness Herbert von Karajan engaged in destroying a singer of whom he did not approve. When conducting singers of whom he *did* approve Karajan could be the most considerate conductor in the business, but every now and then his less kindly side made itself evident. In the instance to which I refer his victim was the highly distinguished German coloratura soprano Erika Köth, who had been cast as the cheeky chambermaid Adele in Johann Strauss's *Die Fledermaus*. I have no idea what Karajan's objection to her may have been, but three times running he let her sing right through her most taxing number, the famous Laughing Song, only to stop each time, leaving her stranded on her crowning high D, because of some minor imperfection which he claimed to have detected in the orchestra. By the time he had finished with her the poor lady was hopping from one foot to the other and I doubt if she could have sung her way through 'Baa baa black sheep'. It was all done with the utmost courtesy, and it was lethal.

To set against this chilling experience, however, the Decca *Fledermaus* also provided some matchless moments. Following the example of those opera houses which habitually invite distinguished guests to let their hair down during New Year's Eve performances Decca engaged a dozen of the world's most celebrated singers to chip in with some unexpected number or other during the party scene in Act II. I was lucky enough to catch Birgit Nilsson recording 'I could have danced all night' from *My Fair Lady*, culminating in one of those high Cs which she used to launch into the auditorium like stratospheric missiles, and though, alas, I missed Renata Tebaldi singing the Vilja Song from *The Merry Widow* I did witness the most egregious turn of all, when Giulietta Simionato and Ettore Bastianini set about the duet 'Anything you can do I can do better' from *Annie Get Your Gun*. Totally at home as these two were when it came to singing roles such as Amneris in *Aida* or Renato in *Un ballo in maschera* they were all at sea when faced with the English language, and it was decided that if they were ever to get their tongues round Irving Berlin's knockabout lyrics they would have to be provided with a phonetic version of the text doctored to suit their natural accents. The task of providing it fell to Decca's Christopher Raeburn, and the opening line read as follows: ENIDING JUKENDU AIKENDU BETTER, AIKENDU ENIDING BETTER DAN JU. Gamely they tackled it, interspersed with a few well-chosen insults in their native tongue, and the final result was something which would have brought down any house in the world.

To attempt to choose peaks of achievement from amongst the operatic recordings issued in recent years would be, for the purposes of this book, a pointless task. To add to the countless full sets which have poured out from leading companies all over the world, sung by the crème de la crème of singers, played by the most illustrious of orchestras and conducted by the starriest of conductors, we have the fact that virtually every important recording from the past (plus some which leave me wondering 'Why?') is re-emerging on CD. At the time of writing the international catalogue is offering, for instance, no less than fourteen complete versions of *Don Giovanni* and twenty-six of *La bohème*; perhaps even more significantly there are four full sets of *Lulu* to choose from, and five of *Wozzeck*. For the operatic beginner who wants to find his or her way step by step the task nowadays must indeed be somewhat daunting. Back in the days when I decided that my next purchase should be the tenor aria from *La bohème* the choice available to me consisted of Gigli, Björling, or Heddle Nash in English; anyone consulting the catalogue today is confronted with 115 different possibilities.* In one other respect, too, life was more straightforward for the non-expert than it is today. When your machine switched itself off at the end of every side, obliging you to get up and either turn the record over or take another one from the shelf, you knew what you were listening to (unless you tangled with the full set of *The Magic Flute*), whereas nowadays those who like to have opera going on in the background tend, I have occasionally noticed, to be unaware whether the band which Pavarotti has just arrived at on a CD of twenty-five best-loved arias is from *Tosca*, *Faust* or *Rigoletto* – not, I suppose, that it matters very much.

Despite the gigantic strides taken by the recording industry in the last few decades it would still be misleading to give the impression that every set which is issued nowadays reaches a pitch of perfection. Contractual obligations often prevent the ideal cast from being assembled, and recordings can suffer, too, from the companies' understandable determination to feature the best-selling singers, whether or not they are familiar with the work in question. More than once in recent years I have had the feeling 'He's singing that phrase because he has reached page fifty-seven of the score, not because he's been shattered by the news of his wife's infidelity', or whatever the dramatic situation might be. Some singers are technically and temperamentally much better equipped to deal with the peculiar requirements of the recording studio than others. If, in an opera house, you are playing a character whose dramatic and musical personality

---

* I settled initially, I remember, for Heddle Nash because his version was cheaper, but there was nothing cheap about the singing, and it came with a wonderfully vocalized account of the Serenade from Bizet's *Fair Maid of Perth* on the other side. I must confess that I could not work out what on earth 'Your tiny hand is frozen' was all about; Nash's articulation was immaculate, but such puzzling lines from the old translation as 'I've wit though wealth be wanting' did not help, and in those days recordings of single arias were not accompanied by any sort of synopsis.

undergoes an extensive change during the course of the piece – let us take Don José in *Carmen* as an obvious example – the development of the role to a great extent looks after itself. In a recording studio, however, you may find yourself having to be the degraded murderer of Act IV in the morning, then switch back to the easy-going fellow of Act I in the afternoon. The characterization must be achieved, so to speak, piecemeal, the voice coloured by conscious technique rather than by the adrenalin flow of a stage performance. It was his skill in meeting these special requirements (as well, of course, as the exceptional beauty of his singing) which made Nicolai Gedda the automatic choice for so many EMI recordings, including two of *Carmen*,* while certain other Don Josés have been known to cause headaches. So, too, have their wives; on one occasion John Culshaw asked Franco Corelli if he felt ready to tackle the Flower Song, only to receive the unequivocal reply from Signora Corelli, 'My Franco maka da song when *I* say 'e maka da song!'

With so many stunning effects available nowadays to recording engineers opinions sometimes vary as to whether their task is to reproduce a performance more or less as an audience would experience it in an opera house, or whether they should exercise their magic and come up with something which only they can achieve. Singers have been known to complain of coming off second best to clever exploitation of the orchestra, and even Birgit Nilsson, who in live performance had no difficulty in competing with the fiercest of operatic accompaniments, used occasionally to feel that on recordings she was being crowded by instrumental sound. More often, though, one encounters the reverse effect, and many an enthusiast who has grown accustomed to having huge operatic voices invading his sitting-room through the good offices of the latest hi-fi equipment has been known to express disappointment on hearing the same performers in the flesh. A stereophonic 'Ride of the Valkyries' may well have Grimgerde brandishing her spear behind your desk,

---

*One of his *Carmen* recordings, under Sir Thomas Beecham and with Victoria de los Angeles in the title-role, had to be temporarily abandoned because de los Angeles found herself so disorientated by the chopping and changing that the schedule required of her. When she informed Sir Thomas of her impending departure he replied 'My dear, you will regret it', but some months later the full team was happily reunited.

Schwertleite leaping through your bookshelf and Rossweisse landing in your lap, their frenzied cries setting your eardrums a-quiver, but from the cheaper sets of the average international opera house they can easily turn out to be nothing more thrilling than distant little figures coping as valiantly as they can with the swirling ocean of sound which engulfs them from the pit. I well remember how surprised I was when, after listening in awe to several of Boris Christoff's recordings, I first heard him on stage. He was singing Boris Godunov at Covent Garden, and though the quality of the sound was everything which his recordings had led me to expect the quantity of it was not; even the mighty Mario del Monaco, when I first heard his celebrated Otello, struck me as being a *tenore* a mite less *robusto* than 'ffrr' habitually indicated, but I am happy to say that in both these instances my ear soon attuned itself to the difference between fact and fiction, and as each of the aforesaid gentlemen gave intensely charismatic performances I did not by any means leave the opera house a disappointed man.

In this respect I differed from one of my favourite figures in literature, the ineffable Uncle Matthew in Nancy Mitford's classic *The Pursuit of Love*. Directly based on the authoress's own eccentric father, Lord Redesdale, Uncle Matthew delights in stumping round the house at five o'clock in the morning, clanking cups of tea, shouting at his dogs and roaring at the housemaids, 'all to the accompaniment of Galli-Curci on his gramophone, an abnormally loud one with an enormous horn, through which would be shrieked "Una voce poco fa", "The Mad Song" from *Lucia*, "Lo, here the gen-tel laha-hark" and so on, played at top speed, thus rendering them even higher and more screeching than they ought to be.' Poor Uncle Matthew; he played these recordings incessantly for years until the fateful day in 1924 when Galli-Curci came to Britain in person and he travelled all the way to Liverpool specially to hear her. So far did the flesh-and-blood diva fall below his heightened expectations 'that the records remained ever after silent, and were replaced by the deepest voices that money could buy'.

Let us not suppose, therefore, that it is only the modern recording engineer, hunched over his bewildering panel with its myriad cables, knobs and dials, or the state-of-the-art technician, his cunning fingers splicing in refulgent high Cs to save the blushes of exhausted tenors and sopranos, whose art has sometimes been known to improve on nature. To judge from the depth of Uncle Matthew's disillusionment it is evident that Fred Gaisberg, heaving Galli-Curci to and fro in front of his old acoustic horn, must already have known a thing or two.

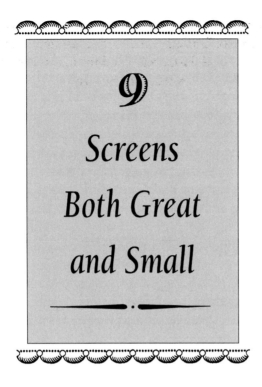

9

Screens
Both Great
and Small

'I can't see that working – who'd want to spend good money to watch the same performance over and over again?' Thus spake myself some twenty years ago when a friend sought my advice about setting up a company for the marketing of opera on video, and I can only hope that there may be some merit in the theory that if you are going to make a mistake you might as well make a big one. Opera on video has turned out to be a triumphant money-spinner, and the selection of available productions grows by the month. It is not just that the *Figaro*s, the *Bohème*s, the *Cav*s and the *Pag*s are to be found in a bewildering variety of versions, but they are joined by rarities which extend from rediscovered masterpieces of the seventeenth century via the more esoteric gems of the Russian repertoire to the most up-to-date offerings by the composers of today. Had I given my friend's question a little more thought I should have realized the immense potential of a technique which perpetuates the outstanding productions of each successive decade, and preserves the visual aspects of many great singers' work as effectively as the gramophone has preserved their voices; but I did not, and now I am happy to say that by ignoring my advice the friend in question has become a much richer man than he was.

The difficulties inherent in adjusting so spacious a form of entertainment as opera to the limitations of the average domestic television screen are many and various. Opera is frequently static, whereas the screen thrives on constant movement and shifts of image; for many people the chief attraction of opera lies in the thrilling sound of great voices accompanied by formidable orchestral forces, effects to which the amplification system of the normal television set is unlikely to do justice; grand opera in a major stage production is a gripping and essentially three-dimensional theatrical event, and how can this survive the reduction to two-dimensional presentation? These and many other ancillary headaches provide the television director with a constant challenge, but compared with that which faced the earliest makers of operatic films for the cinema they are a mere trifle; the director of today at least has access to sound.

On the face of it it may seem extraordinary that film producers of the silent era should have been obsessed with opera; there is an Alice in Wonderland illogicality to the idea, something akin to the production of motor cars with no engines in them. That was not, however, how the situation appeared at the time. The melodramatic nature of so many operatic plots, and the conciseness with which the stories are told (once the time-wasting element of music has been excised) meant that they were peculiarly well suited to the medium of the silent film, and between 1903, when the Pathé Company blazed the trail with a version of Berlioz's *La damnation de Faust*, until 1927 and the coming of sound, so many 'operatic' films were turned out that a comprehensive list would make tedious reading. Music was of course usually tacked on in some form or another. When Pathé followed up their initial successes with a film of *Rigoletto* in 1909, for instance, what it actually consisted of was a potted version of Victor Hugo's *Le roi s'amuse*, the play on which the opera had been based, accompanied by live musicians in the cinema playing suitable passages from Verdi's score. In smaller cinemas the live accompaniment to films such as this would be provided by the traditional cinema pianist, which must at least have made a welcome change from the usual task of instant improvisation, strumming with the left hand as the baddies rode into town, tinkling with the right as the dewy-eyed heroine sank into her lover's arms, and so on.* Sometimes live soloists would be employed who sang along with the 'singers' on the screen, and in the first opera specifically written for the cinema, a German piece entitled *Jenseits des Stromes* (*Beyond the Stream*), musical notes were projected along the bottom of the picture to help the conductor keep the band and soloists in the right place. Several musicians of the highest calibre took an interest in these outré goings-on, one of them being no less a figure than Richard Strauss. In 1926 he appeared in London's Tivoli cinema conducting a specially arranged version of the score of *Der Rosenkavalier* to accompany a film which introduced a number of fascinating new twists to the opera's original plot. Strauss himself was known to feel that the piece had been saddled with 'mistakes and longueurs', and as far as the events at the beginning of Act III are concerned I heartily agree with him. In the film the whole scene was upgraded from the tawdry setting of the inn to the more elevated milieu of a masked ball, which I feel sure can only have been an improvement; and another innovation was to allow the most put-upon non-participant in the whole of opera, the Feldmarschall, to materialize, effect a rapprochement with his errant wife, and thus provide what is so charmingly known in German as 'Das Happy-End'.

Much more peculiar, or so it seems to me, than this partiality for silent films on operatic subjects was the occasional use of famous singers to star in them. I can see the logic of Sam Goldwyn casting Geraldine Farrar as an inaudible Carmen; the public identified her with the role and she was a sufficiently beautiful woman and spirited actress to justify the choice. In any case the end result was a triumph both for her and for the film's budding young director, Cecil B. DeMille, so perhaps it was only to be expected that Goldwyn should travel further down the same road by

---

*By an odd coincidence two of the greatest singers of the century, Rosa Ponselle and Richard Tauber, made useful pocket money as cinema pianists before their voices had been discovered.

engaging Farrar's great rival, Mary Garden, in the sexiest of *her* operatic roles, Massenet's Thaïs. This, however, turned out to have been a mistake. Where Carmen is regularly called upon to rant, rave and dance on table-tops Thaïs is an essentially static seductress, and the heaving bosom of a silent Garden proved to have only limited drawing power. The greater the singer clearly the greater the loss when he or she was reduced to voice-lessness, and when, in 1918, the producer Jesse Lasky made a contract with Enrico Caruso to appear in two romantic comedies at a fee of $100,000, the equivalent to forty of his performance fees at the Met, Lasky soon realized that he had made the most expensive mistake of his life. In the first of the two films, *My Cousin*, Caruso doubled as the world-famous tenor Caroli and an indigent sculptor whose only chance with the girls depends on the fact that he is related to Caroli, but despite massive pre-release publicity the venture flopped disastrously. 'Few films', as the Modern Art Film Library has expressed it, 'ever enjoyed less

The world's greatest tenor in one of the world's worst films. Enrico Caruso adopts a threatening pose in My Cousin *(1918).*

success', and the critic of *Photoplay Journal* was doubtless speaking for many others besides himself when he expressed the opinion that 'you cannot help but wish the star would step through the silversheet and offer just one tiny song'. The second of Caruso's films, *A Splendid Romance*, was never issued in the United States, though Lasky did risk releasing it on a modest scale in Europe and South America.

Predictably the most successful of the silent operas were those shot with the bona fide film stars of the day. Connoisseurs tended to consider that Pola Negri, in a German production of 1919, outshone even Farrar as the best of the many screen Carmens,* and Mary Pickford as Madam Butterfly must have cut an irresistibly vulnerable figure. The 1926 version of *La bohème* starred Lillian Gish, John Gilbert and Edward Everett

FABRICA DE TABACO

Widely regarded as the most effective of silent Carmens – Pola Negri (centre) with the factory girls in the Ernst Lubitsch version of 1918.

---

*It should be mentioned, however, that Farrar made sufficient impact in the new medium to be engaged by Goldwyn for no less than thirteen non-operatic films (including one in which she played Joan of Arc) at the then colossal salary of $125,000 a year.

John Gilbert as Danilo struggles manfully with Lolo, Dodo, Joujou, Cloelo, Margot and Froufrou in Erich von Stroheim's 1925 silent version of The Merry Widow.

Horton, whose double-takes were later to become such a feature of the Fred Astaire films, with designs by Erté, who was destined to create a sensation with his *Rosenkavalier* at Glyndebourne fully fifty-four years later. Of all these classic productions, however, the one I would most like to encounter would be the silent *Merry Widow*, directed by Erich von Stroheim in 1925. By indulging himself outrageously with the camera he managed to make it last for almost two hours, which, discounting intervals, is little less than the length of a normal staged performance, singing and all.

Contrary to what one might assume, once Al Jolson had ushered in the era of the 'talkies' with *The Jazz Singer* in 1927 Hollywood went off the boil as far as opera was concerned; while 'over-the-top' plots were seen to have box-office appeal, 'serious' music clearly was not. *The Merry Widow* reappeared in 1934, given big-budget treatment by Ernst Lubitsch, with Jeanette MacDonald and Maurice Chevalier as his stars, and opera singers such as Grace Moore and Lawrence Tibbett enjoyed widespread popularity in other filmed operettas; but, in the words of Richard Fawkes, one of the leading authorities on the subject, 'it was left to the film-makers of

Looking even more harassed than John Gilbert – Maurice Chevalier (with Minna Gombell) in the Ernst Lubitsch Merry Widow *of 1934.*

Europe to explore the real potential of filming opera with sound.'* In 1933 the great Austrian director G. W. Pabst brought Feodor Chaliapin to the silver screen as Don Quixote, in a film – admittedly not strictly an operatic one – with an original score by the French composer Jacques Ibert; Max Ophuls directed a *Bartered Bride* with the lovely Jarmila Novotna as Marenka, and in Italy Carmine Gallone was responsible for several productions starring the equally glamorous Maria Cebotari, often with Beniamino Gigli as her partner.

For a man whose acting could be described as minimal Gigli ran a remarkably profitable sideline as a film star. Apart from his actual operatic films numerous others were cobbled together as vehicles for the golden voice, usually with a vacuous story-line and an undistinguished supporting cast, but with plenty of excuses built into the script for bring-

*Opera Now, April 1994.

Beniamino Gigli as a remarkably uninvolved Turiddu and Millo Picco as Alfio in a Vitaphone film of excerpts from Cavalleria Rusticana *in the Manhattan Opera House, New York, 1927.*

ing the action to a halt and allowing Gigli to burst into song. Typical of the genre was *Forget Me Not*, in which he plays the part of a world-famous tenor, recently widowed and with one small son; for some un-explained reason, although the great singer has difficulty in expressing himself in any other language than Italian his son's mother-tongue is immaculate BBC English. During dialogue scenes Gigli appears to be sleep-walking, but luckily he seeks solace for his broken heart by giving innumerable concerts, and every time the music strikes up he comes visibly and vibrantly to life. Principally by singing the evocative title-song, 'Non ti scordar di me', at regular intervals he persuades a charming young lady to become his second wife, a consummation devoutly to be wished as far as his son is concerned, because she too speaks BBC English.

During the 1930s the film-going public seems to have developed an insatiable appetite for daft films starring celebrated tenors, and I cannot imagine how much money Caruso and Lasky would have made had

A poster for Carmine Gallone's 1937 film Solo per Te, *depicting a scarcely recognisable Beniamino Gigli and the glamorous Maria Cebotari.*

Caruso lived a little longer, or had sound arrived in time for the making of *My Cousin*. Besides Beniamino Gigli practically every star tenor was at it; John McCormack appeared in the first British film ever to be shot in Technicolor; the Polish tenor Jan Kiepura headed the casts of over a dozen German productions, frequently with his wife Martha Eggerth as his partner, and with scores by Robert Stolz; a film entitled *Abenteuer am Lido* (*Adventure on the Lido*), was written for Alfred Piccaver, the English-born star of the Vienna Opera, and shot, as its title indicates, on location in Venice; Tito Schipa sang his way through a whole string of romances with such promising titles as *Vivere* (*Living*), *Terra di fuoco* (*Land of Fire*) and *Tre uomini in un frak* (*Three Men in a Tailcoat*); and the great Leo Slezak, once he had retired from being Vienna's favourite Lohengrin and Otello, used to amuse himself and the cinema-goers of Central Europe by appearing as the genial old buffer who contributes a

'It is only when
Tauber the vocalist is
in full cry that
proceedings rise above
a level of harmless
banality.' Richard
Tauber, June Clyde
and Jimmy Durante
in Land Without
Music (1935).

couple of sentimental ditties and leaves no eye unwiped.

The attraction of the silver screen to stars such as these was obvious
enough; not only did they earn substantial fees for the films themselves
but they became household names amongst people who would never have
had access to an opera house, and the sales of their gramophone records
rocketed as a result. Richard Tauber, whose all-embracing versatility
enabled him to establish himself as the outstanding tenor of his generation both in the operas of Mozart and the operettas of Franz Lehár, not
to mention his activities as Lieder-singer, operetta composer and orchestral conductor, went so far as to set up his own film production company
in Berlin. Sadly his talents did not extend to entrepreneurial know-how
and he lost a fortune; in any case the timing was disastrous because, being
partly Jewish, he was soon to be declared persona non grata by the Nazis.

In England, however, his movie career took off in a much more encouraging manner. Starting with *Blossom Time* in 1934 – he played the role of Franz Schubert in a version of the composer's life which was sufficiently honest to make no pretence of historical accuracy – he appeared in a string of musical films which brought him such popularity amongst the general public that many people were taken by surprise when Sir Thomas Beecham engaged him for 'highbrow' roles at Covent Garden. Though Tauber was no more of a screen 'natural' than Beniamino Gigli – his greatest admirers, of which I am one, would be hard put to it to deny that he was short, fat and ugly – he was a far more outgoing creature than his Italian counterpart; his acting was wooden and contrived, but he was a man who bubbled with good humour, and his screen persona, though seldom subtle, was never dull. In films such as *Land Without Music*, with a score by Oscar Straus, the plot is as shamelessly devised to lead from one tenor song to another as was that of *Forget Me Not*, and despite the pres-

A scene from the Viennese film Abenteuer am Lido, *produced as a vehicle for the star tenor Alfred Piccaver* (centre), *seen here with Nora Gregor and Szöke Szakall.*

ence in the supporting cast of Jimmy 'Schnozzle' Durante and of Tauber's future wife, Diana Napier, it is only when Tauber the vocalist is in full cry that proceedings rise above a level of harmless banality.

Films such as these do still occasionally find their way onto television, usually in the very early hours of the morning, and though it is tempting to dismiss them as hopelessly dated and 'hammy' one point should not be overlooked. They did introduce many people to the sound of great singing, and thus spurred them on to pursue the subject further. Lord Harewood, a distinguished operatic administrator and as great an expert on singers as one could hope to meet, wrote in his memoirs: 'I think it was listening to Tauber sing Schubert in a romantic film about the composer's life that first turned me firmly towards music, or at least towards singing. I came back from the cinema in a daze of pleasure at what I had heard, and Tauber's records, particularly of Schubert, were very often to be heard at Harewood when I was about ten or eleven years old.'*

On the subject of stimulating interest in singing in general and opera in particular I would hazard a guess that there has never been a more influential film than that highly romanticized Hollywood 'biopic' of 1951, *The Great Caruso*, with Mario Lanza in the title role. I saw it when it first came out, and being already the proud owner of a dozen or more of Caruso's old 78s I remember being somewhat sniffy about Lanza's qualifications for the job. He had a superb natural voice, with a thrilling quality and some splendid top notes, but to compare, for instance, Lanza's rendering of 'O paradiso' from Meyerbeer's *L'Africaine* with Caruso's was to compare promise with fulfilment. Since then, however, again and again I have met people who have told me that it was that film which first kindled their interest in opera. It transmitted something of the passion and excitement so peculiar to the art form, and of the immediacy of communication which can be achieved by that most elemental of musical instruments, the human voice. Lanza, at least at this early stage of his brief career, possessed undeniable star quality; he was joined by two of the Met's most glamorous performers, Dorothy Kirsten and Blanche

---

*I have known several instances, even in recent years, of children becoming 'hooked' on the voice of Richard Tauber. I have a feeling that it is because the man's enormous friendliness is so strongly projected in his singing.

An unexpectedly influential film. Mario Lanza in The Great Caruso.

Thebom, and the operatic excerpts were served up in generous portions. Nor was it only potential opera-*goers* whose appetites were whetted; all Three Tenors admit to having fallen under the film's spell when they were boys, as do that splendid British baritone Thomas Allen and many other prominent singers of today. As in the case of Lord Harewood and Richard Tauber, Lanza/Caruso caught them young and left an indelible impression on their minds. At that age their critical faculties may not have been sharply honed, but their awareness of the potential joys of opera had been well and truly awoken.

Looking back on my own school days I realize that I too enjoyed my first encounter with opera thanks to a Hollywood film, though it was one which presented an even less realistic picture of operatic life than did *The Great Caruso*. In *A Night at the Opera* the cinema public was introduced to a character named Otis B. Driftwood, played by Groucho Marx, who

How to run an opera company. Sig Rumann as the Director finds himself facing a takeover by the Marx Brothers, with tenor Allan Jones in A Night at the Opera *(1935).*

was under contract to promote the social aspirations of a wealthy widow called Mrs Claypool, a role ideally suited to the talents of the stately Margaret Dumont. With unerring perspicacity Driftwood advises her that the most effective way of deploying her millions would be to finance an opera company; enter the World's Greatest Tenor, a fearful cad of whose dastardly character we are left in no doubt by the fact that he takes a whip to his defenceless dresser, Harpo Marx.* I cannot quite recall in what capacity Chico becomes involved, but involved he certainly does become, and the upshot of it all is that the career of the World's Greatest Tenor is brought to a premature close during the opening night of *Il trovatore*, thanks to the chaos caused on stage by the Marx Brothers' zany intervention. Luckily the good guy, clean-cut boy-next-door Allan Jones, is on hand and he knows the role. Taking over in Act IV he scores a

---

*Had I ever been saddled with Harpo Marx as my dresser I might well have taken a pistol to him, but that is neither here nor there.

triumph, and his performance of the Miserere, with Kitty Carlisle as an unusually lissom Leonora, brings the house down. Once I had started going to opera productions of a more conventional nature I realized how unlikely it was that soprano and tenor would sing an encore of their famous duet standing hand in hand by the prompt box; but at least I did notice that *Il trovatore* contained some rattling good tunes.

During the 1940s and '50s Hollywood regularly turned out films with operatic associations, notably several containing tailor-made roles for the genial Danish Heldentenor Lauritz Melchior, and others featuring the glamorous Italian *basso* Ezio Pinza, whose retirement from the Met had opened the door to a dazzling new career on Broadway. Otto Preminger's two sensational 'black' productions, *Carmen Jones* in 1954 and *Porgy and Bess* five years later, won many new friends both for Bizet and for Gershwin, but thereafter Hollywood veered away from anything even verging on the musically highbrow, and once again it was left to European directors to explore the possibilities of opera as a branch of cinematographic art. The Hungarian-born Briton, Paul Czinner, filmed two outstanding Salzburg Festival productions, the *Don Giovanni* of 1955, with Cesare Siepi as a Don to set all female hearts aflutter, Lisa della Casa as a strikingly beautiful Elvira, and Wilhelm Furtwängler in the pit; and *Der Rosenkavalier* in 1961 with Elisabeth Schwarzkopf as an almost unduly glamorous Marschallin, Anneliese Rothenberger as an enticing Sophie, and Sena Jurinac as the red-blooded young gentleman who has to choose between the two of them. Karajan was in musical charge of the *Rosenkavalier*, and although Czinner used a multi-camera technique which in those days counted as revolutionary it was simply not possible for the visual effects of a film made in those conditions to match the quality of the musical performance. When Karajan staged his own *Carmen* at Salzburg in 1967, starring Grace Bumbry and Jon Vickers, two of the livest wires in opera at that time, he transplanted the production into a studio before he filmed it; and during the next two decades directors came up with more and more variations of technique in their determination to solve the problems endemic in the filming of opera. Götz Friedrich's celebrated *Salome* of 1974, for instance, conducted by Karl Böhm, was conceived all along as a studio production – it had had no previous existence on the stage – and the same was the case with Franco Zeffirelli's *La travi-*

*Elisabeth
Schwartzkopf
as the Marschallin
and Herta Töpper
as Octavian in a
scene from*
Der Rosenkavalier,
BBC TV, 1961.

ata in *1982*. It is no coincidence, I feel, that both directors chose the same soprano for their title-roles; this was the Canadian soprano Teresa Stratas, one of the few operatic sopranos able both to sing such highly demanding roles and to look convincing, even in close-up, as a teenage seductress or a consumptive invalid. Not many opera singers truly understand the difference between acting on stage and acting on the screen, but she proved herself to be one of them.

Two of the most successful operatic films, viewed in purely cinematic terms – Joseph Losey's *Don Giovanni* (1979) and Francesco Rosi's *Carmen* (1984) – were shot entirely on location.* Both of these operas are

---

*Zeffirelli's *Otello*, also shot on location, despite the presence in the cast of Domingo, Ricciarelli and Diaz, struck me as being a less successful example of the genre; perhaps because it strayed too far from Verdi's vision of the piece.

Placido Domingo and Julia Migenes in Francesco Rosi's Carmen *(1984), one of the most convincing of operatic films.*

set in Spain, but Losey chose to remove the doings of the evil Don from Seville to the Veneto, where he achieved a series of stunning visual effects amongst the misty canals and soaring architecture of the region. His cast, led by Ruggero Raimondi and Kiri te Kanawa, was a fine one, though no better than the Salzburg team which I have mentioned above; to the cinema-going public, however, there was no contest. Czinner, shackled by the limitations of the theatre, stood no chance against the infinitely greater cinematic potential of Losey's method of production. Even so, if asked to choose between the Losey *Don* and the Rosi *Carmen* I think it would be the latter to which I would hand the victor's palm. While making the fullest use of authentic Spanish locations, again and again displaying the flair of a true man of the cinema, Rosi nevertheless remains utterly true to Bizet, never allowing the exuberance of his visual imagination to deflect us from the tragedy of the principal characters. As Escamillo, Ruggero

Raimondi features once again, a convincingly athletic and predatory tore-ador; in the title-role Julia Migenes catches the wilfulness of a creature whose nature it is to rebel, and as Don José, the real protagonist of the piece, Placido Domingo gives a performance which even he must surely look back on as one of the high spots of his remarkable career. Vocally this production caught him at his peak, the voice fluent and pliable in Acts I and II, but already capable in Acts III and IV of the riveting dramatic cogency which has made him *the* Otello of recent years. Like Teresa Stratas – and for that matter Julia Migenes – Domingo knows how to adapt his dramatic style to the requirements of the screen; to watch his eyes in the final confrontation is to recognize a true actor at work. Add to all this a searing account of the score from Lorin Maazel and a well-balanced sound recording, and I would feel inclined to say that this is as close as anyone has come to a reconciliation between almost irreconcil-able art forms.

With Rosi's *Carmen*, opera shot for the cinema seems at the moment to have run its course. Opera films of this quality are hugely expensive to make, but they cannot be expected to compete with the box-office appeal of other big-budget movies. We may perhaps see a few more examples of the opera-related film, such as István Szabó's 1991 comedy *Meeting Venus*, in which Glenn Close, borrowing the singing voice of Kiri te Kanawa, played the part of a Wagnerian heroine, but actual operas are far more likely to be encountered on video than on film. This is not the place for a detailed treatise on the difference between the two, but suffice it to say that while the type of film needed for the cinema's giant screen is extremely expensive – the cartridges need to be frequently changed, and processing is costly and time-consuming – a videotape, suitable for trans-mission on television, is very much cheaper to buy, it comes in cassettes lasting as long as two hours, and it requires no processing at all. Thus, while the filming of opera has been in decline the videotaping of opera has enjoyed an apparently unstoppable boom.

This does not, however, mean that the headaches which confront the operatic film director are solved when he switches to videotape; the inher-ent discrepancies between the requirements of stage and screen are still omnipresent, and over the years various different techniques have been devised to cope with them. Having myself, in my capacity as a performer, experienced just about all of these techniques I cannot help viewing their pros and cons largely from the singer's point of view, and it is safe to say that our preferences and those of the directors have not always coincided. Like so many things in life the evolution of opera on video has been a history of compromise, cost versus economy, quality versus convenience, artistic aspiration versus commercial interests and so on; in other words, the art of the possible.

In the early days of opera on videotape television companies preferred to mount their own studio productions because it was easier in that way to guarantee higher televisual standards. During a period of three or four weeks the singers would be rehearsed down to the minutest detail while the director worked out exactly how every shot was to be set up, and at the end of that time one or at the most two days would be set aside for the actual filming. I myself first experienced this method of working back in 1962 when the BBC brought me home from Germany to sing the male lead in one of the first operas expressly written for television, a piece entitled *Dark Pilgrimage* by the British composer Phyllis Tate, and my experiences with that production can perhaps be taken as typical of the hazards which the method involved.

Our rehearsals took place during bitter weather in a disused army drill-hall. There were no sets or furniture, but the outlines of where they would ultimately be were marked on the floor by different coloured tapes, red for Scene 1, green for Scene 2 and so on. We would have to remember with absolute precision where our feet were supposed to be at any given moment, because a discrepancy of only a couple of inches would mean that a shot, say, of one singer taken over another's shoulder would be ruined if the placing was not exact. The setting-up of these shots was entirely arbitrary; in the middle of a duet, for instance, where in a staged production you would be doing what comes naturally, namely gazing passionately into your girlfriend's loving eyes, you might have to turn your head away from her altogether during six specific bars while you are being filmed in close-up on a different camera; in other words getting your music right and singing it as beautifully as possible were only two of many things on which you had to concentrate.

Then came the day when we moved into the actual BBC studio and found that the sets and furniture were all just a fraction different from the

The author awaits his death at the hands of three black prostitutes. A scene from the BBC television production of Phyllis Tate's Dark Pilgrimage, *1962.*

markings to which we had been working, so that our moves all had to be marginally readjusted. We had to acclimatize ourselves, too, to a totally new situation as far as the music was concerned. So far we had rehearsed with a piano never more than a few yards away and a conductor comfortably in our vision; now, for technical reasons to do with the sound quality of the recording, the conductor had disappeared to join the orchestra in a different studio, the accompaniment was only audible to us over not very loud loudspeakers, and we could only see the conductor's beat if one of the various monitors dotted around the set happened to be in our natural line of vision. On the day of filming we had to spend several hours standing in costume and make-up under the heat and glare of the lights so that the cameramen could check the effectiveness of every shot; when the evening came, and with it the culmination of all this meticulous and exhausting work, we were no longer as fresh as we might have been.

This was the point at which I made one of the greatest mistakes of my entire career, one which has remained a lesson to me ever since. My role opened with an extended aria containing several challenging high tones which all through the rehearsal period I had sung with no difficulty at all. A few minutes before recording was due to begin a very senior member of the BBC music staff came to see me and said that he had listened to the technical run-through and that in his opinion I did not need to give so much voice in the opening number. 'Take the top a little easier,' he advised, 'it will sound better over the microphone.' These are the moments when there is no substitute for experience, and experience was exactly what I did not possess. I did as he suggested, cut back my energy as I approached the first high B flat – and cracked wide open. There was nothing to be done. The method we were using did not allow us to stop and start again, so I simply had to sing through the rest of the opera knowing that unless we finished well within our time limit I would have no chance to make good my disaster; any run into overtime would have been financially unthinkable. As luck would have it we were well within our allotted time-span, and it was decided that I should take the opening scene again. This time, lacking the vigour to go for the aria with all guns blazing, I took refuge in what was supposed to be an artistic mezza voce, but which I fear emerged more as a sub-standard bleat. The production was the British entry in the prestigious annual Prix Italia, and I have always suspected that I was the main reason why we did not win it. In any case, later that year I went on holiday to the South of France and happened to buy a British newspaper shortly after *Dark Pilgrimage* had been shown on television. My eye, all unsuspecting, fell on the music critic's review. By the time I had finished reading it the wine in my glass had turned to vinegar, the food on my plate had turned to dust and ashes, and the midday sun could strike no hint of sparkle from the cheerless waters of the Mediterranean Sea.

After that the BBC understandably left me out of their calculations for a year or two, but when they did invite me back for the title-role in Lehár's *The Count of Luxemburg* I felt like an old hand, and was ready to defend myself against even the best-meant advice. The only thing that went wrong this time was not my fault, though it was a typical example of the stress which studio production could create. The Count's main aria, in which he tries to determine with which of two ladies he is in love (they are actually one and the same person, and he wins her hand in Act III) was set up in such a technically subtle manner that it had to be shot as a separate entity. I was in a tiny three-walled room, along with two cameras and a microphone boom, and all three walls surrounding me were hung with mirrors. Space was so cramped that my movements were restricted to turning at certain precise moments to address one or other of my three reflections, and as I did so I had to sing an aria containing several abrupt changes of tempo without being able to see the conductor, and only able to hear a very faint version of the orchestral playback. To add to these problems I had to end the aria on a sustained mezza voce high A flat, and all in all the chances of pulling it off were so slender that the director had scheduled sufficient time for three attempts at the scene. Well, a miracle happened. My adrenalin flow was such that for those three minutes it seemed that I could do no wrong; not only did I remember every glance and every turn of the head with immaculate precision, but I even succeeded in capping the aria with a high tone which was, I swear, the finest I ever sang. There was jubilation throughout the studio and I, of course, was over the moon. Then came the sound of a disembodied voice from the control-room: 'Is someone on camera two wearing metal cuff-links? They're catching light in the central mirror – we'll have to take the scene again from the top.' It is difficult to keep smiling at a moment like that; luckily the second take went without any specific hitch, but I knew from the first note that it was out of the question for me to emulate Browning's wise thrush and 'recapture the first fine careless rapture'.

It is, of course, part of a singer's job to sing and act at the same time, but it is asking a lot of us to switch our voices on and off, sometimes after many hours under the lights, during the technical procedures of a television production, and in many countries producers prefer to relieve us of this burden by pre-recording the music and using the playback technique. The sound-track will often have been completed weeks before the filming is due to begin, and the singers can then forget all about vocal and musical problems; they will be sent a tape of their own recording so that they can memorize exactly how they sang it, and when filming begins they simply mime to the sound of their own voices. It is, in other words, a much less stressful procedure than the method which I have described above, but the artistic results seldom strike me as satisfactory. For one thing it is difficult to achieve really precise synchronization; for financial reasons every television studio seems to be permanently working against the clock, and it is simply not possible to repeat tricky phrases again and again until the lip movements are perfect. For another thing, the singing of opera is an energetic activity and if the singers are not seen to be employing a degree of effort commensurate with the intensity of the sound that they are producing the overall effect can sometimes be positively ludicrous. I respect the reverse argument, namely that close-ups of singers in full cry, their mouths agape and the sweat pouring from their brow, does not make a pretty picture, but not for nothing was Caruso reputed to have said that however easy your top notes may *sound* you must make them *look* difficult or the public will feel cheated.

Some television producers today, notably Peter Weigl, take the play-back system to its logical conclusion and habitually use actors and actresses miming to singers' voices. With films such as his *Eugene Onegin*, using a Solti recording as its sound-track, Weigl has achieved many memorable images and in theory this should be the perfect answer, particularly for an opera in which the protagonists are supposed to be very young, or delicate of health, or perhaps belong to a race with specific requirements of physiognomy, such as *Aida* or *Madam Butterfly*. Once again, however, to my way of thinking at least, the match seldom works. No sylph-like fifteen-year-old, which is what Butterfly is supposed to be, could possibly sustain the vocal task which Puccini has set her, and the younger and more childlike a Butterfly looks the less the voice of a Freni or a Gorchakova is going to emerge convincingly from her lips. Similarly a teenage Romeo may be highly desirable in a film of the Shakespeare play, but how convincing will he be in a film of the Gounod opera, when he whispers engagingly to his Juliet and out come the manly tones of a mature operatic tenor?

The only really satisfactory playback production in which I personally have been involved was of Martinů's surrealist opera *Julietta*, shot in Prague in August 1969 – we were originally contracted for August 1968 but the Soviet tanks beat us to it – directed by the then head of the Czech national opera, Václav Kaslík. My role was that of the Director of Dreams, a pernickety bureaucrat with a telephone growing out of the top

A scene from Václav Kaslík's television production of Martinů's opera Julietta, Prague, 1969. *Peter Lagger as the Convict and the author as the Director of Dreams.*

of his hat, to whom anyone wishing for the luxury of a dream must make an official application. There was a lot of tricky text to be sung, which is usually the worst kind of thing for playback, but because at that time man-hours in Prague were, by Western standards, extremely cheap, we were able to work at every scene for as long as necessary until the dubbing was undetectable. There was, however, one feature of Kaslík's production which, for its sheer spookiness, I would not wish to experience again. During one of my scenes he created a nightmarish atmosphere by having some two dozen weird-looking men trudge distractedly round and round in the background indulging in gestures expressive of acute mental disturbance. When I congratulated him on finding 'extras' of such uncanny skill he replied 'They are inmates of the local lunatic asylum; the men in the corner are their keepers.'

By now many works have been written expressly for television, with

Menotti's *Amahl and the Night Visitors*, produced by NBC back in 1951, one of the earliest and also one of the most successful. Probably the most distinguished composer to have accepted a television commission as yet has been Benjamin Britten, with *Owen Wingrave* (1971). It was my good fortune to be selected by the composer for one of the opera's two tenor roles and several of my happiest memories of operatic life date back to this production. It all took place in Britten's favourite concert hall, the Maltings at Snape, near his home town of Aldeburgh on the Suffolk coast; the building was converted into a massive television studio, containing every set involved in the opera, the most imposing of them being the great hall at Paramor, the haunted house in which Henry James's original story proceeds to its grisly end. The opera only calls for a cast of eight soloists (with a brief contribution by a pre-recorded off-stage chorus), Aldeburgh's most congenial hotel stayed open for our benefit out of season, and the rehearsal period was remarkable for its cosy family atmosphere.* Britten himself conducted, and the various sets were cunningly arranged in such a way that he and the orchestra were never far away. His baton could naturally not always be visible to each of us, but the assistant conductor, Steuart Bedford, found ingenious ways to creep about off camera and appear in the corner of the eye just as one needed him, sometimes crouching on the floor, and once, during a duet between Janet Baker and myself, perched on an overhead beam. Indeed, when the production was repeated on BBC television a couple of years ago I was amused to be reminded that at this point I had devised what I hoped would pass as a dramatically excusable rolling of my eyes towards heaven.

I believe that in the process of adapting himself to the stringencies of the unfamiliar medium Britten did have occasional moments of disagreement with members of the BBC's production staff, but as far as we singers were concerned he was a veritable model of tolerance and good will. The only person with whom he occasionally became a trifle impatient was his life's partner and his most celebrated interpreter, Peter Pears. On one

---

*Strangely enough, in Humphrey Carpenter's otherwise authoritative biography of Benjamin Britten (see bibliography) the production period has been described as one of great stress and gloom, but the accuracy of my own memories has happily been confirmed by other survivors from the original cast.

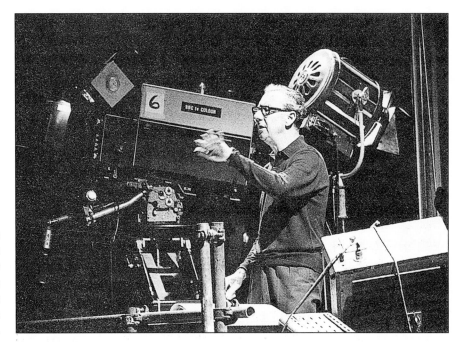

Benjamin Britten conducting the television production of Owen Wingrave, *1971.*

occasion during the rehearsal period he fixed Peter with a beady eye, pointedly muttering 'Some of us had better go home and learn our words'; and it was indeed the question of Peter's words which presented the rest of us with possibly our most challenging task, namely the keeping of a straight face during the Dinner Party Scene. Peter (who was, I must emphasize, regarded by all of us with the sincerest admiration and affection), had, even as a younger man, frequently suffered from memory problems, and over the years he had developed a cast-iron technique for disguising lapses during stage performances by improvising music in the style of Britten to a strange kind of semi-articulated hum which was an invention entirely of his own. This he was able to maintain for as many bars – or, indeed on one or two celebrated occasions, pages – as he needed before slotting himself back into the right groove, and he did it with such consummate skill that even those members of the public who had become aware that something odd was going on were inclined to attribute the momentary fuzziness of Peter's otherwise immaculate diction to some strange flat spot in the theatre's acoustics.

For televisual purposes, however, this would clearly not do, and the knowledge that his words would have to be perfect put poor Peter, at this late stage of his career, under considerable pressure. In the role of the implacable old warrior, General Sir Philip Wingrave, who is suddenly faced with the horrifying news that Owen, his grandson and sole heir, has refused to become a soldier, Peter, during the Dinner Party Scene, had to deliver himself of a vitriolic tirade. Unfortunately the text bristled with pitfalls, notably two lines uttered in reference to the fighting Wingraves of the past – 'Halberds, pistols, daggers were their company; lances, swordthrusts, parted them from life.' The memorizing of a string of nouns would always be easier if librettists would be kind enough to write them in alphabetical order, but they never do, and at every rehearsal, as the lines approached, we could see Peter steeling himself to the inevitable catastrophe. It was not merely that he would put the weapons in the wrong order, which would not in itself have done much damage; far worse was the fact that strange hybrid words would come tumbling out. 'Dagberds', 'haggers' and 'thrustols' did not matter a bit, indeed they sounded interesting things to have as one's company, but it was that wretched first syllable of the word 'pistols' which used to be Peter's undoing; combined with whatever second syllable might leap to his tongue it could have a devastatingly disruptive effect. One after the other we would lower our heads towards our plates – Benjamin Luxon in the title role would invariably be the first to succumb – and strive desperately to keep our laughter silent. Peter, who saw the joke as well as any of us, tried all manner of dodges to help himself out. One was to have a menu card on the table in front of him bearing the words

Halberds
Pistols
Daggers
Lances
Swordthrusts

but it did not help; if the print was large enough for him to read it without his glasses there was a danger that it would be legible on camera. When we came to the actual filming we were all crossing our fingers for him under the table, urging him to succeed; in any case, with a heroic effort he summoned up every ounce of professionalism at his disposal and out the words came, faultlessly.

The impulse to 'corpse', or collapse in giggles at the most tense and solemn moments is, I feel sure, one with which everybody is familiar, and it is one to which opera singers are especially prone. When *Owen Wingrave* reached the Covent Garden stage in 1973 the Dinner Party Scene subjected us to a fresh hazard. Whereas on video it was easily possible, by cutting in and out, to create the impression of passing time, so that it seemed reasonable for us to have eaten our way from soup to dessert before rising from the table, on stage we had to whizz from course to course at a breakneck speed. The Australian soprano Sylvia Fisher, who gave an unforgettable performance as Owen's battle-axe aunt, was seated on my right, and just at the moment when Peter's Waterloo was coming up – he never managed to repeat that one flawless rendering – she and I used to be offered a large and wobbly blancmange by a waiter with severely shaking hands. To this day I can see Sylvia's attempts, her own body rocking with suppressed laughter, to pursue that quivering mass around the dish.

Nowadays the vast majority of operatic videos which come onto the market have started life as a staged production in one or other of the world's great opera houses. Studio productions, like operatic movies, have become too expensive to mount, and by tying up the singers for a period of a month or more they preclude the participation of precisely those stars whose names are needed in the cast-list if the video is to sell. Once again, a willingness to compromise becomes paramount. The video director whose task is to record a performance without altering any aspect of the stage production, and without placing a single camera in a position which might distract or annoy the paying audience, is working within stringent limitations; it will be his main ambition simply to present the viewer with an impression of the production as seen from the best seat in the house. If, however, the production company in question can afford to mount an extra performance specially for the cameras it becomes a very different story. Details of lighting, costume and make-up can be adjusted to meet the video director's requirements, and cameras can roam at will – sometimes they even find their way onto the stage. For the singers this is infinitely the most congenial technique. They may occasionally be asked to make minor alterations to a move or a stage position, but basically it is a question of performing a familiar role in familiar surroundings rather than being exposed to the many inhibiting aspects of the studio method. This, for instance, is how the highly successful Wagner videotapes have been made in the Festspielhaus at Bayreuth, all of them directed for video by an outstanding British specialist in the field, Brian Large, one of whose earliest assignments had been the taping of *Owen Wingrave*.

For those who like to own their favourite operas on video the choice today is, as I mentioned earlier, bewildering. Many of the finest productions of the last thirty or more years, both for stage and screen, have been preserved, amongst them such gems as Ingmar Bergman's *Die Zauberflöte*, Jean-Pierre Ponnelle's *Orfeo*, Peter Hall's Glyndebourne *Fidelio* with the mesmerizing Elisabeth Söderström as Leonore, Visconti's *Don Carlos*, and Andrei Tarkovsky's *Boris Godunov*, to name but a very few. The outstanding singers of yesterday and the day before can still be admired in many of their most famous roles – Tito Gobbi as Rigoletto, Jon Vickers as Peter Grimes, Janet Baker as Giulio Cesare, a choice between Leontyne Price or Renata Tebaldi as the 'Forza' Leonora, the list goes on and on, and for good measure we can even add Toscanini conducting a concert performance of *Aida*. Glimpses can be had of Maria Callas's celebrated Tosca; Joan Sutherland, 'La Stupenda', can be admired in many of her most famous arias; and patient searches will produce fascinating footage of several Soviet artists whom Western audiences were never allowed to admire. It all adds up to being an invaluable treasury, one which, on video, laser disc, or whatever the future may throw up, can only grow and grow.

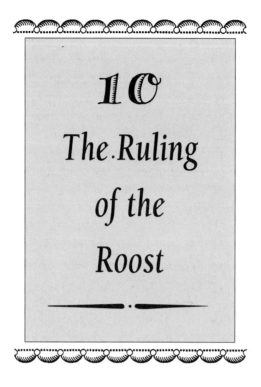

10

The Ruling

of the

Roost

No other art form involves as many different elements as opera – singing, both solo and choral, drama, orchestral playing, sets, costumes, lighting, make-up and frequently dancing as well – and I have often found that members of the public are intrigued to know who, in the preparation of a new operatic production, is really the boss. Is it the director,* is it the conductor, or is it even occasionally the star of the show? After my many years in the firing line the only answer I can possibly give is, 'It depends.' The ideal situation is of course that director, conductor and performers

---

*Complications often arise as to the exact meaning of the terms 'director' and 'producer'. Nowadays in the world of opera we usually call the person who devises the production and directs rehearsals the 'director' – that is how I use the term in this chapter – while 'producer' more usually refers to those members of the commercial theatre and the film world who deal with the money matters.

should all be of one mind as to how the work should proceed, and when that blessed harmony is achieved there is no real need to ask who is wielding supreme power. Like most ideal situations, however, this one rarely occurs, and during the four or so centuries since opera first evolved the pendulum of authority has swung now this way, now that, with much being decided by the strength of the personalities involved.

Many have been the occasions when I have been a bystander, sometimes amused, more often exasperated, while a rehearsal has been brought to a halt so that conductor and director can set about the vital business of establishing the pecking order. 'It is completely unacceptable to have the tenor facing into the wings when he needs that crucial cue!' shouts the one. 'I refuse to destroy the visual effect by having him face out front,' comes the retort; 'we're not in the 1880s!' Sometimes the tenor in question may succeed in quelling this battle of the titans by pointing out that he can manage perfectly all right if he is given a television monitor in the wings, but it is usually best to remain silent and let the power struggle take its course. As I have myself done a certain amount of directing I too have inevitably become involved in the occasional locking of horns. My only serious skirmish was with one of those maddening conductors who absent themselves from production rehearsals only to make life impossible for the singers by setting a mass of unfamiliar tempi at the eleventh hour, and although I would like to think that that particular malefactor benefited from the forcefulness of my views I fear that I would be indulging in self-deception.

Back in the mists of operatic time the situation was simpler. Seventeenth-century operas such as those of Claudio Monteverdi did not use a large enough orchestra to necessitate the participation of a conductor; nor were the musicians in a deeply sunk pit, so that it was enough for the singers to maintain some degree of eye contact with the first violinist or the harpsichordist, who was often the composer of the piece in question. As the size of the operatic orchestra grew so too did the need for a beater of time, and in due course this figure evolved into the fully-fledged opera conductor as we know him today. Prominent amongst the great figures of the past who helped to elevate the status of the operatic conductor, and who presided over an era in which the 'beater of time' could be said to have become king, were men such as Gustav Mahler,

The epitome of the star conductor. Crowds await the appearance of Arturo Toscanini.

Richard Strauss, Arturo Toscanini, Bruno Walter and Sir Thomas Beecham. Mahler used occasionally to extend his authority by also directing the pieces he conducted, as did Erich Kleiber, Otto Klemperer and Herbert von Karajan in later years; and Beecham, though I am not aware that he ever actually directed a production, was certainly seldom short of a pithy comment concerning the proceedings up on stage. My personal favourite amongst the numerous gems attributed to that inimitable character was delivered during a dress rehearsal of *Götterdämmerung* at Covent Garden in the 1930s. In those days when the score called for a horse to take part in the action a horse would be produced instead of merely being left to the audience's imagination, and on this particular occasion Brünnhilde's trusty steed Grane made his presence felt by depositing on the stage a sizeable heap of steaming manure. 'Ah!' said Sir Thomas, temporarily laying down his baton, 'critic as well as artist I perceive!'

My own first experience, as a member of the audience, of the electrifying effect which a great conductor can have on an operatic performance was when Erich Kleiber conducted *Der Rosenkavalier* at Covent Garden in 1950. The resident company in those immediate post-war years had suffered from less than inspiring leadership but the arrival of Kleiber produced a metamorphosis which was nothing short of sensational. When he unleashed the great waltz tune at the end of Act II it was as if the Vienna Philharmonic had slipped surreptitiously into the pit; inspirational brilliance had taken the place of workmanlike dependability. It was a nice coincidence that Kleiber's son Carlos, every bit as gifted as his father and even more demanding, should have made his own Covent Garden debut a quarter of a century later with the selfsame piece. On that occasion he was acting as a replacement for another star conductor who had fallen ill, and although he had had the opportunity to put his forces through several gruelling rehearsals he had omitted to warn them that it was his habit to mount the podium, briefly acknowledge the applause and then launch straight into bar one without that moment of repose, hands raised at the ready, in which most conductors indulge.* The result was a remarkably garbled version of the opening couple of phrases as one musician after another realized that the show had begun, but thereafter all went swimmingly and no one was left in any doubt that an opera conductor of the highest calibre had presented his calling card. This was no surprise to me, because ten years previously Carlos had made his conducting debut in the Opera House, Zürich, with Johann Strauss's operetta *Wiener Blut*, and as I was singing the central role of Count Zedlau I had plenty of opportunity to benefit from his eloquent handling of the score. It is amusing to recollect that when his success emboldened him to ask the Intendant of the Zürich Opera whether in the following season he might be entrusted with an opera he received a negative reply on the grounds that his ability would not stretch beyond operetta.

One of the hardest things for the public to assess is how much difference the conductor makes to a singer's performance, and I have often been asked if it really matters to a seasoned soloist whether it is Maestro A or Maestro B who has the stick in his hand. The answer is that if Maestro A

---

*Herbert von Karajan was a supreme exponent of this 'moment of concentration'. On one occasion at La Scala as he stood stock still, his eyes closed and his arms outstretched, a voice from the gallery was heard to call out 'Coraggio, maestro, coraggio!'

'Critic as well
as artist, I
perceive.'
Sir Thomas
Beecham listens
to a playback of
a recorded talk
on Delius.

is a dyed-in-the-wool opera man and Maestro B is not it makes all the difference in the world. There are some conductors who take the trouble to familiarize themselves with the problems which confront singers and there are others who make one feel that they would be happy to dispense altogether with the goings-on on stage and concentrate all their energies on the orchestra. The true operatic conductor accommodates himself to such things as the singers' need to breathe, and he judges to a nicety when to lead the singers and when to content himself with accompanying them. He knows the vital importance of not varying the tempi from one performance to another; the amount of time available to the singers to perform their actions is dependent on the speed of the music, and in many a complex modern production involving, let us say, some such activity as climbing up a ladder or swinging on a rope it can be extremely awkward to find oneself robbed of a vital half second. The conductor must be conscious, too, of the effect of the considerable distances which have to be coped with in a massive opera house. Sir Charles Mackerras, a singer's conductor if ever there was one, told me recently how often he has noticed that when we opera singers take to the concert platform we tend to be consistently ahead of the beat, because we become so accustomed to the need for anticipation imposed on us by habitually singing at a range of thirty or forty metres from the conductor. The relationship of pit to stage can vary enormously from theatre to theatre, and I well remember one odd situation which arose at a dress rehearsal when Sir Charles was conducting Janáček's *The Cunning Little Vixen*, in which I was singing the part of the Schoolmaster. Because of the depth of the pit in the theatre in question, and the fact that I was flat on my stomach at the back of a steeply raked set, his hands, with somewhat disastrous results, became invisible to me. I asked him if he would mind conducting the passage in question with his baton above his head, a request which a purely orchestral conductor would find bizarre in the extreme, but down went a reminder in Sir Charles's score and in every performance up went his hand.

By concentrating on the degree to which a conductor has to look after his singers I do not want to give the impression that he is solely there to make our lives easier. Obviously one looks to the great conductor for artistic insight into the music, for the shaping of the complex architecture of the score and for that element of inspiration which brings the best out of the performers, but at the same time one cannot overestimate the degree of sheer level-headedness which an operatic conductor sometimes has to display. A scene such as the street fight in *Die Meistersinger* or the naval battle in *Billy Budd* is, both dramatically and musically, an amazingly complex affair, and there is always a chance that somebody somewhere is going to make a mistake. The conductor, faced as he is by some seventy or eighty people up on stage, probably singing at least a dozen separate vocal lines, not to mention the small matter of a hundred or so musicians playing their hearts out in the pit, has to spot where the fault lies and make a split-second decision about how to put things straight again before the performance starts to fall apart. It is at moments like these that singers thank God for a conductor who is truly in charge. I have known some whose faces disappear into the score, not to be seen again until we singers have somehow achieved our own salvation or the curtain has brought the scene in question to a merciful conclusion; and there are others who instantly snap into action and with a couple of quick gestures sort the trouble out. It can be a frightening moment up on stage when you have a vital entry coming up and you realize that the colleague from whom you normally take your cue is, as the Germans put it, 'swimming'. On those occasions the conductor who is instinctively aware of your dilemma, calmly raises his left hand in a 'don't come in till I tell you' gesture, lets the swimmer swim on, and throws you a cue on the right beat, is worth his weight in gold. The conductor who waves his arms around in a series of frantic but meaningless gestures, and then blames you for the ensuing chaos, is a less endearing figure.

In many opera houses these practicalities are left in the hands of the *maestro suggeritore*, or prompter, who sits in the little box at the centre of the footlights. The prompter's job is to give the singers their musical cues (and in the case of many Italian singers their word cues as well), thus leaving the conductor free to concentrate on the orchestra and the broader aspects of musical interpretation. The box is equipped with a mirror, or nowadays more typically a television monitor, from which the prompter can take the conductor's beat. It is an arrangement which can be very helpful to singers, especially in those modern operas which are excessively hard to memorize, but it can also have its disadvantages. It has been known for certain singers, relying on the fact that every cue will be fed to them, to come on stage with a somewhat hazy knowledge of their role, a situation which necessitates their remaining firmly anchored downstage centre. Should they wander too far from the prompt box the *maestro suggeritore* has to start projecting his voice; a state of affairs which has promoted the *maestro* to a position of remarkable prominence in many a live recording.

To revert, though, to the question of who is the dominant authority one point cannot be overlooked, namely that the conductor participates in, and thus exercises his influence over, every performance, whereas it is the normal practice with directors, especially if they belong to the category of international superstars, to disappear after, or even occasionally before, the opening night. One of the staff directors of the company in question will have been assigned the position of production assistant, and it then becomes his or her sometimes unenviable task to monitor the performances and safeguard the director's original intentions; but, human nature being what it is, in those instances where the conductor or the more

A vital link in opera's executive chain. Osie Hawkins, stage manager at the Met.

strong-willed of the singers has not been in total agreement with the director it does occasionally occur that modifications are introduced.

By and large it would be true to say that the emergence of the star conductor started with the operas of Wagner – mid-nineteenth-century critics seldom gave the conductor more than a passing mention – but the emergence of the star director is a more recent development. The Swiss Adolphe Appia (1862–1928), the Englishman Edward Gordon Craig (1872–1966) and the German Max Reinhardt (1873–1943) did much to reveal new possibilities in the visual presentation of opera during the first quarter of the twentieth century, but this does not mean, as many people seem to suppose, that in earlier times no attention had ever been paid to 'production'. This strikes me as being an increasingly popular misconception, as is the theory that it is only opera singers of the last couple of generations who have ever bothered to act. I have even read in a supposedly serious book on Maria Callas the astounding sentence 'She alone has ever conquered the operatic stage', and I am occasionally surprised by the arrogance of those who seem to think that we in our day are the first to have discovered the only True Way. Fashions change in production and in acting as they do in everything else. The clipped tones of the inter-war British film star may fall amusingly on the modern ear (though how I sometimes yearn for them as I sit in a London theatre listening to actors, brought up in the TV era, who are unintelligible beyond Row G of the stalls), and many famous operatic interpretations of yesteryear, such as Caruso's Canio or Claudia Muzio's Violetta would doubtless be regarded as 'hammy' by any audience of today. It is worth remembering, however, that the great Russian director Konstantin Stanislavsky, the progenitor of modern 'method' acting, used to remark 'My system is taken straight from Chaliapin'; and that Feodor Chaliapin, when asked on one occasion to comment on Caruso's histrionic limitations, replied 'Who told you that Caruso is a bad actor? That is nonsense. Caruso has a thousand voices, and each voice has such an abundance of colours and shades! He uses them like a painter. He who can sing like Caruso can act like Salvini.'*

If one delves into the past one finds that innumerable opera singers have been revered by informed and intelligent critics for the skill and expressiveness of their acting – according, of course, to the standards admired in their own generation. The great French tenor Adolphe Nourrit (1802–1839) was famous, as Henry Pleasants tells us in his fascinating book *The Great Tenor Tragedy*,† for being 'ever at pains to make his singing a projection and extension of the actor's art, and he was as attentive to matters of deportment, gesture, makeup, facial expression, and costume as he was to vocalism'. Back in 1850 Giulia Grisi, one of the outstanding vocal technicians of her day, moved the critic of the *Illustrated London News* to describe her physical impersonation of Bellini's Norma as 'grand, terrible and sublime'; and though not many modern designers would have smiled on the fact that 'a piece of costly jewellery was thrown from the grand tier at the end of the first act, the brilliancy of which was displayed by her wearing it in the second', the aficionados of the day were clearly as little disturbed by the anachronism of

---

*Taken from *Chaliapin*, by Victor Borovsky. See bibliography.
†See bibliography.

a Druid priestess wearing a diamond brooch as we are today when we look at a fifteenth-century Florentine painting depicting a scene from the Bible, and spot the city of Florence nestling in the background.

Of course there were plenty of singers around in the past who did belong to the 'stand and deliver' school of performance, but let us not pretend that they have become extinct. Several of the stars who have most deeply endeared themselves to the public during my lifetime have been of the unashamedly non-acting variety. I remember the Swedish director Lars Runsten telling me of the great Jussi Björling that he 'basically just stood on stage, but did so with colossal authority', and that glorious tenor Carlo Bergonzi used to restrict his physical interpretation to the gradual raising of one hand as the Verdian or Puccinian melody climbed its magical pathway to a climactic high B flat. One of the greatest sopranos of my own vintage once said to me 'the public come to my shows because of the

Left 'Grand, terrible and sublime'. Giulia Grisi as Norma.

Right Grisi in less dominant pose, as Pamira in Rossini's Le siège de Corinthe, 16 August 1834.

Always in total control. Herbert von Karajan, Salzburg, 1964.

noise I make, not to see me hopping around', and as they came in their hundreds of thousands she certainly had a point. I remember, too, while I was a student in Vienna, becoming acquainted with an utterly delightful Italian tenor named Eugenio Fernandi who had been discovered by Karajan and brought by him to sing at the State Opera. Fernandi had a resplendent voice but no idea whatsoever of how to comport himself on stage, to such an extent that Karajan, while conducting him as Cavaradossi, used to give him a sign to stand up and bow after the aria 'E lucevan le stelle', followed by another to sit down again and carry on singing. It was decided that Eugenio should be handed over to one of the teachers at the Opera School, Kammersänger Josef Witt, for instruction in stagecraft, and Witt opened the proceedings by saying 'Now, Signor Fernandi, I noticed while you were singing in *Tosca* that from time to time you used a very nice gesture with your left hand. Let's see if you can double your range by occasionally making the same gesture with your right hand.' Fernandi looked at him in deep distress and replied 'With my right hand? But that I do in *Butterfly*!'

Generally speaking, the more gloriously a singer sings the less rigorous will be the public's demand that he or she should also be able to act, and there have without doubt been times during the evolution of opera when production standards have conspicuously yielded to other considerations. The inter-war years, a period of superlative Wagner singing, saw the visual presentation of the Master's works drop to an astonishingly banal uniformity, as permutations of the same star casts travelled the world appearing now in Vienna or Berlin, now in London or Paris, now in New York or Buenos Aires, but seldom with any time to rehearse. When the great Heldentenor Lauritz Melchior made his debut at Covent Garden as Siegmund in *Die Walküre* in 1924 he was given no rehearsal whatsoever, either with the conductor, Bruno Walter, or with a stage director, despite the fact that he had never sung the role before, nor had he even seen the piece performed. During Kirsten Flagstad's sensational opening season at the Met in 1935 she appeared within the space of two months in no less than seven of the great Wagnerian roles, three of them new to her, usually after the briefest of explanations as to where she had to stand and what she had to do. Wagnerian singers of international stature were expected to have immersed themselves in 'the Bayreuth style', and as they would find themselves everywhere in the world with a broadly standardized set to perform on it was up to them to keep out of trouble. Things reached a point at which the young critic Walter Legge, reviewing *Die Walküre* at Covent Garden in 1936, was provoked into describing one of the most passionate passages in the whole of opera, as performed by Elisabeth Rethberg and Lauritz Melchior, in the following terms: 'For the love duet this Siegmund and Sieglinde clambered onto a pile of cushions like a couple of long-married and weary hikers seeking the softest piece of grass on which to rest their limbs before they settled down to their sandwiches.' Opera-goers, one can only assume, were so grateful to hear these alarming roles so heroically sung that as far as the visual side was concerned they were prepared to switch off their critical faculties.

The most fleeting glance at the early days of opera, however, will suffice to show that such slovenliness had not always been the norm; indeed, the lavishness of a production such as that devoted to Cesti's *Il pomo d'oro*, staged at the Viennese court in 1666 on the occasion of the marriage of the Emperor Leopold I to the Infanta Margherita of Spain, was something which would nowadays be totally unthinkable. The scope of this particular undertaking can be gauged from a series of twenty-five engravings, still in existence, depicting such effects as the Glory of Austria descending from the sky on the winged horse Pegasus, a fire-breathing dragon which strikes dread into the hearts of one and all, the goddess Pallas Athene celebrating her birthday by driving around in a chariot of clouds, and many more equally arresting effects. Indeed so paramount was the importance of the stage architect, Ludovico Burnacini, who was not only responsible for designing the necessary mass of machinery but also for ensuring that those whose lives depended on it knew how it all worked, that when the librettist, Francesco Sbarra of Lucca, wrote a postscript to his printed edition of the text giving credit where credit was due, the poor composer was something of an 'also ran'. 'No small contribution to the success', wrote Sbarra, 'was made by the music', an assessment which would have left many a composer with his nose somewhat out of joint. One thing is certain. The production budget, translated into today's terms, would leave any modern Intendant open-mouthed with envy, but priorities in those days *were* somewhat different from our own. Within a few weeks another event was mounted in Vienna to celebrate the same royal wedding, this time a form of horseback ballet, a production which, according to that great expert on the period, Professor Egon Wellesz, 'stripped the Treasury so bare that the means were not left to send even a small troop of cavalry against the Turks, who embarked on a new invasion of Hungary'.

Further evidence of the care invested in the visual aspects of operatic production over the centuries can be found in many other surviving documents, ranging from the detailed stage directions which formed part of the printed score of Gagliano's opera *Dafne* in 1608 to the booklet which the publishing house of Ricordi issued in 1887 setting out the exact requirements for a successful production of Verdi's *Otello*. Nevertheless, I believe it is true to say that the power of the director has never been greater than it is today, and that certain directors, whose views on the entire art and science of producing opera can perhaps best be characterized as revolutionary, are currently alienating the sympathies of a vast majority of opera-goers. Whenever I give a public lecture on opera and arrive at question time the first thing I am asked is almost certain to be some variant of 'What are your views on "concept" productions?', and on one recent occasion a mild attempt on my part to defend the reputation of a certain avant-garde director, who happens to be a friend of mine and a person whose work I greatly admire, brought a positive hornets' nest buzzing round my ears. The secretary of the society in question, normally as peace-loving a bunch of people as one could hope to meet, had to rise to his feet and appeal for order; we might almost have been in the chamber of the House of Commons. The subject is currently the hottest potato in the world of opera, and in Great Britain it reached crisis point in the year 1994, when booing broke out in two places where it had seldom been heard before – at Glyndebourne, and in the expensive seats at Covent Garden. The productions were, respectively, Deborah Warner's updated version of Mozart's *Don Giovanni* and Richard Jones's bizarre approach to Wagner's *Das Rheingold*.

Now there is nothing intrinsically revolutionary about declining to regard the original vision of author or composer as perennially sacrosanct. If we take Richard Wagner as the obvious example of the operatic autocrat – he was, after all, composer, librettist and original stage director in one and the same person – by creating works which are, as George Bernard Shaw so cogently expounded, not so much about people as about ideas, he was challenging every generation to react differently to those ideas and to interpret them in the light of their own experiences and preoccupations. Not for nothing did he himself, with reference to the presentation of his own works, propound the maxim 'Kinder, schafft Neues!', 'Children, create something new!'

It is interesting to note that Wagner, mighty innovator as he was in the realm of music, revealed himself with the premiere of *Der Ring* at the inaugural Bayreuth Festival of 1876 as a far from progressive *metteur en scène*. If you choose to write stage directions such as 'She has swung herself up onto the horse and leaps with one bound into the blazing pyre . . . . At the same time the Rhine, vastly overflowing its bank, has rolled in a flood over the scene of the fire. In its waves the three Rhinedaughters come swimming by . . .', and so on for more than a page, you need a latter-day Ludovico Burnacini to make everything work, and by all accounts the results, during that first production, left something to be desired. The sets, designed by Gotthold and Max Brückner after original sketches by

A truly godlike Wotan.
Hans Hotter in 1961.

the Viennese landscape painter Josef Hoffmann, were literal in the extreme, and the costumes, after much painstaking research into what a prehistoric Norseman might conceivably have looked like, ended up as the kind of thing which used to illustrate Victorian tomes with such titles as *The Schoolboy's Book of Ancient Legends*.

The Norwegian composer Edvard Grieg, who was at Bayreuth in 1876, along with many another eminent musical figure of the time, made a prescient comment when he observed that such a down-to-earth approach to the visual aspects of *Der Ring* held the audience's imagination in a strait-jacket, and that it would be far more effective to allow people to 'create devils and demons in their own minds'. Although, as I have indicated above, the influence of Bayreuth laid a heavy hand on international Wagner productions for many years to come, Grieg's was the path which Wagnerian directors eventually, and inevitably, elected to follow. It is not my intention to attempt a potted history of *Ring* stagings over the cycle's first hundred and twenty years,* but as stepping-stones towards the eruption at Covent Garden in 1994 it is perhaps worth mentioning two particular landmarks in the 'liberation' of *Der Ring* – Wieland Wagner's total re-thinking of the cycle during the 1950s, which 'de-Teutonized' the picture, thus dispelling the aura of Nazism which had bedevilled Bayreuth for so long; and the centenary production of 1976 by the French director Patrice Chéreau, which identified the essential conflicts inherent in *Der Ring* with the effects on society of the Industrial Revolution. As the cycle was subsequently televised, with sub-titles which enabled many people to understand for the first time exactly what the various characters' lengthy conversations are actually about, Chéreau's vision of the Rhinemaidens as three brassy tarts plying their trade alongside a vast hydro-electric dam, of Wotan as a ruthless capitalist in a Victorian frock coat, of Gunter and Gutrune as a nouveau riche couple in dinner jacket and evening gown, and so on, impressed itself forcefully on probably the largest audience ever to see and hear a single *Ring* cycle. In Bayreuth itself the first run led to rioting almost comparable with that which had greeted the public's first encounter with Stravinsky's *The Rite of Spring* in the Paris of 1913.

Now, the audience's reaction to the Royal Opera's *Rheingold* in 1994 achieved nothing like the proportions of a riot, but to those who know their Covent Garden first night stallholders the eruption of boos from so dignified and normally complacent a quarter of the house rates at least as high on the Richter scale as just another demonstration by the excitable people of Paris. The occasion was remarkable enough for the *Financial Times* to report it in the following terms:

> The rowdy reception given to the Royal Opera's surreal new production of *Das Rheingold* marked a novelty in the history of booing in London. It was unusually virulent, wave on wave of baying anger billowing across the auditorium from the highest reaches, aimed mainly at director Richard Jones and designer Nigel Lowery. It was

---

*Anyone wishing to pursue this subject in detail is strongly advised to seek out the book entitled *Bayreuth*, by Frederic Spotts. See bibliography.

Siegfried (Manfred Jung) and the Rhinemaidens in Act III of Götter-dämmerung, Bayreuth, 1980. Director Patrice Chéreau, set designer Richard Peduzzi, costume designer Jacques Schmidt.

also one of those rare demonstrations that unite all classes, price levels and degrees of operatic expertise.

There were immediate repercussions. Lord Young of Graffham, an ex-minister in Mrs Thatcher's government and at that time the chairman of Cable and Wireless plc, was reported the next day to have threatened the withdrawal of his company's sponsorship – a step which he was subsequently persuaded to reconsider – and the management of the Royal Opera came under violent attack in several sections of the press. According to Alexander Waugh of the *Evening Standard*, 'The management of the Royal Opera House should never have allowed a production onto the Covent Garden stage which even ran the risk of being vilified in this way.' The fires of Waugh's fury had evidently been stoked by the manner in which director and designer 'took their curtain-call bows with implacable, smirky sang-froid', and he added the cogent point that 'there is absolutely no justification for receiving any public funding for a show

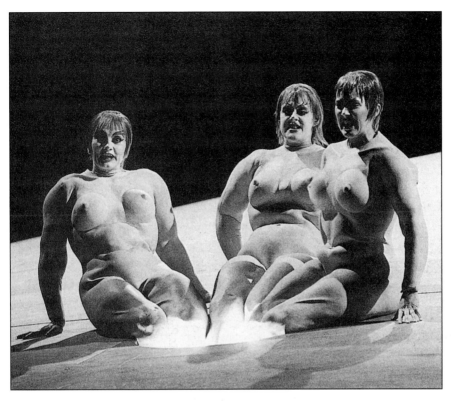

As Alberich puts it, 'How gladly would I slip my arm around one of these slender creatures' ('Wie gern umschlänge der Schlanken eine mein Arm'). Wagner's Rhinemaidens, Covent Garden, 1995.

that is unanimously booed by all those who pay so heavily to go and see it.' In *The Times* that passionate Wagnerian Bernard Levin expressed an opinion with which many members of the audience would surely have sympathized when he wrote of the General Director of the Royal Opera House, 'I cannot even guess why, when Jones showed his first sketches and "ideas" to Jeremy Isaacs, Jeremy didn't throw him down the stairs.'

Far from throwing his chosen director down the stairs, however, Mr Isaacs staunchly defended him against all comers, whether out of loyalty or conviction it would be hard to say. 'This *Ring*, he declared, is one of the boldest things we have ever done. It is not gimmicky . . . and it concentrates on Wagner's text and music'; while Nicholas Payne, who is directly responsible for the operatic side of Covent Garden's activities, said in an interview in the *Financial Times*, '. . . as the abuse rained down at the opening night curtain calls on our brave production team, I

remained convinced that they had created something truly remarkable –
a contemporary response to Wagner's *Ring* which can stand alongside
Wieland Wagner's and Chéreau's in their day.' That was quite a gauntlet
to throw down, and Payne's unwillingness to kowtow to the cash
customer was further emphasized by the words, 'A storm of booing and
some hostile reviews do not automatically signal a good production,
although at least they indicate that our wonderfully quiet audience is
alive.'

I myself attended a later performance at which the production team
was not on show, with the result that not a boo was heard. There were,
however, plenty of people in the audience who felt frustrated by not being
provided with a target for their righteous indignation; they had done the
decent thing by offering sincere applause to the singers and the conductor,
and they were left with a formidable head of steam to release. It was a
production which positively scattered cats amongst the pigeons, and I
scarcely remember a single other instance of opinion amongst the professional critics being so sharply divided.

Prominent amongst the comparatively few champions of the Jones/
Lowery vision were Rodney Milnes of *The Times* and Andrew Porter of
the *Observer* and *Opera Magazine*, two men who are incontestably
experts in their field and, even more importantly, opera-lovers to their
fingertips. To Milnes, who habitually and laudably encourages the novel
if he finds it to be good, the whole cycle was 'provocative yet thoughtful'
and 'deeply satisfying', with 'countless ideas unerringly hitting the mark'.
To Porter, though he openly declared, 'It's not the way I'd produce *The
Ring*', it was refreshing to see something 'often high-spirited and playful'
but not 'unserious'. The visual pictures provided by Lowery and the
lighting designer, Pat Collins, were 'strikingly beautiful', owing much of
their inspiration to Picasso, Klee, Gauguin and Magritte. Porter did
candidly admit, though, that to him one of the chief attractions of the
production was that it was utterly different from the many other *Ring*s
that he had sat through during recent years, brighter than Götz
Friedrich's 'shrouded, subterranean, depressing Berlin *Ring*', livelier than
the 'big, meaningless show' which had been on offer for so long at the
Met, and so on; all of which brings me to the obvious point that there is
one major difference between critics and the ordinary opera-goer for

A deranged dentist or an unemployed hospital porter? John Tomlinson as Wotan in the Jones/Lowery version of Das Rheingold, *Covent Garden, 1964.*

whose edification the reviews are written. The ordinary opera-goer does not receive free tickets for *Ring* cycles wherever in the world they may come popping up. For many people a *Ring* cycle is a luxury to be savoured once a decade if you are lucky; two tickets for each of the four evenings at Covent Garden represents a serious financial commitment, even if you do not aspire to the most exclusive seats; and if you live out of London and have to add to the ticket price such things as rail fares, hotel bills and restaurant meals you may find yourself choosing between a *Ring* cycle and a fortnight's holiday in your favourite Mediterranean resort. Is it reasonable, then, that Covent Garden's first *Ring* for many a long year should be one which the management knows full well will serve as an emetic to many a dedicated Wagnerian? On the other hand should managements permanently play safe by pursuing an Horatian 'auream mediocritatem', or 'golden mean'? It is always easier to ask such questions than to answer them.

To certain of the British critics Jones and Lowery had set up an Aunt Sally of such inviting proportions that there was irresistible fun to be had in taking shies at it. Robert Hartford of *Opera Now*, suspecting that 'the sweetest music to the ears of Richard Jones and Nigel Lowery was the sound of the boos and catcalls', equated them with 'a couple of naughty boys smashing up their toys, refusing to behave, and lying on the floor drumming their heels and screaming "Look at me!" ' The treatment he advocated was that nanny should be sent for 'to sort out the little terrors – a good slapping and off to bed with no banana sandwich ought to do the trick'; while in the *Sunday Times* Hugh Canning, who at the moment has no rival in the art of sticking a witty boot in when he feels the time is ripe, had such a field day that he ended up as recipient of the coveted Critic of the Year award. One of Jones's directorial notions was that the Nibelungs' horde of gold should be converted into female footwear, and presented with a target as inviting as that Canning was quick on the draw:

> My hard-working team of research assistants has revealed to me that the key to understanding Jones's *Rheingold* is the shoe. As all very bright people know, footwear in fairy-tale mythology has psycho-sexual significance: Cinderella's missing glass slipper is a metaphor for lost virginity. By fitting her foot into it when the Prince comes a-courting, she enacts phallic penetration symbolically. By analogy, I am told, the theft of Wellgunde's shoe betokens rape – the despoiling of nature – so the internal logic of the interpretation has Alberich attaining wealth and power by manufacturing gold lamé shoes. For true believers this is evidence of the director's revelatory genius. To others – and who am I to gainsay them? – it will probably seem a load of old cobblers.

Michael Kennedy of the *Sunday Telegraph*, a critic with a well-earned reputation for wisdom and fairness, expressed the hope after *Das Rheingold* that 'Modifications, together with elimination of sheer silliness, could still give this *Ring* credibility', though by the end of *Götterdämmerung* a year later most of his optimism had been dashed. 'The redeeming feature of the production', he wrote, 'is that quite often he [Mr Jones] shows illuminating insight into the characters and tells the story clearly. Unfortunately, he is relentlessly self-indulgent; he cannot resist a joke, good or bad, mostly bad; and he is, in my opinion, traduced by the puerility of Mr Lowery's sets.' Perhaps Robert Henderson of the *Daily Telegraph* summed things up as neatly as anyone when he wrote after the first two operas in the cycle 'It has all added up so far to a production of no real stature. It is thoroughly in keeping with the spirit of the present age in its shallow reliance on instantly arresting but just as instantly disposable ideas.'

Now, I can well imagine any member of the pro-Jones factor leaping gleefully onto this last point and claiming that a production 'in keeping with the spirit of the present age' is precisely what any conscientious director should – no, *must* – be aiming at; and this is a precept which once again leads us into a positive maze of those questions which are easier to ask than to answer. If you live in an age of meretricious values, of crumbling ethics and of visual ugliness are these the qualities which you should seek to reflect in any new production of so universally applicable a work as *Der Ring*, or have you perhaps had a weapon put into your hands which can be used to counteract them with images of higher aspiration? In an era of anti-authoritarianism should you seek to put things straight by extolling the virtue of such concepts as loyalty, patriotism and honesty, or should you echo the drumbeat of the moment and present Wagner's gods, heroes and political manipulators as even more confused and morally compromised a bunch than the composer himself intended? The only answer I can offer is that the proof of the pudding has to be in every individual's eating, and so, having hidden for a while behind the judgements of the professional critics perhaps it is time for me to emerge and declare how the Jones/Lowery *Rheingold* tasted to me.

Let me not beat about the bush – I loathed it. I paid an enormous sum of money for a not very good seat and I left the theatre in a towering rage. Lest anyone should come up with some such irritating cliché as 'Excellent! That was the intention! Odium is better than apathy!', I should perhaps emphasize that I have spent a great deal of my life working in contemporary opera, I have sung in something like fifteen world premieres, I am well acquainted with librettos stuffed with four-letter words, and I do not consider that everything seen in an opera house should be exactly as my great-grandfather would have wished it. What infuriated me at Covent Garden that night was not that I had been brought face to face with innovation, but simply that so much time, so much money and so much talent should have been squandered on such ephemeral childishness.

Too often the motivation seemed not to have risen above the level of 'How is this usually done? Then I shall do the opposite!' 'Most people choose lissom lasses for the Rhinemaidens, do they? Well, I'll have three vast wobbly thunderthighs! Does Donner usually swing a huge great hammer when he gathers up the stormclouds? Well I'll give him a tiny little one!' Let us not mind that the Rhinemaidens' music is sinuously seductive rather than end-of-pier vulgar; what does it matter if at the climax of the thunderstorm music Wagner has written 'Man hört Donners Hammerschlag schwer auf den Felsenstein fallen', 'The heavy blow of Donner's hammer is heard falling on the rocky crag'? (I would not have backed the hammer this poor Donner was swinging to make much of an impression on a two-inch nail, let alone a rocky crag.) Froh could have won prizes as the most gormless yob on the Costa Brava, Freia was a retarded adolescent emotionally inseparable from her truly dreadful little doll, and as for Wotan, some took him for a deranged dentist, clad as he was in a grubby white medical overall, and others for an unemployed hospital porter. The image which he called most strongly to my mind was that of Boris Karloff as the sinister psychiatrist in *The Secret Life of Walter Mitty* – 'an icicle inserted into the brain melts, leaving no trace!' – and his general air of dottiness was underlined by his spear having turned into a measuring pole with a one-way street sign stuck on the end.

Imagery such as this was one of the principal irritants of the production, because by the time you have worked out what on earth this ludicrous prop is supposed to signify – I assumed it was an indication that the gods were heading into a cul-de-sac, which, funnily enough, Wagner makes evident anyway in his own somewhat subtler manner – quite a lot of rather nice music has come and gone. I cannot claim to have read all the references quite that quickly, either. The model aeroplane which flew slowly across the sky baffled me completely – none of the gods took any notice of it, so I supposed that Valhalla, like Kew Gardens, just happened to be on the regular flightpath – but the *ne plus ultra* of dottiness was surely the scene in which the omniscient earth goddess Erda makes her vital intervention. Wagner calls for her to emerge in a shaft of 'bluish light' from a cleft in the rocks, and as her normal residence is somewhere down in the globe's core even those directors who do not favour bluish lights normally go along with the Master's intentions to the extent of bringing her up through a trapdoor of some sort. Not so Mr Jones. He had the singing Erda tucked away invisibly in the wings, while a scene of such peculiarity unfolded on the stage that her all-important messages of doom fell on a houseful of deaf ears. A slinky young lady in a shimmering ballgown, evidently mistaking Wagner's 'open space on the mountain height' for the palm court of her favourite seaside hotel, wandered in for a *thé-dansant*, and selected Wotan as her partner. Now, I yield to no one in my admiration for Covent Garden's Wotan, John Tomlinson. He is a splendid singer, a powerful stage performer and a delightful man, but I never thought that the day would come when I would pay money to watch him dance. Several of the critics referred to him as having joined the mysterious lady in a waltz; this may have been the trouble, as the tempo of Erda's monologue is an unusually stately 4:4.

All in all I was left in entire agreement with Hugh Canning when he summed up in the following terms – 'This arcane "commentary" will, I suspect, be accessible only to a coterie of the director's best friends, the opera house management, the most dazzlingly brilliant critics and Jones's analyst.' It was, after all, 'Kinder, schafft Neues' that Wagner said; he did not say 'Kinder, schafft Blödes' – 'Children, create something daft.'

When the Glyndebourne public booed Deborah Warner's modern-dress production of *Don Giovanni*, I fancy that that was not so much prompted by anger, as by a feeling of betrayal – 'this kind of thing may be considered clever in other places, but we come here to avoid it.' I personally would not rate the evening particularly highly amongst *Don Giovannis* that I have known, because it seemed to me that Miss Warner had thrown out far too many babies with the bathwater, but I suspect that there was a feeling amongst some of the management (though definitely not all) that it would do no harm if, along with the new and enlarged theatre, production values should also emerge as being susceptible to the occasional wind of change. Glyndebourne had come to represent in many people's eyes a temple of that sadly abused word 'élitism'; perhaps now that it was no longer quite so difficult to acquire tickets, some of them at perfectly reasonable prices, iconoclasm should briefly take its place. The production did undeniably achieve something of a *succès de scandale*, and, as in all such cases, the sincerity of the audience's reactions became difficult to assess. People visiting the later performances had to make a decision – do we throw in our lot with the protesters or the progressives? Indifference was no longer an option.

Don Giovanni is another of those pieces like *Der Ring*, or indeed most of Shakespeare's plays, which have so much to offer to the enquiring mind that you can find in them almost anything you are looking for. You can make a case for Giovanni the handsome swashbuckler whose charm outweighs his wickedness; you can make a case for Giovanni the thwarted idealist, eternally seeking the perfect woman and never finding her; people have even tried to make a case for Giovanni the closet homosexual whose whole life is a lie and who is bent on self-destruction. Miss Warner chose to opt for a modern-style layabout with a penchant for changing his shirts, and she made him work well enough; at least he was an immense improvement on the Don Giovanni devised some years earlier by Ruth Berghaus for the Welsh National Opera, the clue to whose sexuality, so a member of the cast reliably informed me, lay in his feet. (Any relation to Mr Jones's Alberich?) This necessitated the stage being littered with odd socks, and oddity was indeed the keynote of the evening. In Miss Warner's case there was a lot of fun to be had with Elvira as an 'if this is Thursday it must be Seville' kind of tourist, and although the working-class members of the cast tended to be indistinguishable from the toffs, and did not appear on their disco outing quite to have got their minds around the minuet, the pace was fast and some of the relationships were handled with challenging originality.

It was of course interesting to be given a woman's view of the arch-seducer. Deborah Warner wrote in a programme note 'we are ravished and find that we can't reject him'; while in the case of Ruth Berghaus we were clearly being invited to share her personal stream of consciousness when confronted with the figure of the Don, rather than any literal interpretation of the text. My main problem lay, as it so often does with 'controversial' productions, in the frequency with which what I was looking at and what I was listening to belonged to different realms of the imagination. To give but one obvious example, there are few scenes in opera more marvellously expressed in musical terms than the arrival of the statue at Don Giovanni's supper table. Leporello, gibbering with fear, announces the approach of the 'man of stone' and gives a graphic imitation of his unearthly footfall. In the orchestra we hear a series of mighty knocks on the door, Don Giovanni opens up, a row of spine-tingling fortissimo chords rings out – and, at Glyndebourne, in walked a middle-aged man in a dinner jacket. As roughly forty per cent of the audience, myself included, consisted of middle-aged men in dinner jackets (admittedly unbespattered with blood) perhaps we should have felt flattered that it was the likes of us who gave the bounder his come-uppance; I could not help feeling, though, that Mozart had been short-changed.

To what extent is it legitimate to tamper with a composer's intentions in this way? This was a question which I found myself mulling over again and again during another more recent 'controversial' production, that of Hindemith's *Mathis der Maler* at Covent Garden directed by Peter Sellars. Hindemith, acting as his own librettist, set this piece very specifically during the Peasants' Revolt in Germany, 1524–5, with the contemporary painter, Matthias Grünewald, creator of the famous Isenheim altarpiece, as his protagonist. The theme, very broadly, is the dilemma of the artist during a period of political intolerance and military upheaval. It was an expression of Hindemith's own predicament in Nazi Germany, and Sellars, choosing to equate Hitlerism with the contemporary political scene in the United States – as he put it in an interview, 'an extreme right-wing movement' was 'wreaking havoc on social legislation' – decided to set the piece in the California of today.

Now, back in the 1930s and '40s there were many people who would have been greatly relieved if Hitler had contented himself with 'wreaking havoc on social legislation'; indeed, several million people might have remained alive who were not allowed to do so, but this is not the place to cross swords with Mr Sellars's view of political history. The salient point, or so it seems to me, is whether or not it is legitimate to hijack a major work of art, particularly one which is unfamiliar to the public in its original form, and re-conceive it as a vehicle for one's own beliefs, however passionately they may be held. For a hijacking is what this was, and a very thorough one. The theatre programme contained Sellars's own synopsis of the action, and aspects of the original which did not fit into his concept had vanished without trace. There was no mention, for instance, of the fact that the emotional kernel of the piece, Tableau VI, consists of a vision in which Mathis himself is transformed into the figure of St Anthony as depicted in his own altarpiece – it would not, of course, be possible for Sellars's modern Mathis to have created such a work. The story was told in up-to-date jargon – the Prefect's soldiers become the 'riot police', the servants who murder Count Helfenstein are 'people who have spent every day of their lives in service-sector jobs' and so on – and it is very neatly done; but will people seeing the piece for the first time have gone home believing that this was *Hindemith's* creation? I imagine that I was one of the few people in the audience who had already experienced the work in a traditional production, in Vienna in 1958, so that I at least could make a mental comparison.

I will pass over the sheer boredom of sitting through scene after scene in the Sellars version in which extras in dingy battle fatigues scampered around the stage waving pistols in the air and trying to look alarming – have we not had enough of that by now? The main pity of it was that so many moments of genuine theatrical impact were tossed into the rubbish bin. There is, for instance, a tiny but memorable role for Count Helfenstein's Piper, who personifies a particularly terrifying aspect of mob violence. Clearly he has spent much of his time at his master's elbow, but when his master is safely blindfolded, bound and gagged it is he – the musician, if you please! – who turns the nastiest of all. 'Oft musste ich stehen bei dir und zu Tanz und Tafel pfeifen,' he sings, accompanying the words with vicious kicks – 'Many is the time that I have stood at your side and played while you danced and you ate; now I'll play you to your doom.' With his final words, a grisly 'Kommt zum Tanz', 'Come to the dance', he picks up his fiddle, strikes up a tune, and accompanies the Count as he is carried off to be lynched. Pre-echoes of the ghastly musical rituals in the Nazi death camps? Well, Sellars's musician did not have a fiddle, he had a gun. He poked it in the Count's ribs, and, surprise surprise, the theatrical effect was nil.

How is it that so much which is supposed to be new and shocking merely ends up being drearily predictable? Later in this scene the singer playing the part of the Piper was prominently placed on the top of a wall.

'Ah!' I thought, 'the only reason he can possibly be standing up there is so that somebody can shoot him,' and, as with Richard Jones's toy aeroplane, my attention was taken right away from anything significant which was going on (the music, for instance), until, a couple of minutes later, the Piper duly crumpled and fell. This, of course, was a peccadillo, but something which occurred later served to crystallize my dislike of this endlessly busy style of production. One of the most beautiful passages in the entire opera occurs as Mathis lulls the lost orphan Regina to sleep with poetically expressed visions of the three angels to which she has just referred in an old folk song. Alan Titus in the role of Mathis was giving a superb performance, his voice, which had rung out during the many dramatic outbursts with a marvellously heroic timbre, now modulated to a deeply moving mezza voce. All that we needed on stage was total stillness, but what did we get? Behind the singer three meaningless television monitors flashed and blinked, while large scarlet surtitles scurried across the tilted panels of a glass-walled skyscraper. (The ordinary surtitles were in their usual place.) At Titus's feet a tall, sinuous extra, clearly symbolizing something, though please do not ask me what, lay writhing on the floor, and weaving his arms around in weird, indecipherable circles. It brought to my mind the one unforgivable offence committed by Deborah Warner at Glyndebourne, who, during Don Ottavio's exquisite 'Dalla sua pace', had a huge false stage rise slowly from floor to ceiling, riveting the audience's attention as it went.

It struck me as ironical that in another part of the interview which I have already quoted Sellars said 'The work does not need a big *Konzept*; I think the content speaks for itself.' Why, then, did he not allow it to do so? Could we really not have built our own mental bridges between the dark deeds of the sixteenth century, those of Hindemith's day, and the many appalling things that still go on in the modern world? I can assure Mr Sellars that in the Vienna of 1958 the message did not pass us by. In any case there were even fewer approving voices in the press for the Covent Garden *Mathis* than there had been for *Der Ring* – Rodney Milnes was moved to write in *The Times*, 'When Sellars gets something wrong he gets it wrong in *spades*' – and I could not help wondering (I went to one of the last performances) whether the three seats empty at my side and the entire row empty at my back would not have had satisfied opera-lovers sitting in them had the production been entrusted to a more conventional director.*

Which brings me back to the old question of the operatic pecking order. Members of the public ask with increasing frequency who is to blame for productions which they so much dislike, and who would be in a position to restore the balance? Could Bernard Haitink not have put his foot down about *Der Ring*? Why did the management choose Jones and Sellars when they must have known what they would get? And, most frequently of all (a question which was also posed by Bernard Levin in his article in *The Times*), why do the leading singers not rebel?

The answer as far as managements are concerned is that when they hire a Jones or a Sellars they are indeed aware of what they are getting, and so one has to conclude that if they know the result will not be to the public's liking they must feel that it will be to the public's good. As far as conductors are concerned it is difficult, unless, like James Levine at the Met, they are in virtually sole charge of the house's artistic policy, to find the right moment for saying 'Enough is enough', because early on in the proceedings the company will have sunk a considerable sum of money in the preparations. Once sets are built and costumes are made there can really be no turning back, though of course in matters of superficial detail it should still be possible for a conductor who possesses the necessary authority to stretch out a restraining hand. During a production of *Salome* a few years back, directed by the Frenchman André Engel, I was required, in the role of Herod, to display my nervousness before the dance of the seven veils by puffing at a cigarette, lit with a petrol lighter. The main conductor of the production, a man of international stature, was incensed by this anachronism and refused to allow it; so Engel made the concession that when that conductor was on the podium I would not light up, but when his assistant was in charge I would.

Those members of the press and public who look to the singers for their salvation are, by and large, in for a disappointment too. I spoke to

---

*Since this chapter was written, the Richard Jones *Götterdämmerung* has been revived for the first time, and though it is a piece which normally causes a run on the box office, the Royal Opera was reduced to offering two tickets for the price of one.

several members of the *Mathis* cast and so great was their respect for
Sellars, not to mention the personal affection engendered by the sheer
niceness of the man, that criticisms of the production were not favourably
received. They had thoroughly enjoyed the process of working with him
and they had been inspired both by his seriousness of purpose and by his
sharpness of mind. The critics' hostility (none of it directed against the
singers) merely served to increase their feelings of protectiveness towards
Sellars and all that he stood for.

I can understand this. Another director with a talent for attracting
odium is Sellars's compatriot David Alden, but a friendlier person would
be hard to imagine, and if you are in one of his productions it would be
difficult to take against him. When I appeared in an Alden version of
Weill's *Mahagonny* some years ago I had only the sketchiest notion of

*The German
Peasants' Revolt
of 1524–5.
Mathis der
Maler, Covent
Garden, 1995.*

why we were all doing the things that he dreamt up for us. The performance opened with Felicity Palmer giving a hilariously improvised TV-style cooking demonstration in a kitchen which subsequently exploded – that was before the music had even begun – and that splendid tenor Alexander Oliver stopped the show at one point by walking across the stage on a barrel, something he had learnt to do as a child, his father having kept a pub in Bridge of Allan. One of the sets consisted of an enormous pile of old shoes (here we go again!), and I spent the final scene as a corpse in a body bag, sticking my head out whenever it was my turn to sing. When asked what it was all about David would give a happy smile and some such reply as 'I think it looks rather nice.' What the public thought, I could never quite make out.

As for Bernard Levin's appeal to John Tomlinson that he should use his position as *the* Wotan of the moment to make a stand against 'slovenly and contemptuously mounted' *Ring* cycles – when he went to the Covent Garden *Rheingold* he had just sat through an equally exasperating version in Bayreuth, also featuring John Tomlinson – here again disappointment awaits. When Tomlinson was interviewed at a meeting of the Wagner Society in London he caused consternation by saying that he welcomed a production such as Jones's because it gave him an opportunity to act 'instead of just standing around looking godlike'. I can imagine that if you travel the world from one *Ring* cycle to another a change might occasionally be as good as a rest, but if Tomlinson is condemned to be a zany Wotan wherever he appears will he, I wonder, ever be given the chance to rank alongside the truly godlike Hans Hotter? In the words of the critic Peter Conrad, interviewing Richard Jones in the *Observer*, 'For Jones, the theatre's purpose is the unleashing of irrationality', and a singer cannot afford to be permanently assigned to the madhouse.

Although the singers engaged for the Covent Garden cycle were questioned in advance about their willingness to submit to the Jones/Lowery concept, one of them, the tenor Robert Tear, emerged from the experience unconvinced. He shed some interesting light on the rehearsal period by keeping a diary and publishing it as part of a book entitled *Singer Beware*. Describing the first costume which was served up to him as having 'the impact of an old and hairy blancmange', Tear flatly refused to wear it; nor does he appear to have been deeply impressed by the concept that he

A style which it would be hard to envisage on any operatic stage in the 1990s. Wagner's 'üppigste Blumenpracht' (lavish abundance of flowers) in Act II of Parsifal, *as envisaged by Tom Mostyn (1864-1930).*

The mammoth set by Stefanos Lazaridis for David Pountney's production of Nabucco, *Bregenz, 1993. Additional lighting effects by Jove the Thunderer.*

Even the seductive wiles of the love goddess can lose their
appeal. Wagner's Tannhäuser tires of life on the Venusberg.
(Willy Pogany, 1911.)

A scene from the BBC TV production of Britten's Owen Wingrave, *with Janet Baker, Peter Pears, Benjamin Luxon and Jennifer Vyvyan (1970).*

'La donna è mobile' on the jukebox. David Rendall as the Duke in one of the many revivals of Jonathan Miller's Mafia Rigoletto. *English National Opera, first produced in 1982.*

*Diabolical goings-on. Anne-Marie Owens as the Witch
and the author as the Devil in David Pountney's
production of Rimsky-Korsakov's* Christmas Eve,
English National Opera, 1990.

Count Boni limbers up with the girls of the Budapest Orpheum Cabaret Theatre. Roger Lemke in the author's production of Kálmán's Die Csárdásfürstin for the Australian Opera, 1990.

The lost jewel of European theatres, La Fenice in Venice. From a painting by Andras Kaldor.

*La Scala, Milan. 'As the theatre originally fronted onto a narrow
street not too much trouble was taken with a façade which no
one would be able to admire from a distance.'*

The opera house of Santa Fe, which makes stunning use of the terrain and night skies of New Mexico.

The Alice Busch Memorial Theatre on the shore of Lake Otsego in upstate New York, home of the Glimmerglass Opera Festival.

'A modern miracle'. The auditorium of the new opera house at Glyndebourne.

All this, and opera too. Glyndebourne, 11 November 1993.

should play Loge as 'a shagged out Philip Marlowe'. All of this doubtless contributed to Tear's distinctly *dégagé* aura during the performance; every time he turned away from the audience I expected to see a large notice pinned to his back saying 'Don't blame me!' One of the most illuminating passages in his book is a description of the moment when Bernard Haitink realized for the first time quite what he had let himself in for: 'Sensitive, he [Haitink] is a fine man who feels music finely and within *its* intellectual parabola. So when BH is faced with RJ the concepts are so different, the solipsism so grotesque that only tears or what passed for them can result. Such I saw today.'*

This was a classic case, though, of the tears coming too late. If BH had only realized a few months earlier quite what RJ had up his sleeve might things have ended differently? Those who wish to rule the roost do need to be crowing as dawn breaks.

During recent years audiences on the continent of Europe have had at least as much cause to vent their fury on idiosyncratic directors as have those in Britain; in the United States, however, there have been remarkably few outbursts of this sort. Peter Sellars to a great extent made his name with a startlingly quirky Mozartian trilogy in the mid-1980s – *Così* set in a neon-lit diner, *Don Giovanni* amongst drug dealers on the Los Angeles freeway, and *Figaro* in a New York apartment block – but these productions started life as part of the Pepsico Summerfare in the village of Purchase, in New York State, which is by its very nature an avant-garde affair, with not too many tuxedos to be seen on first nights. They subsequently reached a wider audience on television, and many people found the *Così*, in particular, vastly entertaining. In any case, opera on television is a totally different matter from opera on stage; if viewers dislike what they see they do not storm and rage, they merely switch it off.

Eruptions at the Met have been few and far between. In the 1980s Peter Hall's *Macbeth* and Jean-Pierre Ponnelle's *Fliegende Holländer* both brought blood to the boil, but it was Francesca Zambello, not regarded

---

*The general public was treated to a glimpse of Haitink's gloom during the television documentary entitled *The House* (see pp. 321–3). For all their subsequent bold words the rest of the management appeared equally appalled by what they had let themselves in for.

by Europeans as any kind of an *enfant terrible*, who really got onto the wrong side of the patrons with her weird new look at *Lucia di Lammermoor* in 1992. In the words of Peter G. Davis in the *New York Weekly*, 'Metropolitan opera audiences tend to be a docile lot these days, and displays of strong emotion, positive or negative, are rare. What a surprise, then, to hear the great howl of rage that greeted *Lucia* on opening night.' During the course of the evening there had been one compensating howl of mirth as well, when that rather nebulous figure Arturo Bucklaw, whose main *raison d'être* is to be murdered offstage by Lucia, was given an unusually tremendous entrance. He rose on a pedestal from beneath the stage, arrayed in a fantastic jewel-encrusted outfit, reminding *The New Yorker*'s critic of the Ingres portrait of Napoleon in coronation robes, and Peter G. Davis of the Bernini statue of the Emperor Constantine. It was bad luck on the singer, Paul Groves, that Zambello should have decided to leave Lucia lying mid-stage, where she had fallen

Salvador Dali's set design for the notorious Peter Brook production of Salome, Covent Garden, 1949.

The Brook/Dali Salome,
Covent Garden, 1949.
Ljuba Welitsch insisted on
wearing her own dress.

at the end of the previous scene, because once Arturo has finished his opening solo his next utterance is 'Dov'è Lucia?', 'Where is Lucia?' The words which Davis used in his review must have been on most of the audience's lips – 'At your feet, dummy!'

There is, however, nothing new under the sun, and controversy has long been a familiar ingredient in the world of opera. The first director-inspired scandal to hit London during my opera-going lifetime was the Peter Brook production of *Salome* at Covent Garden back in 1949, with Salvador Dali as the designer. The singers were accoutred in such astonishing outfits that they could scarcely move, and Ljuba Welitsch in the title-role put her foot down. Years later she described the experience to me: 'It was crazy performance. I could not wear what Dali make me, so I say to Mr Webster [general manager of the Royal Opera] – he was very kind, poor fellow – I have to wear my own dress please. So I had my own dress.' Karl Rankl, the musical director of the company, refused to take a bow although he himself had been conducting, and the upshot of it all was that Brook resigned from his position as director of productions.

Even in those distant days the patience of certain critics was evidently near snapping point. 'How much longer', asked Ernest Newman in the *Sunday Times*, 'will the London opera public tolerate performances and productions that are for the most part an affront to their intelligence? How long, O Lord, how long .. ?'; though it was to be a number of years yet before 'loony' productions proliferated into an epidemic. Another British critic who set his cap unremittingly against what he saw as illegitimate interference with the composer's intentions was Desmond Shawe-Taylor, and I remember one of his *cris de coeur* emerging, thanks to a minor editorial mishap, in an even more trenchant form than he had intended. Reviewing a production of *Il trovatore* directed by the Rumanian Andrei Serban for Opera North in 1983–4, Shawe-Taylor intended to open with the sentence 'Courageously resisting the temptation to set the action in Jane Austen's Bath, Serban has settled for a disused Spanish railway siding.' This elegantly turned piece of sarcasm, which had evidently been dictated over the telephone, acquired an additional piquancy, however, when 'Jane Austen's Bath' was presented to the readers as 'Jane Austen's bath'.

Long before the Second World War techniques for the mounting of opera were being subjected to intense rethinking, and several of the productions seen at Berlin's Kroll Opera under Otto Klemperer in the years immediately before the coming of the Nazis would, by all accounts, still raise conservative eyebrows today. In the immediate post-war years one of the most influential of directors was Walter Felsenstein of the Komische Oper in East Berlin. The clue to his approach was his insistence on the individual singers immersing themselves in the roles that they were playing by drawing deeply on their own personal and psychological experiences, a process which was facilitated by the unusually long rehearsal periods available to him under the communist regime, and which inevitably introduced a strong element of modernity into the style of performance. Felsenstein's principal assistants, Götz Friedrich and Joachim Herz, created something of a stir when they started working in the West, as did Harry Kupfer, whose *Fidelio*, staged by the Welsh

National Opera in 1981, intrigued some opera-goers and outraged others by including in its final scene such unexpected soul-mates for Leonore as the freedom-fighter Che Guevara. Allied to Felsenstein's principles of *Musiktheater* these three had also drunk deep of the Brechtian precepts of ideological involvement and of *Verfremdungseffekt*, or 'alienation', whereby the stage is not seen as a place for the attempted creation of would-be reality, but as an 'empty space' for the presentation of provocative ideas. Those who complain that what they are principally looking for in an opera production is *Werktreue*, or loyalty to the original work, will be asked 'Who is being more loyal to the work, the director who keeps the piece exactly as it has always been, although the audience of today is psychologically, intellectually, socially and politically a million miles removed from the audience of Mozart's, Verdi's or Wagner's day; or the director who discovers within the work the clues to its contemporary relevance?'

The so-called 'tyranny of the director' has largely come about, or so it seems to me, because for many years contemporary operatic composers, with one or two honourable exceptions, have failed to produce new works which have found favour with the public, whereas up until the death of Puccini the composers had been the very people who, by writing new operas which the average opera-goer wanted to see, constantly provided that element of novelty which any art form must enjoy if it is to be preserved from stagnation. Thus it has come about that in recent years a corpus of forty or fifty operas has formed something which never used to exist, known as 'the standard repertoire'. There have been valuable by-products of this phenomenon – a re-examination of operas from long ago, for instance, and a greater willingness to explore such unfamiliar areas as the Slav repertoire – but from it also stems, like it or not, the fact that in the quest for life-giving innovation directors have gained the upper hand. No one objects to modern methods of production being applied to new pieces – that shatters no long-cherished images – but if the new pieces do not exist directors find themselves faced with a dilemma when entrusted with one of the popular favourites. A modern director who presents *La bohème* as it has always been will add no pearl to his crown; if, however, he determines to put his own individual stamp on it by turning it, say, into a blatantly ideological appeal for better social conditions amongst the student population, he will achieve the almost impossible and turn a large section of the public away from *La bohème*. Furthermore, to revert to my previous theme of the pecking order, in the current state of affairs it is inevitable that the impact of the director on the public will far outweigh that of the conductor. It takes a connoisseur to spot that a conductor is injecting fresh ideas into the musical interpretation; when the curtain goes up on *Faust* and you find that you are in a multi-storey car park the element of innovation is not so hard to detect.

There are, of course, different degrees of radicality. As it happens, I made my own professional debut in what was probably one of the earliest examples of a modern-dress *Bohème*, with the Vienna Kammeroper in 1959. Those were the days when there was not much money washing around in Vienna, and the directorial concept was less ideological than economic; if we all wore our own street clothes, for which we were paid a small sum per performance, it would be cheaper for the company than hiring costumes. It could perhaps be said that I provided my own small *Verfremdungseffekt*, in that the overcoat which I wore as the French student Rodolfo was a relic of my days in the British army. The vital presence of the candle in Act I was an anachronism which bothered no one – clearly neither Mimì nor Rodolfo had paid their electricity bills, so they had been cut off – but it is often the purely practical inconsistencies of modernized productions which seem to irritate the public most. I remember an irate opera-goer, after a performance of *Madam Butterfly* which the director had updated in order to emphasize the politically incorrect nature of Pinkerton (colonialist, racist, male chauvinist and so on), complaining bitterly to me that the whole thing was absurd because if it were really going on in the 1990s Butterfly would simply have sent Pinkerton a fax saying 'Baby on the way – send cash.' He had a point; how legitimate is it for a director to use only those aspects of an updating which happen to suit him? In fact the director on that occasion had gone one further by actually inventing a certain subtly effective little touch to assist his argument. At the point in Act I when Pinkerton, shortly before his 'wedding' to the Japanese geisha, drinks a toast to the day of his marriage to 'a real wife in America', he took a photograph out of his pocket and kissed it, indicating a whole new area of caddishness; clearly he already had a trusting fiancée back home, a notion which, I feel sure, had never occurred either to the librettists or the composer. Pinkerton is, of course, an easy target for those directors who wish to display their own caring credentials, but I personally feel that it would be more original by now to take a look at *Madam Butterfly* from a less obvious point of view. How about Pinkerton as nothing worse than a carefree young man who is doing exactly what anyone else would have done at the time in order to make a sojourn in Nagasaki more tolerable, but who has had the misfortune to land himself with the one geisha in Japan who stubbornly ignores the advice of her own countrymen and refuses to stick to the accepted rules of her profession?

Occasionally a radical updating will catch the public's imagination, and there is no doubt that Jonathan Miller's famous *Rigoletto*, which has been revived more often than any other production in the history of the English National Opera, not only delighted many of the most conservative opera-goers, but also brought new enthusiasts into the house. He set it amongst the New York *mafiosi* of the 1950s – it was presumably a coincidence that the previous year, 1981, Jean-Claude Audray had directed a production in Basle which transferred the action to Chicago in the time of Al Capone – and such iconoclastic images as 'La donna è mobile' played on a jukebox made an indelible impression. As in the Deborah Warner *Don Giovanni* there was a mild hiccup in credibility when 'the Dook's' henchmen were obliged to indulge in some courtly dancing, but, as with Mimì's candle, it did not seem to matter. Certain patrons of the English National Opera tended to be less enthusiastic about some of the updatings masterminded by the most controversial of the British directors, David Pountney, during his years of office as the company's director of productions. His opponents will remind one of a *Traviata* in which Violetta appeared to be giving her party in a cornfield, or of a *Macbeth* in which her ladyship's somnambulism was restricted to the confines of a large bed protruding from a wall some twenty feet above the stage. To my mind, however, it is significant that Pountney's controversial productions have usually been those devoted to operas in the standard repertoire. When he is dealing with a piece which is more or less unfamiliar to the public, such as Kurt Weill's *Street Scene* or the various operas in his triumphant Janáček cycle – originally co-productions for Scottish Opera and the Welsh National Opera, several of them still being successfully revived after more than a dozen years – he is (with certain exceptions such as his celebrated *Rusalka*) content to adopt a more traditional approach. The production will always be illuminated by his inventive theatrical imagination but it is unlikely to contain anything which could be described as alienation. Above all – and here he differs from several of those directors whose previous experience has been in the straight theatre – he is always deeply respectful of the music. To quote his own words, 'Contradiction is inherent in opera. Music is a quasi-permanent language, whereas what appears on the stage is a creature of fashion. It's ephemeral, it's made of canvas and bits of wood and it falls to bits after ten years.'

In writing about David Pountney, however, I have to confess to a degree of personal bias, because if he had not requested me for his production of Rimsky-Korsakov's *Christmas Eve* with the English National Opera in 1988 I would have been deprived of the single most memorable remark made in my hearing during the entire course of my career. My role was that of the Devil. I was a seedy, out-at-the-elbow, provincial sort of Devil, as befits one in a fairy-tale about life in a remote Russian village, but it allowed me to fulfil a hitherto frustrated ambition – like Peter Pan I spent much of the evening flying through the air. This is achieved, I discovered, by wearing under the costume a complex and exceedingly uncomfortable harness, onto which two ropes are hooked, one of which determines your height above the ground and the other the speed and direction of your flight. I was surprised to find that this left me no control whatsoever over my movements – you go where the ropemen send you, and that is that. The whole thing is masterminded by specialists in the business, but the actual operation of the ropes is often entrusted to members of the resident stage staff, who supposedly receive special instruction in what is to be done, and upon whom you depend, literally, for your survival. Now, this particular opera opened, once the overture was through, with a witch (the admirable Anne-Marie Owens) flying in from stage left, followed by me flying in from stage right, and the moment I had been deposited on the steeple of a toy-town church, a space roughly the size of an average dinner plate, I had to open my mouth and start singing; it called, in other words, for immaculate precision and split-second timing on the part of my ropemen. At the public dress rehearsal I was, as singers always are, somewhat nervous. I had already been in the theatre for at least two hours, being strapped in, dressed and made-up, and during the whole of the lengthy overture I had had to stand stock-still on my launching-pad waiting for the moment of no return when the stage manager would give the signal 'Go!'. My feelings may perhaps be imagined when, seconds before this was due, out of the darkness where the ropemen stood came the unforgettable words ''Ere, mate, which f***in' rope do I pull to get 'im up?'

Ah, the joy of opera!

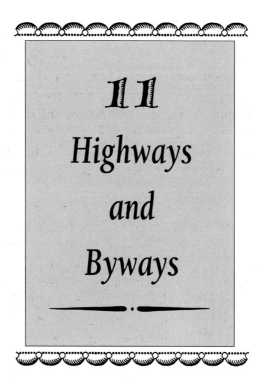

11
Highways
and
Byways

I used to know a German gentleman, now no longer with us, whose passion was the collecting of operatic venues. He had long ago attended performances in every opera house in Europe, I doubt if there were many which had evaded him in North or South America, Australia had been exhaustively covered, so had the Far East, and he was able to concentrate on out of the way festivals and performances which, for one reason or another, were being mounted where opera had never set foot before. I once found myself singing Herod in Joachim Herz's production of *Salome* in a circus big top in Sheffield – the company, Opera North, was contracted to appear in the city but no theatre was available – and I should have guessed: when the performance was over, round to my dressing-room came Herr Schulz.

Although I have never had either the time or the money to emulate his peregrinations, my own career has led me along many of the world's operatic highways and byways, and I do agree with Herr Schulz that one of the most attractive aspects of opera is the fascinating variety of venues in which it is nowadays performed – extending as they do from the historic opera houses of the world via classical Greek and Roman amphitheatres to cunningly devised buildings on the shores of American lakes, and makeshift auditoria erected in the gardens of British stately homes. Each makes its own individual contribution to that special sense of occasion which, to most modern enthusiasts, is so much part of a visit to the opera.

I emphasize the word 'modern', because it was not ever thus; back in 1732 Voltaire was indulging in only mild hyperbole when he wrote, 'The Opéra is nothing but a public gathering place, where we assemble on certain days without precisely knowing why.' Many an old engraving bears him out, with members of the audience clearly seen to be wandering around the auditorium during the performance, or lounging and chatting with their backs to the stage; even as late as the mid-nineteenth century it was not unusual for gentlemen in the semi-seated area which we now call the stalls still to be wearing their exceedingly tall top hats.

When Wagner, in 1876, insisted on darkness in the auditorium of his newly built Festspielhaus in Bayreuth, thereby obliging the audience to concentrate on the performance, it was regarded as a revolutionary measure, welcomed in some quarters and decried in others. Twenty years later those two dedicated artistic disciplinarians Gustav Mahler and Arturo Toscanini were to be found fighting a similar battle, with the main thrust of their campaign directed towards the discouragement of late-comers; wandering in and out of performances was a well-established tradition, and in Vienna the Emperor Franz Joseph reacted to Mahler's insistence that the public should arrive on time and sit in the dark by remarking 'But surely the theatre is supposed to be enjoyable.'* Sir Thomas Beecham still had a fight on his hands at Covent Garden as late as 1934, when a mem-

---

*Franz Joseph made no bones about his lukewarm attitude towards 'serious' music, and once wrote to his mistress, the actress Katherina Schratt, 'I go to the opera as a sacrifice for my country. After all, I function only as an advertisement for the sale of tickets.'

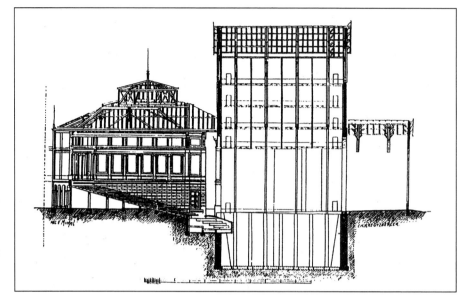

ber of the House of Commons asked a parliamentary question about the new regulation that late-comers should not be allowed into the auditorium until the first interval, describing it as being, in his opinion, 'dangerous'.

The opera houses with which Mahler, Toscanini and Beecham were, between them, most closely associated were the Vienna Hofoper, the Teatro La Scala, the Metropolitan Opera, New York and the Royal Opera, Covent Garden, and although one of these institutions is nowadays newly housed and another has changed its name they remain, I would guess, at or near the top of anyone's list of Great Opera Houses. The Vienna Opera, indeed, is far more than a mere theatre for the performance of opera and ballet; both geographically and in terms of national pride it is the city's focal point. Whatever Franz Joseph's personal feelings, when he decided to have the old city walls dismantled and replaced by the sweeping new boulevard known as the Ringstrasse, he recognized that of all the magnificent buildings which were to be raised as emblems of the Habsburg Empire's greatness – the new Parliament, the Rathaus, the University, and so forth – the most vital of all would be a new opera house. When building began it was, regrettably, typical of Vienna that the

'I go to the opera as a sacrifice for my country.' Emperor Franz Joseph at the time of his sixtieth jubilee.

intensity of the public's interest soon spilt over into criticism and intriguing of such viciousness that one of the two architects, August von Siccardsburg, hanged himself before the building could be completed, and his colleague, Eduard van der Null, died only a couple of months later – officially as the result of an operation, but basically, as most people felt, because he had lost the will to struggle on. Be that as it may, with its two creators safely in their graves the new opera house was promptly hailed as a triumphant achievement, and under a series of outstanding directors, with Mahler's tenure of office (1897–1907) the most distinguished of all, it established itself as one of the great musical institutions of Europe.

Twice during the twentieth century the Viennese have given remarkable proof of the importance which they attach to the well-being of their Opera. At the end of the First World War the city was reduced to a sad shadow of its former self; the capital of a small republic instead of a far-flung empire, it suffered from shortages of every kind – food, fuel and clothing – and the value of its currency plummeted. These are not normally the circumstances in which people will countenance the expenditure of vast sums of public money on opera, yet from 1919 onwards the Vienna Opera – now no longer the Royal and Imperial

The new Vienna Hofoper (Court Opera), 1869.

Court Opera but the rather plainer-sounding State Opera – enjoyed one of its many periods of glory; with Richard Strauss and Franz Schalk as its directors, and with such stars in the company as Maria Jeritza, Lotte Lehmann, Elisabeth Schumann, Alfred Piccaver and Richard Mayr, to name but a few, it established itself as the one national institution which could still look anyone in the eye. Politics unfortunately decreed that this state of affairs should not last. The coming of the Nazis signalled the end of the old ensemble, with half the most famous stars seeking asylum in England or America; then an air raid on 12 March 1945, only two months before the end of the Second World War, went one further by signalling the end of the building itself; it received a direct hit, and although the façade and much of the great staircase survived, the stage and auditorium were almost totally destroyed.

   During the immediate post-war years, while Vienna was under quadri-partite occupation, the company of the State Opera performed in two of the city's smaller theatres, but once again the agonies of a decade had done nothing to diminish its status. Under the guiding hand of conductors such as Josef Krips, Karl Böhm and Clemens Krauss a new ensemble was built

The Vienna State Opera, March 1945.

up which, when it came for a season of guest performances to Covent Garden in 1947, left no one in any doubt that the Viennese still knew a thing or two about how to sing Mozart, Beethoven and Richard Strauss. Then, on 5 November 1955, shortly after the Russians' sudden withdrawal from Austria, came the event which, to the people of Vienna, was the final milestone on the road to peace and normality; the newly restored State Opera was reopened with a performance of *Fidelio* under the baton of Karl Böhm. The invited audience included not only numerous visiting heads of state and other prominent figures in the world of international politics, but also – and this was of no less significance to the people of Vienna – two of the great stars of yesteryear, returning from voluntary exile in America and England, Lotte Lehmann and Alfred Piccaver. Lehmann recalled the occasion in a talk given shortly afterwards to the Opera Guild of Southern California: 'Our box was decorated with roses,

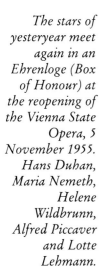

The stars of yesteryear meet again in an Ehrenloge (Box of Honour) at the reopening of the Vienna State Opera, 5 November 1955. Hans Duhan, Maria Nemeth, Helene Wildbrunn, Alfred Piccaver and Lotte Lehmann.

and we were in a crossfire of popping flashbulbs. There we stood, Alfred Piccaver and I . . . He is now old, and I am old – but I certainly did not feel it at all at that moment.' There were, of course, very few tickets available that night for the ordinary opera-goers, but a vast crowd assembled in the streets outside, where the performance was transmitted to them over loud-speakers; and there they stood in the cold night air listening to Beethoven's immortal tribute to the concept of liberty.

No one, I think, visiting the Vienna State Opera today, could fail to be impressed by the lavishness of the building's interior. Some might, however, be surprised that in the 1950s a decision should have been taken to keep so closely to the original scheme of an auditorium designed to meet the social requirements of the 1860s, including as it does a large number of boxes whose occupants, instead of facing the stage, look straight across the horseshoe towards their counterparts on the opposite side. Indeed, the occupants of the backs of these boxes, despite being provided with specially raised chairs perched up on stilt-like legs, have to settle for seeing virtually nothing. I remember that while I was a student in the opera

Crowds assemble outside the Vienna State Opera on the occasion of its reopening, 5 November 1955.

school of the Vienna Music Academy (from 1956 to 1959), a very elderly Viennese Countess once explained to me how vital the boxes in the old house had been to her and the rest of her heavily chaperoned contemporaries. 'The lobbies leading into the boxes', she told me, 'were the only places where one could enjoy a tête-à-tête with an admirer. A scene as long as the second act of *Tristan* would be enough to send your grandparents to sleep in the box, and then you could sneak out to the lobby.' At that point her eyes took on a happy, far-away look. 'You know, it's a funny thing,' she added, 'but in the love duet Wagner got the rhythm quite wrong.'

It often amuses me now to hear the 1950s referred to as a golden age of opera in Vienna, because at that time if ever I enthused about, say, a *Figaro* with Lisa della Casa, Irmgard Seefried, Sena Jurinac, Paul Schoeffler and Erich Kunz, I could be sure that someone would say 'Ah, yes, but of course you never heard Lotte Lehmann, Vera Schwarz, Elisabeth Schumann, Alfred Jerger and Richard Mayr.' In Vienna there has always been a better yesterday, and the selfsame people who used to assure me that Sena Jurinac was no match for Lotte Lehmann as the Composer in *Ariadne* were quick to decide that this new girl Christa Ludwig would never be a second Jurinac. The truth of the matter is that there were indeed many marvellous singers to be heard in Vienna at that time, and as there was a generous allocation of standing-room tickets to the students in the opera school I was lucky enough to hear them all. Apart from those named above there are others who remain with particular vividness in my memory – Elisabeth Schwarzkopf, whose performance in *Capriccio* offered a perfect blend of exquisite vocalism, physical elegance and musical sovereignty, with the patina of artificiality which almost always characterized Schwarzkopf's interpretations ideally exploited to express the self-consciousness of the Countess Madeleine; Hans Hotter, surely as godlike a Wotan as any mere mortal could hope to be; Julius Patzak, the reediness of his tone not to everybody's taste, but to his admirers quite simply *the* Florestan; then amongst the representatives of the up-and-coming generation Eberhard Waechter, a singer who never did himself justice in London or New York, but whose death scene as Posa in *Don Carlos* was one of the great moments of my opera-going life; Fritz Wunderlich, accurately described by Dietrich Fischer-Dieskau after his tragically early death as having been 'in a class of his own'; and Graziella Sciutti, a Zerlina as irresistible to the audience as she was to Waechter's or George London's swashbuckling Don Giovanni.

The list could go on and on, with names such as Lucia Popp and Gundula Janowitz just around the corner, and still today during a year's zealous opera-going you would hear at least as many of the world's leading singers in Vienna as you would in any other single city. Indeed, there is no other opera house in the world which claims to offer so consistent and varied a fare as the State Opera. Where many houses today work on the 'stagione' system, whereby a cast will be assembled for a certain piece which will be concentratedly rehearsed for several weeks, performed perhaps ten times in the next month and then 'mothballed' until it is due for revival, the State Opera keeps a running repertoire of some forty-five to fifty productions rotating through a ten-month season, and in the course of any normal week it is likely to be offering four or five different operas, probably with an evening of ballet thrown in for good measure.

The pressures involved in this relentless turnover are mainly sustained

The Vienna State Opera from the air. It is widely believed that the American pilot who picked it as his target shortly before the end of World War Two had mistaken it for a railway station.

by the singers and conductors, who are constantly required to give of their best despite minimal rehearsal; and, perhaps even more so, by the stage crews whose routine of setting up and clearing out productions is a never-ending process. One might expect the culmination of this frenetic workload to be a series of damagingly under-rehearsed performances, but somehow this is not the case, and one of the principal ingredients for keeping the pot so effectively on the boil is the contribution made by the orchestra, no less a body than the Vienna Philharmonic. One visiting singer after another will bear witness to the 'Vienna Phil's' extraordinary adroitness in the art of accompanying voices, something which is assisted by the fact that the pit is placed unusually high, so that the musicians can always hear and often even see the singers. A few years ago the Opera's then director, Claus Helmut Drese, gave a piece of very sound advice to one young man who was about to conduct his first performance there without having had a single orchestral rehearsal. 'Lassen Sie sie nur spielen,' he said – 'Just let them play.'

The expense of running an opera company on these lines is colossal, but the Austrian government provides a guarantee of $150,000 a night, by far the highest level of financial support for any company in the world. It might be supposed that such extravagance as this would meet resistance from the ordinary taxpayer, but I have been assured by Austrians who are in a position to know that if any political party nailed its flag to a reduction of this subsidy it would lose a mass of votes. Even amongst residents of the Austrian provinces this would be regarded as a savage dent in national pride. Though there are plenty of Austrians who are not interested in opera with a small 'o', the Opera is a different story, and in Vienna itself the latest *Opernskandal* is far more likely to be the stuff of coffee-house gossip than anything which the politicians may be getting up to. People do not need to have attended last night's performance to be aware that the tenor was not up to scratch, and the best informed amongst them will know that his vocal decline is not unconnected with the demands made upon him by the red-haired *première danseuse* in whose company he has been frequently seen of late. The hounding of the Opera's administration, too, is a keenly followed national sport, one to which men of the calibre of Böhm, Karajan, Drese and Lorin Maazel have all fallen victim since the new house was opened. When Eberhard Waechter was appointed General Manager in 1991 he wrote me a letter saying that he regarded it as 'the most wonderful job in the world, but the job one is most likely to lose in a hurry'. His words were sadly prophetic, though not in the way he expected; after less than a year at the helm he dropped dead of a heart attack while walking with his wife in the Vienna Woods.

I cannot leave the subject of the Vienna Opera without mentioning one other vital function which it fulfils in the city's life; for one night every year, during carnival time, it becomes the scene of the Opera Ball. The seats are removed from the stalls, and a false floor is put in at the same level as the stage to form one gigantic space for dancing. This is where one sees the essential conservatism of the Viennese at its most unassailable; the *sine qua non* for the young couples who are selected to open the proceedings in their long white gowns and white tie and tails is that they should have fully mastered the elegant art of dancing the *Linkswalzer*, the quick waltz with the gentlemen spinning to their left – and a very fine sight they make. I was lucky enough to be invited to the first opera ball held in the new house, and it was an occasion second only to the re-opening itself. Everyone who could possibly scrape up the money for a ticket did so, and in those hard-up days many of the ladies' dresses and even some of their shoes were home-made – a fact which became evident when the revels ended and we found that there had been a massive fall of snow during the night. Even those few people who possessed cars in the Vienna of February 1956 were unable to dig them out, and during the trudge home many a lady parted company with her carefully glued-on high heels.

Vienna is not, of course, the only city whose opera house can be described as the principal shrine of its civic pride; in the lives of the Milanese the Teatro La Scala plays precisely the same role. The instinctive reaction of anyone approaching La Scala for the first time is likely, I think, to be one of disappointment. As the theatre originally fronted onto a narrow street not much trouble was taken with a façade which no one would be able to admire from a distance; and today, standing in the Piazza della Scala, which was created in 1857 in order to provide so prestigious a theatre with a worthier setting, one could be forgiven for wondering which is the star of the show, La Scala or its neighbour, the Banca Commerciale Italiana. Nor does the entrance to the theatre provide instant reassurance; it cannot even remotely be compared with the visual pomp and circumstance which greet you as you enter the Vienna State Opera or the Palais Garnier in Paris, now freshly restored to its pristine glory. It is when you first set eyes on the auditorium that you feel convinced; it is vast and it is magnificent, and there is no longer any doubt that you have arrived at the true home of Italian opera.

La Scala boasts one of the world's largest stages – the auditorium, though it seats almost three thousand people, would fit onto it twice* –

---

*It is an interesting thought that when the original theatre was built the total population of Milan numbered 150,000. At a rate of one seat per fifty members of the population a modern opera house in London would need to have some 200,000 seats.

The great staircase of the Palais Garnier.

and certainly the world's largest orchestral pit. To the singers the conductor may seem to be an alarming distance away, but to the audience the clarity of sound arising from this *golfo mistico*, or 'mystic gulf', as it is picturesquely dubbed, is truly remarkable. During a recent performance of *Madam Butterfly* I found myself hearing orchestral details of which I had never previously been aware, and although some of the credit for this should of course go to the conductor, Riccardo Chailly, and to the orchestra itself, the *golfo* was certainly playing its part.

If the boxes in Vienna are known to have been put to certain non-operatic uses, those in Milan have an even more esoteric history. They were originally the personal property of the families which subscribed for them, and they would be used very much as a home from home, especially during the cold winter months. Each family would install the furniture and decorations of its own choice, frequently including a stove on

The epitome of operatic grandeur: the Paris Opéra, known in honour of its architect as the Palais Garnier.

which the servants could do some cooking; and until 1830, when it was decided that the practice encouraged immorality (here we go again!), curtains could be drawn to close the box off from the auditorium. Today the Scala's architectural features include a clock above the proscenium arch – I can think of no other opera house so thoughtful as to keep its patrons *au fait* with their chances of catching the last bus home – and a stupendous chandelier comprising 365 light bulbs, one for every day of the year. The theatre also boasts the most up-to-date box-office in my experience, with a computer screen set into the outside wall enabling passers-by to discover at any time of the day or night, and in any of five different languages, what seats are available during the coming week, and how much they will cost. I was also amused to see, during my most recent visit, that above the actual counter inside the box-office an electronic signboard flashed up the running message 'Sabato completamente esaurito – prego di non insistere!', which can perhaps be most effectively

The auditorium of La Scala in 1811, the boxes curtained off to oblige those patrons who required privacy.

translated as 'Saturday completely sold out – please don't make a fuss!'

To attend a performance at La Scala is to participate in the history of opera itself. I doubt if any other house in the world has witnessed as many significant premieres as La Scala, ranging from Rossini's first success, *La pietra del paragone* in 1812, via numerous new works by Bellini and Donizetti, to such pieces as Poulenc's *Dialogues des Carmelites* in 1957, and more recently the various days of the week which constitute Stockhausen's massive project entitled *Licht*. The story has naturally not been one of unremitting triumph, and one man who felt impelled to turn his back on La Scala, though happily not for ever, was no less a figure than Giuseppe Verdi. Back in 1847 Verdi expressed himself with typical trenchancy in a letter to his publisher, Ricordi:

> Do not permit this *Macbeth* to be performed at La Scala. Far too many examples already have persuaded me that they either can't or won't produce operas decently, especially mine. I cannot forget the foul manner in which they produced *I Lombardi*, *Ernani* and *I due Foscari* etc. And I have another example before my eyes with *Attila*.

Ask yourself if, despite a good company, this opera could have been worse staged!

Stinging words, and the premiere of *Macbeth* duly went to the Teatro della Pergola in Florence. Forty years later, however, the management of La Scala succeeded in reassuring the revered maestro that all was well again, and the premieres of his last two masterpieces, *Otello* and *Falstaff*, were to be numbered amongst the most triumphant evenings the opera house had ever witnessed. Only a few years later, though, in 1904, another keenly anticipated premiere turned out very differently – *Madam Butterfly*, of all pieces, was one of the most complete fiascos in operatic history. Incessant jeers and catcalls rendered most of the second act inaudible, and the piece was withdrawn after only one performance. Puccini made some revisions, the new version was produced three months later in Brescia, and within a couple of years the international popularity of tragic little Butterfly rivalled that of her predecessors Mimì and Tosca. It was not until 1925, though, that the piece found its way back to La Scala, with Arturo Toscanini on the podium, since when it has been

Opera-goers enjoy a stroll in one of the foyers of La Scala, Milan.

*A unique event
in the long
history of
La Scala.
La traviata
performed with
Maestro
Riccardo Muti
at the piano,
2 June 1995.*

revived there in no less than twenty-four different seasons.

The public at La Scala has always been notoriously hard to please, indeed one of the present artistic directors of the company described it in a recent BBC radio programme as 'merciless'. If the claque decides to swing into action against an individual singer – perhaps one who has not crossed the palm of the *Capo del claque* with the requisite quantity of silver, or one who is suspected of trying to step into a local favourite's shoes – it can be a fearsome experience, with the booers running from one part of the gallery to another, creating the impression of being several times more numerous than they are. When offered truly great singing, however, the Milanese have usually recognized it, and there is an anecdote in the memoirs of one of the theatre's most celebrated directors, Giulio Gatti-Casazza, which dramatically illustrates the point. During the season of 1900–1901 a new comic opera by Mascagni flopped disastrously, and Gatti, together with his music director, Toscanini, decided to offer a new production of Donizetti's *L'elisir d'amore* as a stop-gap. The piece had long fallen out of favour, being considered excessively trivial, and the notoriously haughty subscribers at the first night made a point of expressing their disapproval; throughout the first half of the opera they resolutely refused either to laugh or to clap. Early in the second half comes an important scene for soprano and tenor. The soprano, though she acquitted herself well, failed to find favour, and now it was the tenor's turn. This was Enrico Caruso, a newcomer who had started badly in Milan by singing Rodolfo in *La bohème* while suffering from the aftermath of a feverish cold, but now his hour had come. As Gatti himself expressed it:

> Who that heard him would not remember? Calm, and conscious that at this point the fate of the performance will be decided, he delivered the reply 'Chiedi, al rio perchè gemente' with a voice, a feeling and an art which no word could ever adequately describe. He melted the cuirass of ice with which the public had invested itself, little by little capturing his audience, subjugating it, conquering it, leading it captive. Caruso had not yet finished the last note of the cadenza when an explosion, a tempest of cheers, of applause and of enthusiasm on the part of the entire public saluted the youthful conqueror.

At no point in the house's history has it stayed out of the headlines for long. In the 1950s La Scala was the scene of the great confrontations between the Callas and Tebaldi factions, and as recently as 1995 an unique event occurred, when the orchestral musicians called a strike. The Music Director, Riccardo Muti, rather than cancel a performance of *La traviata*, decreed that it should go ahead with himself joining the singers up on stage and accompanying them at the piano. 'The strike', Muti declared in an interview in the *Corriere della Sera*, 'is a tragic episode and should never have taken place in a theatre where people queue from five o'clock in the morning to hear *La traviata*, and where foreigners come to fulfil the dream of a lifetime. Indeed, I would have to say that we have made typical Italians of ourselves.' The stand that he took made him the hero of the hour and the problems with the orchestra were soon resolved, but, as any foreign singer performing at La Scala rapidly recognizes, the Italians do have their own way of doing things. Again and again first nights which seem doomed to disaster, with the scenery arriving late and the costumes not ready by the final dress rehearsal, emerge miraculously as artistic triumphs – in the words of the American bass Samuel Ramey 'In the end you always complete the trip, but the road getting there is very, very bumpy.'

In a chapter such as this there is naturally not room to cover all the great opera houses of Italy, but at the time of writing the news has just broken of the destruction of that jewel amongst theatres, La Fenice in Venice, and I feel impelled at least briefly to salute its memory. Like La Scala it was the scene of many an historic premiere, and, again like La Scala, of one historic fiasco – *La traviata*, no less. Perhaps by the time this book appears plans will have been completed to enable La Fenice to live up to its name and arise from the ashes – if so, let us hope that both its beauty and its acoustics will have been preserved. It was a theatre much loved by audiences and by singers alike, though I do have one less than rosy memory of the sole occasion on which I sang there, on tour with the English Opera Group. The opera, appropriately or not, was Britten's *Death in Venice*, and the character I was playing, Gustav von Aschenbach, opens the proceedings, standing all alone on stage and singing an extended and virtually unaccompanied recitative. In one of the boxes close to the stage an Italian couple, instantly recognizing that this was going to be a far cry from *Tosca* or *La bohème*, started discussing whether or not it might be more amusing to spend the evening elsewhere; and as sounds in that lovely old theatre carried as clearly from auditorium to stage as they did from stage to auditorium it took all my concentration to continue singing Aschenbach rather than joining in their conversation. There was one other strange aspect to that particular engagement, too. Shortly before the company was due to leave England we were warned that some suspected cases of cholera had been reported in Venice and that we should all have ourselves innoculated forthwith. As one of the salient features of the opera's plot is an outbreak of that very disease my injection seemed almost like the ultimate 'method' preparation for immersing myself in my role.

Reverting to the subject of acoustics, I was interested, when re-reading the memoirs of Beniamino Gigli a couple of years ago, to find that he had described the Teatro Massimo Bellini in the Sicilian city of Catania as 'the most beautiful and most acoustically perfect in the world'. It so happened that at the time I had just been singing there myself, and it was indeed remarkable how little voice was needed in that huge auditorium. There was, however, one other aspect of performing in Catania which impressed itself equally on my mind. In most places guest singers are paid either by having their fee handed to them in cash during the interval, or else it is transferred to the singer's bank account. Catania, however, operates on different lines. There the singers have to collect their fee for the whole engagement from a certain bank, situated in a dingy side-street, on the morning following the final performance. Thus every local villain is aware that at a certain hour sundry foreigners will be heading for their hotels with millions of lire stuffed into their pockets, and it is a golden rule not to attempt the journey in groups of less than three or four. During the rehearsal period for the production which I was in a gruesome Mafia assassination had taken place within a couple of minutes' walk of the opera house, and on pay day it was noticeable how everyone kept close to the burlier members of the cast.

It would be hard to love opera without also loving Italy. It was, after all, the Italians who invented opera and there is something intrinsically operatic about so many aspects of Italian national life. It is not always easy, however, for non-Italians to adapt to the volatility of their methods, and to find an opera house which offers the very antithesis to Samuel Ramey's 'bumpy road' one could scarcely do better than to visit his native land and take a look at the Metropolitan Opera, New York. There are few opera houses in the world which run on such well-oiled wheels as the Met, and perhaps even fewer which contain so many employees who openly profess to be contented with their lot. To quote a British bass this time, Robert Lloyd, the Met is 'a self-contained opera town', a house in which everything required for a performance, from the prima donna's jewellery and the leading tenor's shoes to the rifles for the firing-squad in *Tosca*, are manufactured on the premises; and it would amaze the production staff in many a European house to know that one of their opposite numbers at the Met felt able to state in a recent interview, 'When I need to ask for something, whether it is from the props department, the stage management or whatever, I never need to ask twice.'

There are some members of the public, I know, who still lament the

*The Met's
Diamond
Horseshoe
during the
Good Old Days.*

passing of the old Met. It was a theatre with a history glorious enough to rival even that of La Scala, and it boasted a company whose cast-lists, taken from virtually any of the eight decades of its existence, make truly mouth-watering reading. Furthermore it was the favourite gathering place of New York's plutocrats, a number of whom had clubbed together to finance its construction, and newspapers would often devote as much space to the social reporting of evenings at the Met as they did to their musical reviews – 'In Colonel John Jacob Astor's box, No. 7, were Mrs William Force and her daughter, Miss Katherine Force, and a party of young men. Miss Force wore white brocade'; and so on round the so-called Diamond Horseshoe. The decision to desert this treasured place cannot have been an easy one, but the stage mechanism was woefully inadequate for modern purposes, the rehearsal facilities even more so,*

---

*As a typical example of rehearsal practices at the old Met during the inter-war years, when Lauritz Melchior made his debut there in 1927, singing the Paris version of *Tannhäuser* for the first time in his life, he was allowed one brief musical run-through, which took place in the chorus ladies' dressing-room.

and there was no space whatsoever for the storage of scenery. If, let us say, *Tannhäuser* was given as the Saturday matinée, to be followed by *Aida* in the evening, the Royal Palace of Memphis would spend the afternoon out on the street.

Never having visited the old Met I carry with me no backlog of negative comparisons when I visit its replacement, and though I can imagine that any habitué of the original theatre might lament a certain loss of atmosphere I find the new Met hard to fault. Proudly dominating the Lincoln Center Plaza with its marble façade and five towering arches – if only there were space enough to view certain of the great European cathedrals at such a distance! – the exterior of the Met is an arresting sight. Through its acres of glass two vast Chagall paintings announce that this

Despite the Depression there was still no shortage of sartorial display amongst 'Knickerbocker Society' at the Met's opening performance in 1931.

Five Met immortals let their hair down: Giuseppe de Luca, Giovanni Martinelli, Maria Jeritza, Frances Alda and Arturo Toscanini.

is a building in which nothing has been done by halves, an impression confirmed by the generous sweep of the double staircase. The auditorium itself is even larger than that of La Scala, containing no less than 3,788 seats, and its many touches of luxury include twelve crystal chandeliers, an inaugural gift from the Austrian government, which rise gracefully towards the ceiling as a sign that the performance is about to begin.

Unlike several of the other prominent opera houses built since the Second World War, the most obvious example being La Bastille in Paris (whose auditorium could well be that of an expensive cinema), the Met was designed on the traditional lines of the curved amphitheatre. At the same time, however, care was taken to ensure that all but a few of the very cheapest seats should offer a clear view of the stage, and indeed the degree of consideration which has been given to the convenience of the patrons, even those who are sitting in the upper reaches of the house, is one of the building's most attractive characteristics. Where those who have bought cheap seats at Covent Garden, for instance, are segregated from the rest of the house, using an uncongenial side staircase and having to make do during the interval with a bar so small and overcrowded that no drink could assuage the thirst engendered by the battle to acquire it, their opposite numbers at the Met enter by the same lofty portals as everyone else, have just as much access to any foyer they may choose to explore, and if they feel averse to climbing five flights of stairs they can do the journey by lift. Once in the topmost balcony they will find plenty of space for the leg-stretching so essential during the intervals of some of the more extended works in the repertoire, and – the ultimate touch in what would nowadays be termed 'user-friendliness' – for those who do not want to add to the expenses of the evening by buying a drink there are water fountains on every floor.

Although the Met maintains a repertoire, and undertakes a workload, second only to those of the Vienna Opera, less than 1 per cent of its total budget is directly funded by the government. This apparent meanness is seen by the general manager, Joseph Volpe,* as a distinct advantage, because it protects the institution from the unpredictability of political decision-making. In fact, if one examines the situation a little more closely it becomes evident that the government *does* provide support, but by an indirect route, cutting out much of the tiresome bureaucracy which bedevils the system in many other countries. Out of the Met's total annual budget of $130 million some $50 million is provided by fund-raising, and in the States donations to a foundation such as the Met are tax-deductible. It may surprise Europeans to know that around 80 per cent of the fund-raising money comes from private individuals rather than public corporations; subscriptions start at a level of $1,000 a year and extend upwards to members of the 'Golden Horseshoe' scheme who donate $150,000 over a three-year period – and even to one particular patron who contributes $100,000 a year out of his own pocket. Most remarkable of all, perhaps, is the fact that there are numerous subscribers who have never even set

---

*Joseph Volpe is the only opera manager I can think of who has spent his entire working life with the same company. He started at the Met as an apprentice carpenter and worked his way to the top.

foot in New York, their access to the Met being limited to Saturday matinée broadcasts and regular television transmissions. These reveal that in comparison with certain of America's smaller opera companies the Met's house style is still largely conservative, as is the choice of repertoire, but the management is never slow to point out that any house which needs to earn $85 million a year is well advised to leave experimentation to others. It would be fair to mention, too, that the Met caters to an exceptionally conservative public; there are not many European houses in which the sets of an elderly production would be greeted with warm applause at curtain-up, a rather charming phenomenon which I recently experienced at a Met revival of Donizetti's *La fille du régiment*.

There was a time – it extended with one or two gaps from 1883 to 1986 – when the Met used to reach out to the nation by mounting a massive annual tour; the company habitually visited a dozen or more cities in the

The Met's new manager ruminates over seat prices. Rudolf Bing, New York, 1950.

process, and in 1900 it managed to find its way to no less than twenty-three. The logistics of these peregrinations were daunting. Special trains would take the entire company, the orchestra, the costumes and the scenery as far afield as San Francisco (where in 1906 it lost all its equipment, though luckily none of its singers, in the earthquake) and even, on one occasion, to Mexico. The 'togetherness' engendered by these tours has been referred to in the memoirs of several singers as having cemented the family feeling which so strongly characterized the old days of the Met, though life at such close quarters could also have occasional disadvantages. I was once told by a retired member of the company about an evening when the amorous Ezio Pinza had forgotten to note down the compartment number of a certain young lady with whom he had arranged a tryst on the post-performance train, an oversight which resulted in his having to knock on every door down many a lengthy corridor until the right voice murmured 'Come in!'

Many factors contributed to the end of the Met tours. Transport costs

The new Metropolitan Opera, New York.

*The spacious foyer of
the War Memorial
Opera House,
San Francisco.*

became prohibitive, especially after complex sets had started to replace the primitive backdrops of the previous era; and with the jumbo jet making it a simple matter for the Met's international stars to flit back to the summer festivals and recording studios of Europe, several cities which had regularly featured on the Met's itinerary were beginning to field equally attractive casts in their own local companies. There had of course for many years been a busy operatic life beyond the confines of New York, with Chicago and San Francisco sharing the principal honours, but even so the burgeoning of operatic activity in the States since the Second World War has been spectacular. Up until 1964 there were only twenty-seven operatic organizations in the whole country which ran on an annual budget of $100,000 or more; within twenty-five years that number increased to 209. By the end of the 1980s five companies besides the Met were exceeding the $10 million mark – New York City Opera, San Francisco, Chicago, Houston and Los Angeles – with several others only a short distance behind. Most of these cities boast theatres of considerable splendour, notably San Francisco, whose War Memorial Opera House was inaugurated on 15 October 1932 with a performance of *Tosca*, starring that most compelling of operatic tragediennes, Claudia Muzio.* By the end of the 1995 Autumn season the San Francisco Opera had presented no less than 174 different operas, including twenty-four American premieres, and the singers who have made their American debuts there have included such names as Birgit Nilsson, Leontyne Price, Renata Tebaldi, Boris Christoff, Tito Gobbi and Mario del Monaco.

In Chicago the resident opera company has had a confusing habit of changing its name at regular intervals throughout the twentieth century. Starting life as the Chicago Grand Opera Company in 1910, with the indomitable Scottish-born soprano Mary Garden as the most glittering of its acquisitions, it reached exalted heights during the period 1921–32 as the Chicago Civic Opera; artists of the calibre of Amelita Galli-Curci, Conchita Supervia, Tito Schipa, Titta Ruffo and Feodor Chaliapin gave some of their greatest performances there. In 1954 Chicago brought off a tremendous coup by securing Maria Callas's first appearances in the United States – they achieved it by the simple means of offering a higher fee than the Met – and in 1956 the company assumed yet another name, Lyric Opera of Chicago, under which it has gone from strength to strength.

Apart from the various traditionally designed opera houses situated at the hearts of its wealthiest cities the United States also offers several operatic venues of startling originality, created to capitalize on the varied glories of the American countryside. One such is the theatre of Santa Fe, situated seven miles outside the capital city of New Mexico in the foothills of the Sangre de Cristo mountains. Since its inauguration in 1968 this has been the home of an annual summer festival,† and its special

---

*The first act of this historic performance was broadcast, and the transmission has now found its way in mildly truncated form onto CD as part of a Muzio recital (Romophone *81015-2*). The sound quality is naturally nowhere near that of a studio recording, but it has been skilfully remastered and it does give a precious glimpse of a great prima donna in the white heat of action.
†The festival itself had been inaugurated back in 1957 in a 480-seat wooden theatre which was destroyed by fire in 1967.

features include a stage which can be left open at the back, thus making stunning use of a vista of rolling desert, distant mountain tops and whatever the night sky may have to offer in the way of sunset and evening stars. Unfortunately August is a month in which it has also been known to offer an occasional downpour, and as some 350 of the almost 1,800 seats were, up until 1995, open to the elements, the enthusiasm of the patrons, as well as the patrons themselves, have occasionally been dampened. In 1996, however, a new roof was installed, and now Jupiter Pluvius can wreak no further damage. The Santa Fe Festival was, and has remained, the brainchild of one man, John Crosby, who provides his audiences with a cunning mixture of the novel and the familiar. Over the years he has attracted the active collaboration of such august figures as Stravinsky and Hindemith, and his roll-call of American and world premieres makes impressive reading. At the same time it was a typical Crosby touch to open the 1995 festival with Emmerich Kálmán's Austro-Hungarian operetta *Gräfin Maritza*, and to conduct all eleven performances himself.

Another collector's piece for those who like to enjoy their opera in original surroundings is to be found on the shores of Lake Otsego near the village of Cooperstown in upstate New York. The most celebrated scion of this breathtaking terrain was James Fenimore Cooper, creator of *The Last of the Mohicans*, and it was he who bestowed upon Lake Otsego the fictional name of Glimmerglass. In 1974 the Glimmerglass Festival was inaugurated with four performances of *La bohème* in the Cooperstown High School, mounted on a budget of $14,000; within twenty years the turnover had risen to $3 million. Every summer four different operas, ranging once again from the adventurous to the bankable, are presented in a theatre ingeniously designed to blend, barnlike, into its surroundings, and the sale of tickets has risen from 1,200 in 1974 to a little under 30,000 at the time of writing. The principal roles are largely cast with up-and-coming American soloists under the guiding hands of directors who are not afraid of innovation, and the whole project has been presided over since 1979 by the same general manager, Paul Kellogg.* Glimmerglass is a festival for those who appreciate a blend of artistic and

*Mr Kellogg's appointment to the management of the New York City Opera was announced shortly after this chapter was written.

pastoral joys, and anyone who is stirred by unspoilt countryside will find it around Cooperstown in copious quantity. Apart from the Baseball Hall of Fame, which commemorates the fact that America's answer to cricket was invented just around the corner, the Alice Busch Memorial Theatre, with its 920 seats and its sides that roll up to give the auditorium a blast of fresh air during the interval, is the only tourist attraction for miles around. Traffic jams are more likely to be caused by wandering deer than by the intrusion of other motorists, and the choice of picnic sites is unlimited.

To British opera-goers the word 'picnic' is liable to conjure up one specific image, that of the gardens of Glyndebourne; and indeed, Glyndebourne's joyously eccentric founder, John Christie, must, I think, be saluted as the original progenitor of the modern predilection for opera in unlikely spots. The manner in which he incorporated an auditorium into his Sussex home as a showcase for the talents of his wife, the soprano Audrey Mildmay, has been chronicled often enough, but even so fresh anecdotes about his idiosyncratic methods do still come to light. One such was recently related by the nonagenarian British baritone, Roy Henderson, who was summoned by Christie to audition for the role of Count Almaviva in the inaugural performance of *Le nozze di Figaro* in 1934. The people whom he had to convince of his suitability were the newly appointed heads of music and production, Fritz Busch and Carl Ebert. When he had sung a couple of arias they expressed satisfaction with his voice, but asked what evidence he could give them that he could also act. The matter was clinched by a retort from Christie, which I imagine must have left those two eminent Germans too perplexed for further deliberation – 'Of course he can act; he's a cricketer!'

Back in my undergraduate days, when I was President of the Oxford University Opera Club, I invited Mr Christie to come and give one of our monthly lectures, and thereafter he and Mrs Christie, a truly lovely lady, greatly befriended me. I remember asking Mr Christie why he insisted that his audiences should wear evening dress, and he told me that when he dreamt up the festival it was his intention to make it as difficult as possible for people to come to it – he would, he assured me, have liked to surround the place with barbed wire – so that only those with a genuine hunger for operatic excellence would bother to buy tickets. In this respect things did not quite work out as he intended, and for those who wish to go on attaching to opera that tired old label 'élitist', Glyndebourne is understandably one of the most tempting targets. The sight of people in long dresses and dinner jackets gathering on Victoria Station during the early afternoon has long been one of the more bizarre characteristics of the London summer; and as Glyndebourne has never taken one penny of the taxpayer's money, thus making itself (once it had outgrown Mr Christie's ability to pay for it out of his own pocket) heavily dependent on corporate sponsorship, the accusation that a disproportionate number of its visitors are there for business or social reasons has, at least until recently, been a hard one to deny. The desire to increase the size of the auditorium, and thus make it possible to offer a number of seats at less daunting prices than of yore, was, however, partly responsible for the dramatic decision taken in 1992, under the leadership of Mr Christie's son George, to tear down the old theatre and replace it with a modern building containing 1,200 seats rather than the previous 800.

The fruits of this decision are a modern miracle – an opera house which opened on time, within budget and to virtually unanimous acclaim. The new Glyndebourne, now boasting facilities on both sides of the curtain which should carry the festival far into the foreseeable future, is as easy on the eye as it is on the ear. Eschewing the regal plushness of most metropolitan opera houses, the auditorium remains loyal to its rural setting by appearing to be constructed almost entirely of exquisitely polished wood relieved here and there by open brickwork, the effect of which manages to be both intimate and spectacular. There are those who regret the fact that bats can no longer gain admittance, adding local colour by flitting over the heads of the audience after the long supper interval; but no one, I feel sure, could carp about the ingenious mechanism which supplies fresh air through the stem of every seat, thus dispelling the stuffiness which, in the old days, used to help set so many heads a-nodding.

At Glyndebourne it is the picnic supper which takes place under the sky, but in many places on the continent of Europe it is the opera itself. Amongst these open-air venues I suppose the palm for the sheer size of its auditorium has to go to the Arena in Verona, the scene of one particularly happy memory from my early opera-going days. It was (I think) in 1950; I was on a motoring holiday with two undergraduate friends and when our rickety Ford 10 landed us in Verona I found that there was to be a performance that night of *La Valkyria* by Riccardo Wagner. Neither of my friends had ever been to an opera and they had no idea what I was letting them in for – hours and hours on a stone seat, a long way from the stage. Eventually, in the early hours of the morning, Wotan reached his heart-rending Farewell. He called upon Loge to surround Brünnhilde's rocky fastness with impenetrable fire, and the resultant smoke, billowing from a range of mountains on either side of the stage, disturbed the slumbers of an elderly cat, which had apparently been ensconced there for most of the performance. Slowly and deliberately, yawning and stretching itself as it went, this cat walked straight across the stage behind the luckless Wotan, who was standing in a traditional operatic pose, gazing upwards with arms outstretched, at a total loss as to why the audience should be greeting one of the most moving passages in the whole of opera with peals of laughter. After a moment or two of indecision he reached down towards his nether regions; the only explanation, he had evidently decided, was that his trousers were falling down.

Even on occasions when nothing so untoward occurs, there is always a certain holiday atmosphere, a feeling of informality, about open-air performances, and this was typified for me during a more recent visit to Verona to see *Rigoletto*. The title-role was taken by that admirable baritone Leo Nucci, and at the end of his tragic *scena*, 'Cortigiani, vil razza dannata', he received a well-deserved ovation. He was kneeling downstage centre, a broken man, humiliated and submissive, and as the waves of applause rolled over him he was faced with an age-old dilemma – do I remain as I am, in character, and let the clapping subside, or do I step out of character and acknowledge the audience's appreciation? At Covent Garden the solution expected of him would have been the former, and at La Scala probably the latter. In the Arena he went one further. After raising his head and bowing repeatedly to the public he turned towards conductor and orchestra, and himself began applauding them.

On a smaller scale than Verona, but with room for 6,000 visitors nonetheless, is the Sferisterio in Macerata, the capital city of the province of Le Marche. Originally built in 1829 as a place to play the game known as *pallone*, it was converted to operatic use in the 1920s, and inaugurated, as a plaque still informs us, by the local-boy-made-good, Beniamino

Gigli, 'col suo canto divino', 'with his divine singing'. The main characteristic of the Sferisterio is the width of its stage, fully ninety metres, and
in comic operas the singers have a delightful habit, when applauded after
a concerted number, of holding hands and scampering from one side of
the stage to the other, to ensure that all the audience is adequately thanked
for its appreciation. Musical standards are high; soloists of international
calibre are supported by a locally recruited chorus, and in a gloriously
spirited performance of _L'elisir d'amore_, which I saw there in 1994, the
difficulty with which some of the choristers resisted the temptation to
wave to their sisters and their cousins and their aunts added greatly to the
jollity of the whole proceedings.

Turning from comedy to tragedy, another open-air production which I
recall with particular vividness was Cherubini's _Medea_ in the classical
Greek amphitheatre of Epidauros, with Maria Callas in the title-role and
Jon Vickers as Jason. There was a strange sense of continuity through the
centuries as the most famous Grecian performer of modern times – I
know Callas was born American, but both her parents were Greek –
bestrode a stage which had been inaugurated by her predecessors some
two thousand years before. To be candid, on that occasion her acting was
more remarkable than her singing, though even her riveting stage persona
was not enough to achieve suspension of disbelief when she made her first
entrance as the sinister stranger whose identity is known to no one,
swathed in black and with her face concealed, only to be greeted with a
roar of welcome from several thousand enthusiastic admirers.

I have happy memories, too, of audience participation during performances on another classical site, the Baths of Caracalla in Rome, where
opera used regularly to be on offer during the summer months until it was
found that the fabric of the buildings, which had been opened for their
original purpose in 217 AD, was being endangered – even more, I believe,
by the trampling feet of the visitors than by the decibels produced on the
stage. I have never known any other auditorium in which the members of
the claque were so immediately identifiable. Cunningly dotted throughout the vast auditorium the same twenty or thirty voices would obedi-
ently shout 'Bravo' each time the tenor hit a high B flat; it was almost as
if with every climactic tone he had scored the clinching goal.

One of the most imposing historical (as opposed to classical) sites to have been converted to operatic purposes is the Felsenreitschule (Rocky Riding School) in Salzburg. This mercifully possesses a roof, because when it rains in Salzburg it really rains, and I well remember how, the first time I ever went there – the opera was *Die Zauberflöte* – the unscheduled contribution of Jove the Thunderer to the first appearance of Wilma Lipp as Queen of the Night was something of which no mortal *régisseur* would dare to dream. I have one other strange, lingering memory of that performance, too. The role of the Sprecher was taken by Paul Schoeffler, an artist whose aura of benignity, quite apart from the splendour of his singing, made his great duet with Tamino into one of the many high points of the evening. Re-entering the Temple of Wisdom after his valedictory utterance, he evidently had a long walk back to his dressing-room, which took him along a gallery skirting the side of the auditorium. He was behind a stone wall, invisible to the public, but we could exactly

Graziella Sciutti, sauciest of Despinas, enjoys a refreshing glass of wine after a performance of Così fan tutte, *Salzburg, 1961.*

trace his progress because with every step he took one of his shoes let out an extraordinarily well-projected squeak.

The Salzburg Festival was initiated in 1920, in the aftermath of World War One, and must, I suppose, by now be regarded as the premier music festival of Europe. Not to be overlooked, however, is that other Austrian success story, the festival at Bregenz, on the shores of Lake Constance. This started immediately after the end of World War Two, and after the humblest of beginnings – a presentation staged on a large boat – it has grown with such leaps and bounds that today it offers a programme of some seventy performances of opera and operetta in a five-week season. Some of these can be enjoyed in the Neues Festspielhaus, opened in 1980, and others in the lakeside auditorium, which boasts some 6,300 seats, and faces what is generally reckoned to be the largest performing area in the world. By making use of island stages, floating platforms and stretches of water in between, directors such as Jerome Savary with *Die Zauberflöte* and *Les contes d'Hoffmann*, and David Pountney with *Nabucco*, *Der fliegende Holländer*, and *Fidelio*, have devised some of the most spectacular productions of the century. Pountney's designer, Stefanos Lazaridis, believes his sets for Bregenz to be the largest ever built, and looking at them it would be hard to suppose him wrong. In any case, for the growing number of travel companies which specialize nowadays in opera tours the little town of Bregenz (population just under 30,000) has become something of a Mecca.

The association of opera and water brings me to what is, I should imagine, the most readily recognizable building in the world, the Sydney Opera House. As with the original Glyndebourne, so much has already been written about the extraordinary circumstances of its construction – the gigantic over-running of the budget, the confusion as to which of its auditoria was to be the concert hall and which the opera theatre, and so on – that the story needs no re-telling. Externally, perched as it is in a position of breathtaking beauty, it makes an ineradicable impression; internally, it does present undeniable problems. When I directed a production of Kálmán's *Die Csárdásfürstin* for the Australian Opera in 1990 – one of the most enjoyable assignments of my career – I was immediately confronted with the same problem as everyone else who works for that delightful company. As the traditional wisecrack has it, 'Australia can claim the best opera house in the world; what a shame that the inside and the outside are five hundred miles apart.' In other words, any production devised for the Australian Opera Company has to be equally at home on the huge and splendidly equipped underground stage of the Victoria Arts Centre, Melbourne, and on the cramped and technically challenging space provided by the Sydney Opera House. Ironically it was not the stage mechanism in Sydney, though that caused headaches enough, but one of the lifts in the auditorium which almost proved my undoing. To achieve my curtain call on the opening night, slipping out of my end-of-the row seat in the circle shortly before the end of Act III, I had to descend to stage level in a lift and walk through a pass door. I took the trouble to try a few dry runs, because it is hideously easy to get lost in unfamiliar theatres, and there appeared to be no problem – until the first night, when the lift declined to open. This left me with less than two minutes to hare down several flights of stairs to the main entrance, out onto the walkway, round the building to the stage door, past the stage-door keeper, who took me for some lunatic interloper and did his best to block my path, up several more flights of stairs and eventually into the wings – where I arrived just in time to present myself to the public, most of whom must have imagined that the performance had left me in the grip of over-whelming emotion.

There are many other theatres of which I have fond memories, and though the confines of this chapter prevent me from going into detail about them all I cannot refrain from mentioning that magnificent old house, the Teatro Colón in Buenos Aires, with acoustics to rival those of Catania; the late lamented Gran Teatre del Liceu in Barcelona, like the Fenice the victim of a devastating fire, but now, according to all reports, about to be resurrected in greater glory than ever; the Maltings at Snape, with its indelible memories of Benjamin Britten, the creator of a whole new gallery of fascinating tenor roles, and a man whom I revered; the dear old rabbit-warren known as Sadler's Wells, where I have both sung and directed on numerous occasions; and the many theatres in Britain's lead-ing provincial cities in which I have spent happy hours with touring com-panies such as Scottish Opera, Opera North and the Welsh National Opera. One of my few remaining ambitions is to see the Welsh National installed in a worthy home of its own – if by then my singing days are over perhaps they might allow me to carry a spear on opening night. Of all the many companies I have worked for this is the one to which I feel most attached, and I rate two of its productions, Michael Geliot's *Billy Budd* and David Pountney's *From the House of the Dead*, as the finest in which I have ever appeared. Then, what about the innumerable historic houses in which I have never even managed to set foot? The Semper Oper in Dresden, the Mariinsky in St Petersburg, Drottningholm in Sweden, Olavinlinna Castle in Finland – I shall never catch up with Herr Schulz.

So, in conclusion, to the theatre which, to many a British opera-lover, must surely rate as the most precious of them all, the Royal Opera House, Covent Garden. Although it is the third theatre to occupy the site – the previous two, as opera houses have a habit of doing, went up in smoke – Covent Garden embodies the history of opera in London as solidly as the Tower of London embodies the history of the city itself. In the original

J. Cruikshank Del.

The famous actor John Philip Kemble, in his capacity as joint manager of Covent Garden, faces an irate public during the Old Price riots of 1809.

theatre (1732–1808) several of Handel's operas received their first airing; in the second (1809–1856), which opened to a month of sustained rioting in the auditorium because of a steep rise in ticket prices, Carl Maria von Weber held the post of music director, living just long enough to see his last opera, *Oberon*, open there, and stars such as Wilhelmine Schröder-Devrient, Maria Malibran, Giulia Grisi and Pauline Viardot established themselves as the favourites of the London public; while the third, which opened in 1858, has contrived to remain ever since, despite many vicissitudes, the virtual flagship of opera in Britain.

Unlike an institution such as the Vienna Opera, which, first under the patronage of the Emperor and then of the State, has enjoyed a solidly established existence, Covent Garden has had a motley history. Initially it passed through the hands of a series of commercial managements, culminating in the most successful of their number, Augustus Harris, whose

Opposite £2,000 of damage was inflicted on the Covent Garden Theatre by a gang of rowdies at the revival of Arne's Artaxerxes *on 24 February 1763 because the management had discontinued the custom of charging half-price for those only wishing to attend Act III.*

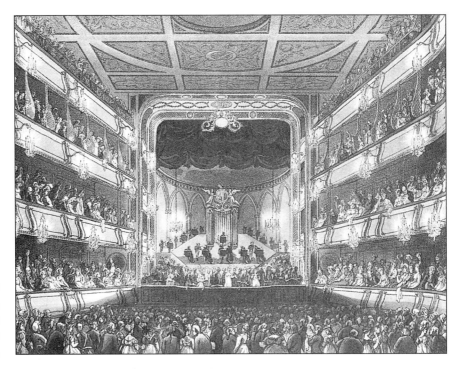

The Covent Garden auditorium in 1808, showing Handel's organ placed centre stage.

Grand Season, mounted every summer, became a social 'must' for London's high society. After his death in 1896 control of the theatre was undertaken by successive syndicates of its wealthiest patrons, and this remained the basic system until 1939. Between the two wars the mercurial figure of Sir Thomas Beecham dominated the scene, as lessee and head of his own company while his money lasted, as principal conductor after it had run out, and as artistic director from 1932 onwards. From time to time Covent Garden would be leased to visiting companies, during the First World War it was requisitioned by the government and used as a furniture store, and during the Second World War it reached its artistic nadir, serving as a dance-hall.

It was not until 1946 that Covent Garden first became the home of an established opera company and the unprecedented degree of continuity which it has enjoyed since then can be judged by the fact that it has had precisely three general directors in fifty years. Although during that period standards have naturally varied, and artistic policy has undergone

Covent-Garden Theatre.

Closed for One Week

ADDRESS.

WHEN the brilliancy of GAS illumination attracted Public admiration, the Proprietors of this Theatre anxious to adopt every Improvement which would give brilliancy to the Scenery, and the appearance of the Theatre, introduced it; and to prevent the accidents which the best Street illumination is liable to, they at a great expense constructed Gasometers: finding however that with the utmost care and skill, the introduction of Gas in the audience part of the Theatre, produced an offensive odour, and the Public having suffered inconvenience and disappointment in their amusements, by the mischievous agency of some malignant and interested Persons; the Proprietors have determined to remove the Gas, not only from the Box Circles, but from all internal avenues leading to them, as well as to the Pit and Galleries.

But as this important Alteration cannot be effectually done, while the Theatre is nightly open, without the Public being put to inconvenience, the Managers have determined to submit to the heavy loss of Closing their Theatre, rather than allow the Public to suffer any drawback to their Theatrical Enjoyments.

The Public is in consequence respectfully informed, that as the proposed Improvements cannot be executed in less than a Week, the Theatre will remain

CLOSED TILL MONDAY,

THE 24th INSTANT;

when they hope to welcome the Public to a Theatre, where no Expense will be spared, or Zeal remitted, to render it worthy the liberal Patronage it has ever enjoyed.

J. FAWCETT, Stage Manager.

Printed by W. REYNELL, Broad Street, Soho.

The inconveniences of modernization. A solicitous management presents its case.

the occasional change, Covent Garden can claim an undisputed right to be regarded as one of the world's great operatic institutions. This is no mean achievement when one considers that several of its competitors at the top of the operatic tree have the advantage of vastly more generous finances; the Royal Opera's annual grant from the Arts Council may be large enough to ensure its position as a favourite whipping boy amongst those who decline to recognize the value to Britain of our expertise in the performing arts, but on the continent of Europe the directors of many theatres considerably less prestigious than Covent Garden would scratch their heads if they had to make both ends meet on so tenuous a budget.

In recent months the mystique which has traditionally attached to the inner workings of the Royal Opera has been blown apart by an extraordinary piece of investigative television, namely a series of six programmes entitled *The House*, made over the period of a year by 'fly-on-the-wall'

Royal Italian Opera, Covent Garden.

Copy   **RETURN.**

"Tristan und Isolde"

37th *performance of Royal Italian Opera.*

Wednesday Evening,   28th June 1893

	£	s.	d.
Grand Entrance	8	3	6
Amphitheatre Stalls	3	.	.
Amphitheatre	69	5	6
Money taken late			
Money in Boxes			
Total of doors	80	9	.
Box Office	123 14 .		
Libraries :—			
Deal	361 1 3		
Extras	71 13 9 432 15 .		
Subscriptions	198 2 2		
		754 14 2	
Books of Words and Scores	. . .	835 3 2	
Cloak Room Fees, &c.	- . .		
Final Total, £	835	3	2

Then as now, one of any management's chief concerns. The takings for Tristan and Isolde, *Covent Garden, 28 June 1893.*

cameramen, who were apparently allowed to go anywhere they liked and film anything that took their fancy – even confidential conversations between members of the management about key figures on the staff. These programmes have reputedly riveted six million British viewers a week to their television sets, and are expected to achieve the same result in numerous other countries. To me, watching with incredulity, it seemed that the management had shot itself in the foot with a howitzer. Those in charge were depicted either as being grumpily inept, lurching in an apparently rudderless manner from one unexpected catastrophe to the next, or else as being machiavellian intriguers, frequently close to the edge of hysteria, and only happy when sliding the knife into an unsuspecting set of ribs. Performances appeared to take place largely by coincidence, thanks to the production of last-minute rabbits out of providential hats; and to those of us who know that for dedicated professionalism it would

*Sir Augustus Harris,
financially and artistically an
outstandingly successful
manager of Covent Garden
from 1888 until his death in
1896, as portrayed by Spy.*

be hard to beat the hundreds of people whose working lives are spent backstage in the Royal Opera House, the decision to allow such a selective impression to be disseminated throughout the world is baffling in the extreme. It seems, however, that we are wrong. After every one of these no-holds-barred exposés hundreds of people (we are told) rang the opera house asking to become subscribers. The old cliché must indeed be true – there really is no such thing as bad publicity.

Covent Garden is shortly due to close for a massive programme of rebuilding and refurbishment; for months the newspapers have been full of conflicting reports on whether or not planning permission will be obtained, and whether or not the money will be forthcoming. As far as the backstage facilities are concerned it is as urgently required as was the

Cavalleria Rusticana. *How, one wonders, did a story of seduction, adultery, unwanted pregnancy, drunkenness and murder appeal to the elderly Queen Victoria?*

move from the old Met to the new; I devoutly hope, though, that renovations in the auditorium will take the form of a face-lift rather than major surgery. Still presided over by the profile of the young Queen Victoria, the Royal Opera House, with the regal red of its furnishings and the gold and cream of its decorations, breathes an air of imperial greatness, and while we all know that this is but the ghost of an illusion, is illusion not the very stuff of opera?

My personal memories of the house go back to the first opera which I ever saw, *The Magic Flute*, nearly fifty years ago as I write, and to many performances in the late 1940s, while I worked there during university vacations as assistant to the house's first official archivist, Harold Rosenthal. Kirsten Flagstad as Isolde, Ferruccio Tagliavini as Nemorino with the visiting company of La Scala, Tito Gobbi as Renato, Callas as Norma, Victoria de los Angeles as Manon, Beecham conducting *Meistersinger* – they are all still clear in my mind's eye and ear. So, too, are many treasurable performances by members of the resident company –

Marko Rothmüller as Scarpia, Rigoletto, Jokanaan and Wozzeck, Adèle Leigh as Oscar and Susanna, James Johnston as Calaf and Don José, and Geraint Evans as Figaro to name but a few. I remember, too, that harrowing evening, 8 June 1952, when Britten's *Gloriana* was given its premiere in celebration of the Queen's coronation, and fell with a thud to the floor in front of the most glittering audience to have assembled in any theatre within living memory. Heaven only knows what the crowns, tiaras and necklaces gathered there that evening must have been worth – even up in the gods (ten shillings a seat) I was wearing white tie and tails – but I suspect that by the time the performance was over their wearers would have happily hocked the lot rather than sit through another half hour of 'modern music'.*

Dire as that particular evening was in terms of audience appreciation, it was undeniably an historic occasion, and it is the sense of history which makes Covent Garden so special. Unlike many of the great houses on the continent of Europe it was mercifully spared from the ravages of the Second World War, and it is still the self-same place in which successive generations of the world's most fabled singers have given of their best. One may no longer have to pick one's way through a teeming vegetable market to get there, and the air of Floral Street may no longer be thick with the smell of rotting cabbages, but this is still the place where Adelina Patti, with her bewitching smile and flawless vocalism, broke many a Victorian heart, where in Edwardian days Nellie Melba ruled supreme, and where, between the two wars, people queued all night to hear Jeritza sing Tosca. I remember feeling a sense of awe when I found myself for the first time singing the starring role at Covent Garden – it was my old friend Aschenbach again – and I mentioned to a colleague how disappointing it was that the number one gentleman's dressing-room should contain little else but an ancient chair with a broken arm. 'Ah! Yes,' he replied, 'but don't forget – it could have been Caruso who broke it!'

---

*There is, of course, nothing unusual about going to the opera without knowing much about it. A couple of years ago, when Covent Garden performed Rossini's *Mosé in Egitto* (*Moses in Egypt*), a lady rang the information desk seeking enlightenment about 'this new piece *Moses in his Ghetto*'.

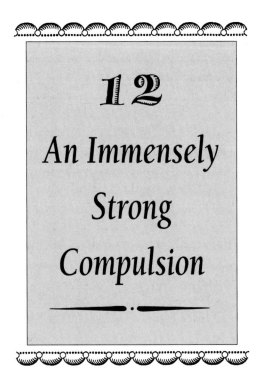

12

An Immensely
Strong
Compulsion

'Ah, how I envy you being a singer! It must be marvellous to spend your life doing something you enjoy!' Yes indeed, quite right, but whenever these words are addressed to me my instinctive reaction is one of mild irritation; they inevitably contain – or am I being oversensitive? – the hint of an implication that singing is fun, not work, and we singers like to think that we work very hard. The words are naturally that much more irritating if they are spoken by someone who would be shocked at the suggestion that he should exchange the comfort of his luxurious office for the cramped quarters of a pokey little opera house dressing-room (probably shared with several other people), but there we are – if we succeed in creating the impression that the glamour engendered by the operatic stage bathes the whole of our lives in an iridescent glow we should doubtless take it as a compliment. We are, after all, illusionists, and the wider-ranging the illusion, the better we must be doing our jobs.

I know, of course, that this irritation of mine is an unworthy reaction, because *au fond* the words are true. We *are* lucky people, and if ever I hear colleagues grumbling about how much they are having to travel, how many new roles they have to learn in the next six months, or what torture it is to sing under the celebrated Maestro X, a neat little Neapolitan saying comes to my mind – 'Chi te lo fà far'?', 'Who makes you do it?' Because the truth of the matter is that very few of us, however burdensome certain aspects of the operatic profession may be, would dream of trading it in for a different way of life. I have known people who could have been lawyers but decided to become accountants, I have known people who could have been engineers but decided to become farmers, I have known people who could have been secretaries but decided to become shop assistants – I have seldom, though, known anyone who could have been a professional singer but preferred to become something else. The desire to sing is an immensely strong compulsion; I imagine psychologists would say that it has something to do with our instruments being a part of ourselves, and with the fact that singing was one of the original, primeval forms of man's artistic expression. The act of singing comes, both physically and emotionally, from deep inside us; as Ralph Vaughan Williams put it 'The human voice is the oldest musical instrument and through the ages it remains what it was, unchanged; the most primitive and at the same time the most modern, because it is the most intimate form of human expression.' It could without doubt be argued that as far as opera is concerned singing has moved a long way from its natural origins, and that when a human voice has been trained to cover two octaves or more and to make itself heard in a vast auditorium over an orchestra of more than a hundred people it cannot be said that it has remained unchanged through the ages. The vocal method of the medieval troubadour would certainly have had little in common with that of the modern Wagnerian tenor, but one basic feature remains the same – total dependence on those two little folds of mucous membrane which extend across the interior cavity of the larynx and which are known as the vocal cords.

In the English-speaking world one particular stereotype of the opera singer has impressed itself over the years so deeply on the public consciousness that it appears to be all but ineradicable; to be a *real* opera singer you must be fat, flamboyant and foreign. There are of course plenty of us who do meet these criteria in varying combinations, and in any case even if every other member of the profession were to be a slender, self-effacing Anglo-Saxon, there is always Luciano Pavarotti, who embodies every aspect of the blueprint to such perfection that he would single-handedly keep the myth alive. In general, though, despite the enormous growth of interest in opera as an art form during recent years, there is still only a vague perception amongst the British public of the sort of creatures we singers are and the kind of lives that we lead. In the course of this chapter, leaning heavily on personal reminiscence, I will try to shed a little light on the species *homo cantans operaticus*.

The first thing I would emphasize about us singers is what very different animals we are from our opposite numbers in the straight theatre. By this I mean in no way to denigrate the noble army of thespians, but whereas most of my actor friends had a more or less firm idea quite early on in their lives that the theatre would be their destiny,* there is no point in setting your heart on a career in opera until you have reason to believe that you possess the necessary strength for it, strength both of voice and of body, and this cannot be established until you have achieved a certain degree of physical maturity. For the male sex there is also the question of the voice having to settle down after it has broken. Although I know few successful male opera singers who did not have beautiful voices when they were boys, the converse cannot be taken for granted, and many a twelve-year-old who has brought tears to the eyes of one and all with his yearnings for the Wings of a Dove finds a few short years later that his chirrup has turned to a croak, and he has lost the power to enchant. It is always dangerous to generalize and I know that a number of famous opera singers have started surprisingly young – amongst the men Titta Ruffo, Tito Schipa and Jussi Björling had all made their professional debuts before they were twenty-one, and amongst the women we find even more extraordinary examples of precocity. To mention four nineteenth-century prodigies, the fabled Maria Malibran

---

*Ballet dancers, too, have usually decided at a very early age on the careers they intend to pursue.

was singing Rosina in *The Barber of Seville* at seventeen, at eighteen Giulia Grisi had an extensive repertoire, Adelina Patti undertook the title-role in *Lucia di Lammermoor* at sixteen, and Luisa Tetrazzini took the Florentine and Roman publics by storm at nineteen; though all of them have to yield to Conchita Supervia, the great Spanish mezzo of the inter-war years, who made her debut in the Teatro Colón, Buenos Aires two months short of her fifteenth birthday. Nowadays, however, such instances are unheard of, and it is rare indeed for women of under twenty-one or men of under twenty-four or so to make a successful debut in opera.*

The principal explanation for this change lies in the modern view of what should constitute a singer's training. Most of the great stars of the past had certainly worked hard in order to perfect their vocal techniques, but they were usually privately trained. Malibran, for instance, was taught by her own father, the celebrated Spanish singer and teacher Manuel García; she traipsed around wherever his busy career happened to take him, and so harshly did he treat her that she plunged at the earliest opportunity into an unhappy marriage in order to escape his tyranny. Patti's training was a family affair too – she studied with her half-brother, Ettore Barilli, in New York – and the most glaring exception was the inimitable Luisa Tetrazzini, who sprang fully armed into the arena after only the sketchiest of training.† Today, however, few people enter the operatic profession other than through the opera school of one or other of the established musical colleges or academies, after a course, probably lasting three years or more, which offers training not only in vocal technique, but also in such ancillary subjects as acting, languages, musical theory and so forth. Many of these students will have been through university first – it is noticeable how many of the young men entering the profession in recent years have had choral scholarships from leading universities – and so, before the hopeful young singer has had a chance to set foot on a professional stage, quite a number of years have rolled by.

---

*One notable exception to this generalization is Placido Domingo, who made his debut as an operatic tenor at twenty, after singing in *zarzuelas* as a baritone. Pavarotti, on the other hand, did not face the public until he was twenty-five.
†See p. 64.

*Maria Malibran
(1808–1836), who made
her debut as Rosina in*
The Barber of Seville *at
the King's Theatre,
London, aged only
seventeen.*

Looking back on my own student days in the opera school of the Vienna Music Academy I would say that the hardest nut which the operatic student has to crack is the task of learning to act and sing at the same time. Here again I would like to emphasize the contrast between us and our opposite numbers in the straight theatre; where they are encouraged early on to be looking for emotional truth in the roles that they are playing we are principally concerned with the sheer mechanics of getting it right, because unlike them we have to cope with the impositions of the music. We cannot choose our own timing in the delivery of a line or the performance of a specific action – the composer has decided all that for us. Until one has become accustomed to opera's peculiar demands there is a bewildering amount to think about all at the same time, and I often compare the complexity of the task with that which faces anyone in the early stages of learning to drive a car. You approach a crossroad where you are to turn right, and what has the instructor told you to do? You must look in the rear mirror to see that there is no one behind you trying to overtake, you must pull across into the middle of the road, with your right hand you must put out your indicator and with your left hand you must change gear, but you must not do these two things at once because one hand must always remain on the steering-wheel. Meanwhile with your left foot you must operate the clutch, with your right foot on the brake pedal you must slow the car down and then stop it, while looking right, left and straight ahead to observe the positions and speeds of any oncoming vehicles. Initially it seems scarcely possible that you can simultaneously master so many different actions performed by so many different limbs, and yet within a couple of months the miraculous moment arrives when you realize that you have negotiated some overcrowded city centre during rush hour without giving a moment's conscious thought to either hand or foot, and you are still alive to tell the tale.

So it is with opera, and to illustrate what I mean I would like to quote a passage with which I regularly had to grapple in the Vienna Academy. This is the scene of Rodolfo's first encounter with Mimì in Act I of *La bohème*. It is a scene which, when mastered, comes across as the most natural piece of conversational singing that one could possibly imagine, but I can only say that hardly a young soprano was put through this particular mill without being reduced to tears at least once – not *only* because of my ineptitude as her partner – and that the same would certainly have been the case with me had it not been for the stiffness of my masculine upper lip. Let me put just eight bars under the microscope. The situation is that Rodolfo, a penniless young poet, is sitting in his cheerless garret in Paris when to his delight a pretty young girl knocks on his door and announces that she is his neighbour from over the way and she has stupidly let her candle go out – can he please relight it for her? To his consternation, though, no sooner does she enter the room than she is convulsed by a coughing fit and then faints away. She is clearly sick and he is at a loss to know what he should do. He sprinkles some water in her face, and as she comes to herself again he suggests that she should move closer to the stove. Then we come to our eight bars. Rodolfo has a bright idea – he will offer her something to drink. 'One moment,' he sings, 'a drop of wine...' 'Thank you,' she replies, so he says, 'Here you are.'

OPERA SCHOOLS AT WORK. Opposite *Students of the Vienna Music Academy (the author, Cato Brink and Peter Felsenstein) in a dramatized version of Bach's 'Coffee Cantata', part of a presentation in the Schubert Saal of the Konzerthaus, 1957 . . .*

. . . followed by Paul Hindemith's one-act comedy Hin und zurück. *The composer, apparently amused by what he had seen, with Helen Richardson, the author (as the deaf old aunt), Raimund Herndl and Peter Felsenstein.*

Left *Anthony Besch directs a scene from* The Barber of Seville *at the London Opera Centre. To judge from the formality of the students' clothes it must have been a special occasion.*

Before he says that, though, he must remember to pick up the glass and give it to Mimì, whose next utterance is 'Just a little', whereupon he must immediately pour out the wine – which he will not be able to do unless he has meanwhile remembered to have the bottle ready in his pouring hand. 'Like this?' he asks as he pours, to which she replies, 'Thank you'; whereupon he murmurs as an aside, 'What a pretty girl!'

Now, this may sound very straightforward, but what I have not yet mentioned is that while you are doing all this you are also having to concentrate on the music, and every time you go wrong you will bring proceedings to a halt. You have, for instance, precisely a beat and a half, round about one second, between 'A drop of wine' and 'Here you are', and having once come in late you decide to play safe by keeping your eye firmly fixed on the pianist's left hand, which (you hope) will give you the cue. But standing there watching his hand and counting out the rests between your phrases you are a beat behind in picking up the glass, so you cannot pour out the wine at the proper moment, Mimì fails to come in with 'thank you' because she has nothing to thank you for, and you are left having to sing the line 'What a pretty girl' straight into Mimì's left ear because if you turn away to sing it as an aside you will miss the glass and the wine will end up in her lap. The one time you get it all right your Mimì is shouted at by the pianist for forgetting that Puccini has marked 'Just a little' pianissimo and staccato, the director in charge of the class begins to show signs of impatience and Mimì starts to cry. Ah! the dreams you have always cherished of standing on stage in the role of Rodolfo modestly acknowledging the cheers of a packed-out house, as Giuseppe di Stefano did last Tuesday – will they ever be fulfilled?

The answer to that last rhetorical question is 'almost certainly not'. A minute proportion of those who once harboured the ambition to sing in opera actually end up by doing so, and of those only a very few reach the topmost heights. I used to reckon that of the young hopefuls who auditioned for the Vienna opera school perhaps one in five was accepted, and of those who were accepted perhaps one in ten ended the course by winning a contract with a professional company; and looking back on those days now with the hindsight of nearly forty years in the business I can see that those who did eventually make steady careers were by no means always those of whom it was expected. So often the possessors of the God-given voices lack certain other qualities needed for survival in the hurly-burly of international opera, and they fail to stay the course. Perhaps they do not have the self-discipline required to look after themselves properly, to turn down tempting invitations the night before a big performance, or to have their roles properly prepared every time rehearsals start for a new production. Perhaps they suffer from the curse of shaky nerves and cannot stand the strain of being so regularly put to a make-or-break test, which is what every performance really amounts to until you have been singing for long enough to establish a track-record and a reputation. There are some who quite simply feel out of place on stage – to quote yet again the contrast between us and straight actors it is to be assumed that anyone who sets his or her heart on an acting career will be someone who feels at home in a theatre, whereas an exceptionally beautiful voice in no way guarantees that its possessor will be what the

Germans call a *Bühnenmensch*, a 'stage creature'. The British bass, Michael Langdon, who used to run the National Opera Studio in London, once said on one of my radio programmes 'There is a tendency among young people to feel that opera singing is all about making beautiful sounds, and it is not. It's all about acting with the voice. One does, of course, have to make beautiful sounds, that is the basic requirement, but one has to learn to portray emotions within the voice, and for this to be done the person has to have a certain *craft*, a certain *foxiness*, a certain ability to pick it up.' Those were the words of a real dyed-in-the-wool old pro, who had started his singing career in pantomime, and then worked his way up from the Covent Garden chorus to become one of the most sought-after interpreters in the world of that highly demanding role, Baron Ochs in *Der Rosenkavalier*, and they are words which continue to ring very true.*

How, then, does any beginner manage to cross the no-man's-land between the territory marked 'student' and that marked 'professional singer'? For many people the first step consists of securing the services of an agent. This need not be too agonizing an experience, as those agents who interest themselves in beginners will probably have attended student performances and will already have formed an impression as to which of the up-and-coming crop of youngsters they might like to represent. To take my own case, I was approached by one of the Viennese agents before I had left the Academy – any young tenor has the advantage of a certain rarity value – and I relied on him for advice as to what my next step should be. Now this is the point at which my personal experiences diverge from those of most of my compatriots, because the opportunities available to a young singer in the German-speaking countries have always been vastly more numerous than they are in Britain, which was why I spent the early years of my own career largely in exile. The explanation for this state of affairs is simple. In Germany (limited at that time to the Western sector), Austria and Switzerland every town with a population of

---

*To pursue the theme of 'many are called but few are chosen', Michael Langdon told me that to select fifteen students for the National Opera Studio he would audition 120, and of them he would expect five to be still making a living in opera by the age of forty.

more than one hundred thousand or so has its own full-time opera company. That meant that in my young days there were over sixty companies in the German-speaking countries which offered steady employment to singers, whereas in Britain at that time there were precisely two, Covent Garden and Sadler's Wells (later to become the English National Opera).* The gallant Carl Rosa Company was in its death throes, the Welsh National Opera was a small local group struggling to survive its chronic under-funding, Scottish Opera was still but a twinkle in Alexander Gibson's eye, Glyndebourne was only in action for a few weeks during the summer, and Opera North would not be called into existence for another twenty years.

The prevalence of opera in the German-speaking countries does not, to my mind, indicate a greater degree of musical appreciation than is to be found in Britain. It came about because so many of their cities were in earlier times the capital of some small Kingdom, Princedom or Bishopric, and they all maintained their own Court Theatres, which in due course passed into the hands of the municipalities;† it is simply the view in those countries that any self-respecting community should provide its citizens with access to the performing arts, just as it does to those amenities offered by institutions such as schools, hospitals, libraries or swimming pools. I often think of the operatic profession in German-speaking countries as being similarly structured to professional football in Britain – there are, so to speak, first, second, third and fourth division opera houses, and thanks to the agents, who flit busily from one to another, young singers hope to be talent-spotted up the professional ladder. At the outset they are faced with one tricky decision – is a beginner better advised to attempt his or her entry into the profession via small roles in a

---

*Even today German-speaking Switzerland, with a population roughly two-thirds the size of London's, maintains as many full-time opera companies as the whole of Great Britain.

†One typical instance of this is the Stadttheater (Municipal Theatre) in Koblenz, a city of 120,000 inhabitants on the confluence of the Rivers Rhine and Mosel, where I spent my second year in the profession. The theatre, which maintains an opera company, a theatre company and a ballet group, has 500 seats and was first built in 1787 under the patronage of the local ruler, Kurfürst (Elector) Clemens Wenzeslaus.

large house or vice versa? Some feel that the consummation most devoutly to be wished is to get a toe into the door of a house such as the Vienna State Opera, even if it means singing nothing more arduous for the foreseeable future than 'My lady, supper is served.' Others prefer the prospect of being a big fish in a small pond, and I personally served the first year of what I look back on as having been my apprenticeship in a tiny one.

It would be difficult, I think, for anyone not involved in the operatic profession fully to appreciate the sense of relief felt by any young singer when he or she secures that longed-for first contract. If your agent decides that you are the right material for the big fish option he will send you off to audition for the various small houses which are looking for a soloist of your type. The process is agonizing. You arrive at the railway station of some town in which you know no one and have no idea how to find your way around. You ask hopefully whether the Municipal Theatre is within walking distance and if it is not you grit your teeth and face up to the cost of a taxi. You arrive at the stage door to be told that four other tenors are also auditioning, and no, unfortunately there is not a room with a piano free in which you can warm up. As you find your way round the spider's web of corridors which lead to the cheerless room in which the little gang of hopefuls is assembled you pass numerous irrepressibly confident people humming, singing snatches of this and that, or simply greeting each other with such mundane phrases as 'Guten Morgen, wie geht's?', 'Good morning, how are you?', but all so resonantly projected that every chorus member in the place appears to be a Melchior or a Chaliapin. Faced with your competitors you can see at a glance that you are in trouble – they are all burly, self-assured fellows who clearly have at least a dozen leading roles already under their belts – and then the ordeal begins. One by one you are escorted onto the stage, and a bored voice out of the darkness asks 'What is your name?' and 'What are you going to sing?' To your surprise the two confident figures who go on before you turn out not to be so marvellous after all; one, God bless him, cracks on a high note and the other makes two serious musical mistakes. Your turn comes and on you go. You have long ago learnt not to try being clever by offering unfamiliar arias which do not go above an A flat, because when you have finished the bored voice will simply ask

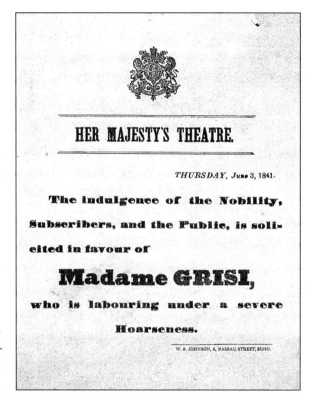

HER MAJESTY'S THEATRE.

THURSDAY, June 3, 1841.

The indulgence of the Nobility, Subscribers, and the Public, is solicited in favour of

Madame GRISI,

who is labouring under a severe Hoarseness.

W. S. JOHNSON, 6, NASSAU STREET, SOHO.

'A singer hatching a cold is a pitiable specimen of humanity.' Evidently it was ever thus.

'Have you brought any Mozart?' and 'Do you have a high C?'; so you start with Tamino's aria from *The Magic Flute*, and follow it with Rodolfo's from *La bohème*. To your amazement you sing rather well – not as well as you habitually do at your singing lessons, but much better than at your last three auditions. You are told to wait behind because the Herr Intendant and the Herr Generalmusikdirektor wish to speak to you. Can this be it? Is this where your glorious career is destined to begin? The two gentlemen speak kindly to you. They have liked your voice and are satisfied with your appearance; but then comes the moment you are dreading. 'How many roles have you sung on stage?' they ask. 'I am afraid I have not sung any as yet, Herr Direktor,' you reply, 'because I am only in my last year at the opera school.' 'Ah, that's a pity,' one of them says, 'because here, you see, we can only afford two principal tenors, which means that you would have an extremely heavy workload and we cannot risk engaging a singer who has not yet proved that he can stand up to it. Do come and sing for us again when you have a full season's experience behind you.' Back you go to the railway station, walking this time, as the prospect of earning your first fee has receded once again, and back in Vienna the agent's voice is beginning to lose its quality of friendliness as you report the failure of yet another mission.

The circumstances of my eventual breakthrough remain etched on my mind with a rare degree of clarity. It was at the beginning of February 1959, and virtually every opera director had completed his team for the season which would start the following August or September. I had more unsuccessful auditions behind me than I cared to contemplate, and my time in the opera school would end in June. Out of the blue my agent rang me once again. The director of the smallest of all the established opera companies was coming to Vienna the following day to audition young singers in the agent's studio, and one of the vocal categories which he was still looking for was 'principal tenor'. The company was that of the Städtebundtheater in Switzerland, jointly run by the two small cities of Biel (Bienne) and Solothurn (Soleure), and the director's name was Herr Markus Breitner. This time a feeling of desperation must have given my performance an extra edge – there would not be another chance after this – and when Herr Breitner said, 'You are exactly what I am looking for; I will make a contract with your agent, so please come back tomorrow and sign it', I had difficulty in not embracing him. My agent, Herr Alois Starka, smiling at me benevolently, said, 'So we see each other tomorrow at 10.30', and I headed for home.

Home at that time was a rabbit-warren of a flat in Vienna's VIIIth district, known as the Josefstadt, which I shared with a fellow student, the Finnish baritone Tom Krause. Tom, blessed with outstandingly the most beautiful voice in the opera school, had only needed to audition once to be snapped up by the Berlin Opera, and he had become almost as concerned as I was by my failure to secure an engagement. 'This evening', he stated, with an air of authority, 'we shall celebrate' – and we did. Anyone who has visited Vienna is likely to be familiar with that admirable local institution, the Heuriger, a form of picturesque wine-garden to be found in suburbs such as Grinzing and Sievering, where fresh local wine is drunk, a quarter of a litre at a time, cold food is served, and to the accompaniment of fiddle and squeeze-box Viennese songs are sung. It was to a favourite Heuriger that a small group of us repaired that evening and it was not long before people started asking us to sing. Tom, in particular, possessed the gift of winning all hearts whenever he broke into song, and as he was in generous voice that evening glass after glass of wine was passed up to our table by enthusiastic revellers. When we eventually made our way home the ninety-eight stairs which led to our flat had seldom seemed so steep.*

At 8.30 the next morning the telephone rang. It was Herr Starka. He was very sorry, but Herr Direktor Breitner had decided that as I would be the only principal tenor in his company, and as I would have an enormously heavy workload, he just wanted to reassure himself as to the quality of my top notes; so could I please present myself at 10.00 ready to sing the tenor part in the *Madam Butterfly* love duet, high C and all, as that would be the first of the seven leading roles which I would be expected to sing during the eight-month season. So voiceless was I that I only just managed to explain to Herr Starka the impossibility of my being able to sing the humblest octave scale until I had had a couple of days to recover, whereupon he pointed out that the decision was mine – did I want the job or didn't I? Thus it came about that an hour and a half later, green and shaking and leaning heavily against the piano for support, I launched into 'Un po' di vero c'è', or rather ' 'S'ist schon was wahres dran', as we sang everything in German. It was perfectly evident to me that I was not going to survive this second round with Herr Breitner, but after I had made my first gallant attempt at a high note he interrupted me with a happy laugh, saying 'If you can reach even a *middle* C looking as ill as that I think I've got the right man', and the contract was settled then and there.

It would be impossible to describe how much I learnt about the busi-

---

*The lift was one which would nowadays have a preservation order placed on it. It dated from before the First World War and contained the maker's brass plate headed 'K.u.k. ausschliessliches Privilegium', indicating Royal and Imperial patronage. When I had taken the flat three years earlier I was assured that this historic object was to be restored to working order 'within a few days'. The prophecy was fulfilled just before I left Vienna three and a half years later, but meanwhile the stairs had done wonders for my breath control.

ness of being a singer during that one season in Biel-Solothurn. The theatre in Biel (population 75,000) held 280 seats, that in Solothurn (population 18,000) held 300. The singers were based in Biel, the actors, whom we never actually met, in Solothurn. On the evenings when we were singing in Solothurn they were acting in Biel, and we would wave at each other as our coaches passed on the main road; we also gave occasional performances in several other small towns in the Canton of Bern.* The orchestra, if I remember rightly, numbered around twenty, with occasional reinforcements in the brass section for the more richly scored pieces, and the chorus numbered a dozen or so, almost all of whom were also expected to undertake small roles. The theatre in Biel was a little gem, cunningly tacked onto part of the medieval city walls, and the windows of the male principals' dressing-room were arrow slits. The workload was indeed remarkable. The musical standard required of us singers was high and though the style of production was distinctly conservative the sheer fact that for most of the season we were performing one opera, doing the stage rehearsals for the next and the musical preparation for the next but one meant that time did not hang on our hands. By the end of my eight months in Biel I had sung Pinkerton in *Madam Butterfly*, Don Ottavio in *Don Giovanni*, Alfredo in *La traviata*, Almaviva in *The Barber of Seville*, Rossillon in *The Merry Widow*, Ishmaele in *Nabucco* and Ritter Hugo in Lortzing's *Undine*. Each opera was performed about ten times, so by the end of that one short season I had notched up some seventy performances, a harvest of experience which would have been out of the question for any young British-based singer.

It is doubtless because of this baptism of fire that I have always been somewhat intolerant of those singers who feel that they are being put under excessive pressure if they are required to perform more than two or three times a week. The workload in Biel was admittedly rather a make-or-break affair, and my soprano partner, a highly talented young American, buckled under it and had to be replaced after the first three productions. I do feel, however, that if you do not possess the vocal and nervous stamina for what is an undeniably strenuous profession it is best

---

*One of them was Burgdorf, birthplace of Lisa della Casa, who had made her own professional debut with the Städtebundtheater in 1941.

to establish the fact sooner rather than later, and it was one of the great comforts of starting a career in so small a theatre that we were performing to audiences who understood our circumstances and were ready to forgive the occasional shaky performance. They understood, too, that we were not paid very much, and it was an endearing habit amongst many of the season-ticket holders to reward us for our efforts not with the customary bouquets of flowers but with gifts of a greater practical value such as baskets of groceries and bottles of wine. On one memorable occasion as I took my final curtain after a performance of *La traviata* I was handed a gift-wrapped parcel which felt slightly soggy and left traces of blood on the palm of my hand. The butcher from whom I regularly bought my meat had attended the performance with his wife and the parcel contained two superb beefsteaks.

Five years after I had moved on from Biel, Herr Breitner came to see me after a performance in the Zürich Opera House. He was crowing with delight, because he had been sitting next to the director of a small German theatre, who was one of the many people for whom I had done an unsuccessful audition in my student days, and who had apparently warned Herr Breitner that he had made a big mistake in engaging me. So this evening Herr Breitner had been rubbing it in. 'There you are!' he told his companion. 'Just look at him up there! You could have had him, I got him, and now you wouldn't be able to afford his fee!' It gave me the greatest pleasure thus unwittingly to have repaid Herr Breitner for the faith that he had shown in me.

In his book *The Perfect Wagnerite* Bernard Shaw wrote, 'It is possible to learn more of the world by producing a single opera . . . than by ten years reading in the library of the British Museum', and I would feel inclined to say the same thing about performing in one. I suppose it was during those months in Biel that I first became aware of the exceptional variety of human experience which is to be encountered in our profession. It is by its very nature remarkably free of those barriers which usually exist between people of different nationalities, different age groups or different social backgrounds; the one unifying factor between us all is the desire to sing, and what people will want to know about us is not where we come from or what our previous lives have consisted of, but whether we have the ability to step on stage and deliver the goods. There is, for instance, no such thing as a senior member of the profession being able to rest on his laurels; he may trail clouds of glory from his distinguished past but it is tonight's performance which counts, and he will be well aware that he is sharing the stage with people who have fresher voices, younger lungs and probably more retentive memories than he. Conversely he will have the advantage over his younger colleagues in terms of knowing the tricks of the trade – how to carry on unperturbed if something is going wrong, how to husband his resources through a taxing role when he is not feeling at his best, and so on. Indeed whoever it was who first coined the aphorism 'Se il giovane sapesse, se il vecchio potesse', 'If the young man had the knowledge, if the old man had the strength', might have done so with the operatic profession in mind. For reasons such as these self-importance is a characteristic which one seldom encounters amongst opera singers. When you are liable to be shouted at in front of the whole company by a conductor thirty years your junior for coming in a beat late at a rehearsal, self-importance is really not an option.*

During my many years in the profession my mind has often turned to one senior colleague who made a deep impression on me during my days in the Städtebundtheater. His name was Egon Waldmann, he played comic roles in the six or seven operetta productions which also featured in the company's schedule, and being an innately modest man he would have been amazed to know that he had exercised any influence on me. *The Merry Widow* was the only piece in which we worked together; I was the young Frenchman Camille de Rossillon, he was Njegus, the old embassy clerk, a role which he played to perfection, and on *Widow* evenings my place was next to his in the principals' dressing-room. He was German by birth, and I have no doubt that it would originally have been his ambition to end up in a more exalted theatre company than that of Biel, but he was also Jewish, so back in the 1930s he had been obliged to flee from the Nazis and he was grateful to have found a refuge. He was

---

*When Leonard Bernstein conducted a recording of *West Side Story* some years ago with Kiri te Kanawa and José Carreras in the leading roles, the sessions were filmed and shown on television. I remember how astonished many people were by the brusqueness with which Bernstein treated Carreras.

*Stars of two genera-
tions share an auto-
graph session.
Lotte Lehmann and
Lisa della Casa in the
Palais Auersperg,
Vienna,
2 November 1955.*

small and neat, his natural expression was a welcoming smile, his air was one of old-world courtesy, and his attitude towards those of us young-sters who were clearly hoping to treat the Städtebundtheater as the first step in a more ambitious career appeared in no way to be tinged with envy. While putting on his wig and make-up it was his invariable habit to look wistfully into his mirror, ask 'Ist das ein Beruf für einen erwachsenen Mann?' – 'Is this a profession for a grown man?' – and then with a merry chuckle carry on with what he was doing. I have often thought of this little ritual of his, because by immersing ourselves in a world of make-believe we do undeniably retain some of the trappings of early youth. The atmosphere when a cast assembles to start rehearsing a new production is strangely reminiscent of the first day of term at a new school, especially if the company is one for which you have never sung before. What will the colleagues be like, will they be convinced by you, have you got Act I securely by heart, and, most vital of all, how are you going to get along with the director and conductor? For colleagues read fellow pupils, for

Act I read your holiday task, and for director and conductor read your new teachers. Herr Waldmann had been in the theatrical profession all his adult life, and I have no idea how many hardships, dangers and sorrows he had gone through before ending up where he did – knowing what happened to so many other Jewish artists I imagine they would not have been trivial – but he never lost his youthful relish for the job in hand. He was a *Bühnenmensch* if ever I saw one.

David Webster, for many years General Manager at Covent Garden, used to say that the vital thing for a singer is to be liked by the right people at the right time, and to that I would add that it is equally vital to fall into the right hands early on. There are opera managers who understand how to nurture a budding talent and there are those who do not – indeed there are those who have no interest in doing so. If a young actor is given a part which is beyond his capabilities it may set him back for a while in his self-confidence and in his reputation, but it is unlikely to do him any lasting physical harm, whereas a young singer who is persuaded by an unscrupulous management to undertake a role which is too heavy for him may do his voice irreparable damage. He will get through the half dozen performances which are all the management is concerned about, but he will pay a heavy price for 'singing on his capital rather than his income', to quote a familiar operatic saying. Managers who possess the perspicacity accurately to assess a young singer's potential strengths and weaknesses are few in number, and in my own case it was my very good fortune to attract the attention early on in my career of exactly such a one, Dr Friedrich Schramm, Intendant of the Stadttheater, Basel. Observing in me the rudiments of a theatrical talent he advised me to abandon those roles in which ninety per cent of the requirement was pure *bel canto*, and to my surprise he offered me a guest contract as the Drum Major in *Wozzeck* and Danilo in *The Merry Widow*. These are two roles which nobody would normally dream of casting with the same singer, but he was right – for some reason they both suited me admirably, and for many years thereafter my career ran along what most people would have called incompatible paths, those of twentieth-century opera and Viennese operetta. The first two roles which I sang back in my native Britain were the title-role in Johann Strauss's *The Gipsy Baron* for the Sadler's Wells Opera and Britten's *Peter Grimes* at the Edinburgh Festival, a highly unlikely right and left, and one which I owed entirely to the sagacity of Dr Schramm.

It was the opinion of no less an authority than Enrico Caruso that the requisites for a great singer are 'a big chest, a big mouth, ninety per cent memory, ten per cent intelligence, lots of hard work and something in the heart'. With all of this I would agree – who would dare disagree with the King of Tenors? – but I would add one other attribute; an opera singer has to maintain a precarious balance between self-confidence and self-criticism. Without the former you could scarcely pluck up the courage to stand in front of a couple of thousand people and risk making an idiot of yourself, but without the latter you stand no chance of artistic development. One problem is that you do not hear yourself as others hear you; your own voice comes to your own ear via so many different internal points of resonance. This means that there must be people in your life on whose advice and expertise you can totally rely. Initially this is likely to be your singing teacher – and even the most celebrated singers usually continue to work with a teacher long after they have achieved fame and fortune – then later on probably one or two favourite coaches, known in the business as repetiteurs.

These invaluable people are the unsung heroes and heroines of our profession, because whereas it is possible to memorize spoken dialogue sitting by oneself in a comfortable armchair it is very hard for any except the few musical geniuses in our ranks to memorize an operatic role without the assistance of a coach. A coach will not only play the orchestral part on the piano and make sure that you hit the right notes at the right time, but also sing in the vital vocal cues which you need in the duets and ensemble passages. Even those singers who are themselves capable pianists still need the services of a good coach, because the coach will know from past experience such things as which instruments you can hear in the orchestra at a given moment and which you cannot. Especially in modern music those of us who are not blessed with perfect pitch need all the help we can get, and many is the time that patient coaches have explained to me some such solution to a problem as 'The only way you will ever find the F sharp at the beginning of this phrase is by listening to the brass chord two bars before, trying to hang onto the trumpet's A natural and coming down a minor third – but whatever you do don't let the oboe put you off, because it plays a loud F natural half a beat before your entry.' Not many of us

The phenomenal Jussi Björling (1911–1960) appeared in no less than forty-four different roles with the Royal Opera Stockholm before reaching his twenty-fifth birthday.

would be able to work that out for ourselves, and though it is obviously a great advantage to be what most people call 'a musical singer' this question of musicianship in opera singers is an intriguing one. I have known colleagues who can pick up a score by Berio or Stockhausen and sing it at sight, but the most facile readers often find it hard to memorize their music. Similarly those who are able both to read and to memorize with enviable ease may not necessarily possess the gift of bringing their music to life in performance. Sometimes the sheer fact that the less gifted amongst us have had to spend longer learning the role with a patient coach means that we have also had longer to ponder the part, store it away in our subconscious minds and ultimately serve it up to the public as a natural part of ourselves.

Something which few people realize is how much more of our time we spend in studying, rehearsing and travelling than we ever do in performing, and the structure of a successful singer's life can become quite bewildering. Nowadays it is not the fashion for opera houses to maintain a large permanent company – it is too expensive for them to have artists under contract who may only be needed irregularly. At the time of writing the British company with the largest staff of principal singers is the English National Opera, but even there there are only nineteen soloists under regular contract as against some forty or so back in the 1970s; none of the other established companies has more than half a dozen, though they do maintain a permanent chorus. This means that the majority of British soloists operate on an independent basis, which has the advantage that they are free to appear with whatever company, at home or abroad, may seek their services, but which also leads to some very complex situations. Whereas a successful actor may perhaps be playing just one role for a whole year in the West End of London, a comparably sought-after singer may well appear during the same period in as many as a dozen roles with, say, half a dozen different companies and in several different countries. He or she will be unlikely, though, to be involved in more than a maximum of seventy or eighty actual performances during the course of any one year, because none of the operas in question will be given more than seven or eight times and several of them only once or twice.

To take a hypothetical case, let us say that you have a contract to sing in a new production of Opera A with one of the leading German houses. This will involve you in rehearsing in the city in question for around five weeks, followed by the first night, another two performances during the following week or so, five more at irregular intervals during the rest of the year, and possibly two or three a year as long as that particular opera remains in the house's repertoire. During that rehearsal period, however, you have two performances of Opera B in a Swiss house and one of Opera C in an Austrian house, in productions in which you originally appeared one year ago and two years ago respectively, and the dates of which were cleared by your agent as N/As (non-available dates) when settling your contract for Opera A. Once Opera A is launched in Germany you fly home to Britain, where, after ten days' break, spent largely in brushing up your next new role with your favourite coach, you are due to begin rehearsing Opera D with one of the British regional companies. There you will be based for eight weeks (the company having engaged one of those tiresome new-wave directors who evolve their 'concept' during rehearsals) and your agent has secured you two N/As for performances of Opera A in Germany and one for a concert in London. Once Opera D has had its premiere it is featured once a week in each of the six cities which comprise the regular touring circuit of the company in question, and each of these dates has been cleared as an N/A from your rehearsals for Opera E in London, as have the dates of one further performance of Opera B in Switzerland (where you are needed for two days of rehearsal before the performance because several members of the cast have been replaced since you last appeared there), and the final performance of Opera C in Austria.

Now, any reader who has followed me thus far will see that this is a peculiar way of life, and that it contains several glaringly disadvantageous factors. One is the question of home life. Our putative singer may have been able to return to the bosom of the family for a few days here and there when he or she had not been called for rehearsals, but most singers agree that these fleeting visits can be as disruptive to domestic bliss as the extended absences.* Then there is the question of clashing dates. The jig-saw which I have postulated in fact represents an unaccustomedly obliging schedule – a rather more likely situation is that our singer loses one of the new productions altogether because the date of the dress rehearsal clashes with one of the performances to which he is already contractually committed elsewhere, and as a freelance singer is paid by the performance it is a bitter experience to lose a string of evenings in one place because of one single evening in another. There is also the problem that travel is not always as simple as I have made it sound, and it is both fatiguing and risky to undertake a journey of any length on the day of a performance. Sometimes it is inevitable, and strangely enough one such occasion in my own career provided me with an experience which I look back on with particular gratification, as it culminated in my achieving an unlikely victory over that popular bogeyman, the tax inspector.

The gentleman who presided over tax affairs in the London district in which I was resident at the time was self-evidently of the opinion that

---

*The incidence of enduring marriages in the operatic profession is depressingly low.

anyone connected with the entertainment industry was likely to be a mendacious layabout, and it was his habit to go through my claims for expenses with nit-picking exactitude. One day my accountant rang to warn me that I had played into this gentleman's hands by committing an error of great foolishness; I had claimed expenses for two hotel rooms on the same night, one in Amsterdam and the other in Leeds. In normal circumstances such a telephone call would have made me quail but this time officialdom had in fact played into *my* hands and I was able to prove the following unlikely tale. The Welsh National Opera's production of *Billy Budd*, in which I sang Captain Vere, was being revived in the Grand Theatre, Leeds, and on the one free day between the dress rehearsal and the first night I had long been contracted to sing the title-role in a modern opera called *Ein Engel kommt nach Babylon* with the Deutsche Oper am Rhein in Düsseldorf. The Welsh National Opera would not normally have accepted these very tight travel arrangements but they had no understudy for the role of Vere and decided to take the risk.

It was in the late autumn, and when the time came not only was there widespread fog in England and in Germany, but the British air-traffic controllers were indulging in an on-and-off strike. I managed nonetheless to fly without trouble from Leeds to Düsseldorf after the dress rehearsal, but the return journey looked problematic. I decided that the safest method would be to hire a car in Düsseldorf, drive the 140 fog-ridden miles after the performance from there to Amsterdam airport, pick up a couple of hours' sleep in an airport hotel, hope for an early morning flight to Heathrow, take the train from London to Leeds, climb straight into bed as soon as I arrived there, and thus achieve the sleep which I would need in order to sustain the taxing role of Captain Vere. The Queen's Hotel in Leeds, however, told me that if I arrived during the course of the morning they could only guarantee me instant access to a room if I had booked it for the previous night, hence the expenses claim which had so aroused the tax inspector's suspicions. By a miraculous chance the journey, though strenuous, went without a hitch and the upshot of this curious affair was a performance in which, to quote Richard Fawkes's history of the Welsh National Opera,* 'near-perfection was achieved'. Whether

---

*See bibliography.

or not it had anything to do with the fraught circumstances – had I failed to arrive the performance would have been cancelled – I really cannot say, but I am entirely of one mind with Thomas Allen, the evening's Billy Budd, who looks back on it as having been one of those very rare occasions when a special kind of magic seemed to descend on the entire company; it is remarkable, too, how often members of the public have told me that they were there that evening and that it had left an indelible impression on them.

Beside the threat of clashing dates there is always one other potential spectre lurking in the life of every freelance singer. Ask any of us what we will be happiest to say goodbye to when the day of retirement finally dawns and you will be likely to receive the same reply – what a relief it will be no longer to live in dread of that nasty little tickle in the throat which heralds the arrival of a common cold. Partially, I dare say, for psychological reasons it has a devastating habit of making itself felt three or four days before some vital performance, and the threat can assume chimeric proportions. These are the moments when you realize that 'the voice',* however well you may have learnt to deploy it, is in fact only minimally under your control. If the vocal cords become swollen and inflamed you suddenly find that the instrument with which you are so familiar has been surreptitiously replaced by some hideous mockery of its usual self. It is as if a violinist were to find that his beloved Stradivarius has been strung with coarse household string; however great his skill the required sounds will simply not emerge. A singer hatching a cold is indeed a pitiable specimen of humanity. He is like a person in the grip of some nightmarish obsession – will the infection go to the nose, will it descend to the chest, will it strike the larynx? Hour by hour the victim waits and observes its stealthy invasion, knowing that he is totally in its power, and that if it chooses the wrong day to strike with its full force,

---

*People are often surprised by the habit, common amongst singers, of referring to 'the voice' rather than 'my voice', as if it were some object that we keep in a cupboard to be brought out when required. There is a tendency, too, to regard singers as fussy or self-centred if they complain of a draught or refuse to sit in a smoke-filled restaurant, but we do not see it in that light. We are not doing it for our own sakes but for the sake of 'the voice', just as anyone else would be careful in his treatment of some valuable precision instrument.

months of study and weeks of rehearsal may turn out to have been in vain.

There are, of course, other tribulations to be encountered in the profession. There are the star conductors who are too busy to attend production rehearsals, so sweep in at the last minute changing the tempi and upsetting all concerned. There is the occasional vicious review to be survived. Most singers accept reasonable criticism with equanimity, but personal attacks can be deeply wounding and in certain cases, particularly where young performers are concerned, potentially devastating. From time to time comes the hideous realization that one is locked into a new production under a director whose view of the piece in hand is either inept or perverse, and that one must choose between a course of endless friction or of devoting one's energies to an interpretation which one profoundly feels to be wrong; for most of us the third alternative, walking out, is not financially viable.

If these, then, are the sorrows, or some of them, what are the joys? Perhaps having just addressed the question of what most of us would be happiest to turn our backs on after retirement I should try to express what I personally shall miss the most when that day comes. It would be hard to put into any order of precedence the many compelling features of what has been for nearly forty years not merely a job but a way of life; high on my list, though, I would have to place the companionship of the profession. Contrary, perhaps, to the impression made by familiar titbits of backstage gossip singers are by and large the easiest of people to get on with.* Most of them are open-hearted, generous people, frequently with a refreshingly childish sense of humour,† and the nature of the work we do leads to easily formed friendships; you could sit next to someone ten times at formal dinner parties and not establish the bond with them that you do in one rehearsal of a big duet.

Furthermore this sense of companionship is not limited to one's fellow singers. Before you go on stage to give a performance a whole army of

---

*The colleagues with whom I have run into trouble during all these years can be counted on the fingers of one hand – for the curious they have been two mezzos, two tenors and one baritone.

†I remember the great American mezzo Frederica von Stade telling me that one of the things she treasures about the profession is that 'singers are such fun to be with – like a bunch of third-graders'.

people has been beavering away to make your life as easy as possible. The people in the costume department who make sure that nothing will inhibit your movements and nothing will be too tight round your throat; the lady in charge of shoes who has bought you a new pair because the ones you wore at the dress rehearsal pinched your toes; the girl who spends half an hour getting your wig and make-up exactly the way the designer wants it; the member of the music staff who bobs into your dressing-room to wish you luck and remind you not to drag the tempo at the beginning of Act II; the man from props who lets you know that your walking stick is ready on the table backstage left; the stage manager who has a glass of water waiting in the wings for your brief exit after the aria; the dresser who remembers that you do not like to put the heavy cloak on until just before your first entrance; the chorus singer who knows that you hate to have your concentration disturbed by talking as you wait in the wings, so gives you a silent smile and a thumbs-up – all of them, and many others too, provide the back-up to your own contribution, and it is a very special feeling to be amongst so many people whose whole energy during those few hours is solely directed to ensuring that the performance should be a good one.

There are several other features of a singer's life, too, which I shall be sorry to say goodbye to. On a superficial level there is the applause, which I would never deny enjoying, particularly on those rare occasions when I feel that I have deserved it. It is a fickle yardstick of a singer's worth, as it so frequently reflects the attractiveness or otherwise of the role in question rather than the true merit of the performance, but when colleagues try to give the impression that their vanity has remained untickled by a spontaneous roar erupting from every corner of the house they may deceive themselves but they do not deceive me. Then there is the sheer fact that the very tools of our trade are so often works of surpassing beauty. When I was young I used to think that I was well acquainted with certain operas – *Don Giovanni*, let us say, or *La traviata* – because I had seen them a couple of times and was familiar with many of the most famous numbers on gramophone records; but when I came to grips with these pieces with a view to performing in them myself, and when my insights into the genius of Mozart and Verdi were illumined by the guiding lights of the various coaches and conductors with whom I worked I realized that it was a very privileged path that I was treading. The actual process of memorization can have tiresome side effects. When all day your subconscious mind has been fed with new notes and words to be stored away it has a habit of not resting at night; you wake up, frustrated by a scrap of melody to which you cannot find the text, and you will not get back to sleep until you have turned on the light, fetched the score, and found the answer. If, however, it is an inspiration as sublime as 'Il mio tesoro' or 'Parigi o cara' which is robbing you of your slumber you are not entirely to be pitied – it could, after all, be the neighbours' barking dog.

Another element of the singer's life which I imagine it will be hard to shrug off is the danger. All of us in the world of opera are aware that we permanently skirmish with disaster. Anyone who has cracked on a high note in an aria which the entire audience knows by heart, or whose memory has suddenly gone blank, leaving a void where words and music are supposed to be, will remember those moments as long as they live, and the knowledge that they could occur at any time is, I think, in the backs of all our minds when we look at each other five minutes before curtain-up on a first night and ask each other 'Why on earth do we do this?' And yet if ever I am not nervous before a performance I know that I must take care – it can only mean that I am tired or in some way distracted. Stage fright such as Maria Callas used to suffer from as she stood in the wings drawing blood with her nails from the arm of anyone gallant enough to support her, or which used to assail the great Rosa Ponselle with such force that she would walk round and round the block trying to summon up enough courage to enter the theatre, must be a fearful burden to carry; but the nerves which concentrate the energy and set the adrenalin flowing, uncomfortable though they may be at the time, are, I would say, essential to any singer who hopes to make a mark on the public.

Which brings me to what is, without a scrap of doubt, the greatest joy of the operatic profession, and that is the actual function of singing to an audience. Singing in an opera is one of the very few activities which call for a person's maximum physical, emotional and intellectual output all at the same time. To sing a vocally glorious passage in a role which you love on an evening when everything seems to be going right is an experience of extraordinary completeness. I remember my old friend Tom Krause saying to me 'When I'm singing well it's like an inner force, something that takes over', and I know exactly what he meant. To be for those precious moments the mouthpiece of whichever composer you are interpreting, to be at one and the same time expressing the emotions of the character you are playing and expressing yourself, to hear that mighty orchestra cushioning your endeavours as you send your voice to the back of a vast, sold-out auditorium – it is an intensely exhilarating experience. It happens, of course, far more regularly to some other singers than it does to me, but I can make do with certain happy memories.

* * *

A couple of years ago I presented a series of BBC radio programmes in which I talked to twelve of my friends in the operatic profession about

Nicolai Gedda, the beau idéal *of lyric tenors.*

the business of being a singer. One of them was that *beau idéal* of lyric tenors Nicolai Gedda, a man who possesses the ability to express himself fluently in nine different languages. On that occasion, though, my last question reduced him to a brief, shocked silence. 'Before you became a singer', I said to him, 'you worked in a bank. Can you imagine what your life would have been like without the coincidence of a wonderful voice?' A moment's pause, and then the reply – 'I could imagine; but I prefer not to think about it.'

Select Bibliography

Alda, Frances: *Men, Women and Tenors*, Houghton Mifflin, Boston, 1937.

Benke, N. E.: *Ljuba Welitsch*, Dachs-Verlag, Vienna, 1994.

Blyth, Alan: *Opera on Video*, Kyle Cathie, London, 1995.

Borovsky, Victor: *Chaliapin*, Hamish Hamilton, London, 1988.

Cairns, David: *Memoirs of Hector Berlioz*, Victor Gollancz, London, 1977.

Carpenter, Humphrey: *Benjamin Britten*, Faber & Faber, London, 1992.

Chamier, J. Daniel: *Percy Pitt*, Edward Arnold, London, 1938.

Christiansen, Rupert: *Prima Donna*, Bodley Head, London, 1984.

Clément, Catherine: *Opera, or the Undoing of Women*, Virago Press, London, 1989.

Cone, John Frederick: *Adelina Patti*, Scolar Press, Aldershot, 1994.

Culshaw, John: *Putting the Record Straight*, Secker & Warburg, London, 1981.

Dent, Edward J.: *Mozart's Operas*, Oxford University Press, London, 1947.

Douglas, Nigel: *Legendary Voices*, André Deutsch, London, 1992.

Douglas, Nigel: *More Legendary Voices*, André Deutsch, London, 1994.

Einstein, Alfred: *Mozart*, Cassell, London, 1946.

Emmons, Shirlee: *Tristanissimo*, Schirmer Books, New York, 1990.

Endler, Franz: *Das Walzerbuch*, Verlag Kremayr & Scheriau, Vienna, 1975.

Faris, Alexander: *Jacques Offenbach*, Faber & Faber, London, 1980.

Farrar, Geraldine: *Such Sweet Compulsion*, Greystone Press, New York, 1938.

Fawkes, Richard: *Welsh National Opera*, Julia MacRae, London, 1986.

Gaisberg, F. W.: *Music on Record*, Robert Hale, London, 1946.

Gattey, Charles Neilson: *Luisa Tetrazzini*, Scolar Press, Aldershot, 1995.

Gatti-Casazza, Giulio: *Memories of the Opera*, John Calder, London, 1977.

Glass, Beaumont: *Lotte Lehmann*, Capra Press, Santa Barbara, 1988.

Gobbi, Tito: *My Life*, Macdonald and Jane's, London, 1979.

Grun, Bernard: *Gold and Silver*, W. H. Allen, London, 1970.

Hamilton, David (ed.): *The Metropolitan Opera Encyclopaedia*, Thames & Hudson, London, 1987.

Harewood, Lord: *The Tongs and the Bones*, Weidenfeld and Nicolson, London, 1981.

Heyworth, Peter: *Otto Klemperer*, Cambridge University Press, Cambridge, 1983.

Holden, Amanda (ed.): *Viking Opera Guide*, Viking, London, 1993.

Hughes, Spike: *Great Opera Houses*, Weidenfeld and Nicolson, London, 1956.
Hughes, Spike: *Glyndebourne*, Methuen, London, 1965.
Hussey, Dyneley: *Verdi*, J. M. Dent & Sons, London, 1940.
Kelly, Michael: *Reminiscences*, Oxford University Press, London, 1975.
Kemp, Peter: *The Strauss Family*, Omnibus Press, London, 1989.
Kennedy, Michael: *Britten*, J. M. Dent & Sons, London, 1981.
Leinsdorf, Erich: *Cadenza*, Houghton Mifflin, Boston, 1976.
Leitich, Anna Letizia: *Lippen schweigen*, Forum Verlag, Vienna, 1960.
Marek, George R.: *The Eagles Die*, Hart-Davis, MacGibbon, London, 1974.
Merrill, Robert: *Between Acts*, McGraw-Hill, New York, 1976.
Moore, Gerald: *Am I Too Loud?*, Hamish Hamilton, London, 1962.
Morley, Sheridan: *Spread a Little Happiness*, Thames & Hudson, London, 1987.
Newman, Ernest: *Wagner Nights*, Putnam & Co, London, 1949.
Newton, Ivor: *At the Piano*, Hamish Hamilton, London, 1966.
Osborne, Charles: *The Opera House Album*, Robson Books, London, 1979.
Pleasants, Henry: *The Great Tenor Tragedy*, Amadeus Press, Portland, Oregon, 1995.
Prawy, Marcel: *Johann Strauss*, Verlag Fritz Molden, Vienna, 1975.
Rosenthal, Harold D.: *Two Centuries of Opera at Covent Garden*, Putnam & Co, London, 1958.
Rubinstein, Arthur: *My Young Years*, Jonathan Cape, London, 1973.
Rubinstein, Arthur: *My Many Years*, Jonathan Cape, London, 1980.
Sadie, Stanley (ed.): *The New Grove Dictionary of Opera*, Macmillan, London, 1994.
Schwarzkopf, Elisabeth: *On and Off the Record*, Faber & Faber, London, 1982.
Shaw, G. B.: *The Perfect Wagnerite*, London, 1898.
Slezak, Leo: *Song of Motley*, William Hodge & Co, London, 1938.
Spotts, Frederic: *Bayreuth*, Yale University Press, New Haven and London, 1994.
Steane, J. B.: *The Grand Tradition*, Duckworth, London, 1974.
Strauss, Richard/Krauss, Clemens: *Briefwechsel*, Verlag C. H. Beck, Munich, 1963.
Tear, Robert: *Singer Beware*, Hodder & Stoughton, London, 1995.
Traubner, Richard: *Operetta – A Theatrical History*, Victor Gollancz, London, 1984.
Tuggle, Robert: *The Golden Age of Opera*, Holt, Rinehart & Winston, New York, 1983.
Wellesz, Egon: *Essays on Opera*, Dennis Dobson, London, 1950.
Wilson, Conrad: *Scottish Opera*, Collins, Glasgow, 1972.
Witeschnik, Alexander: *Dort wird champagnisiert*, Neff Verlag, Vienna, 1971.

Index